The Longing

A CANADIAN FAMILY'S WORLD WAR II ODYSSEY

The Longing

A CANADIAN FAMILY'S WORLD WAR II ODYSSEY

Dorothy Mandy

MW Publishing
Nanaimo, British Columbia

Copyright © 2024 Dorothy Mandy
All rights reserved

Canadian Cataloguing in Publication Data

Mandy, Dorothy 1937 -
    The Longing: A Canadian Family's World War II Odyssey
    Dorothy Mandy - - 1st ed

Ebook ISBN 978-1-7381678-0-7

Hardcover ISBN 978-1-7381678-1-4

Softcover ISBN 978-1-7381678-2-1

Cover photo by Dorothy Mandy

Cover Design by Richard Hoedl & Jackie Boucher

MW Publishing
5234 Sherbourne Drive
Nanaimo, BC V9T 2J8

To The People of Poland

*"In that year (1939) they decided to make a trip to Germany, where Werner's mother is still living, in Hamburg. They did not sell their land, as this trip was intended as a visit rather than a migration. They sailed on the ship **Hansa** from New York. Ten days after their arrival in Hamburg, World War II broke out.*

Jacob Ulmer, 1956

Table of Contents

Acknowledgments

Foreword

Preface

The Longing..1

Leaving Canada..5

Map..12

Rostock..13

A New Home in Ziegelhof...40

Life in Ziegelhof..49

Leaving Ziegelhof..80

Goldenitz..101

On the Move Again..114

Life in Norderney...128

Preparing to Leave..236

Sources...246

About the Author..247

Acknowledgments

My mother often apologized for her clumsiness at letter writing—she had no idea what a treasure she was creating. My grandfather knew the value of a recorded history, and I appreciate his wisdom and forethought in collecting the letters written to the many family members over the years. By doing so, he helped to preserve our story.

Many others have played a part in this journey and I want to acknowledge and thank them.

My children, Carla and Adrian, were my captive audience when they were small, and they always made me feel my stories were worth telling. I hope my younger sister, Helga doesn't think I have made us look too much like *The Five Little Peppers, and How They Grew*. My older sister Heidi enriched my memories with her joyous reminiscing.

My dear friends of more than forty years, Rozina Janmohamed, Janie Cawley and Judy Doll, continue to be my greatest cheering section.

In the last few years I have been fortunate to know a number of accomplished women who have helped me improve my writing and made me believe that I can tell my story.

Lois Peterson, author, artist and writing instructor inspired me with her talent and generosity of spirit. It was through Lois that I became involved with Nicole (Nikki) Tait-Stratton, another accomplished author. As host, instructor and leader of the writers' group, *Writers on Fire,* Nikki and members Carol Thornton, Brenda Verwey, Kathi Pointen and Chris Nykoluk have been unstinting in their help and support.

Every manuscript benefits from the keen eye of a good editor and I was fortunate enough to work with two. Sarah Harvey helped me find the gems in my mother's letters while whittling my manuscript down to a manageable size. Sheila Cameron patiently worked with the many idiosyncrasies in both my mother's writing and mine. She also cajoled me into present-day grammar, making my book so much better and easier to read.

I am honoured to have my long-distance friend Sieneke de Rooij write the Foreword. It was also she who made it possible for me to consider publishing my story by introducing me to Sabine Bode's book, *Grandchildren of the War, The Forgotten Generation.*

I must take care how I acknowledge my life partner, Larry. He is formatting and preparing my book for printing and he has the power to delete this.

For the past forty-five years Larry has been my companion, my mentor and my constant source of support. He has witnessed my struggle with this writing journey over many years and has never doubted my ability to get it done. Once he read the manuscript, he insisted it deserved a wider readership than just my family and friends.

Larry is always helpful, providing useful information and bringing his considerable skill to bear. If you are reading this, it is because he got it published.

Thank you.

Foreword

Family stories are fascinating. For elderly people who recognize themselves in them and who want to record their history for their children and grandchildren. For young people who are curious about stories from the past because they know nothing about them. And for people in the middle of their lives who want to preserve their parents' stories before they fade away forever.

I am a creative writing teacher and a writer of two novels based on family history from World War II. One based on a four-sentence story from my father's family. One based on only five letters from my husband's father's family. Almost every European family has stories from the Second World War. In my father's family it was a story of which only the one-minute version circulated: a drama in the Dutch Hunger Winter, my father as a twelve-year-old boy travelling alone from Voorburg to Friesland, my grandmother cycling on a hunger journey and surviving a ship disaster on the IJsselmeer, she still comes home with food, in one shoe and a clog. That's about it.

As a child I had heard this compact summary many times. But it wasn't until I was forty that I suddenly became really interested. How had that all worked? What had my father experienced as a child during the war? Would that period have influenced his life, his personality? Suddenly I wanted to know. I took action out of passion. I researched the story and provided background in a novel form and it was a fascinating revelation to my much younger nieces and nephews

Dorothy Mandy started telling her fascinating story on the basis of letters written by her mother to her relatives in Canada, during the family's time in Germany. Some family history transcends the family because it tells a universal story. The flight of hundreds of thousands of German civilians, who were hunted from the east to the west at the end of the war, is one of them. Dorothy's family story has been lived by thousands of families, each in their own way.

German journalist and writer Sabine Bode wrote extensively about 'Kriegsenkel' in her book *The Forgotten Generation, The War Children Break Their Silence*. She explores inherited trauma in Germans that were born after the Second World War. Inherited trauma that results in uncertainty about their roots, their place in the world and their future. For Germans and their descendants all over the world, the Second World War presents a specific trauma. This is because the civilians had to deal with being the perpetrators, but also victims. And the world has not been ready to see the children and grandchildren as victims for a long time, for many decades. I see this inherited guilt as a kind of "double survivor's guilt." Children and grandchildren of Nazis and other civilians in the Third Reich had played no active part in Nazism and the Holocaust, yet they feel unease and discomfort, rooted in their DNA, to the present day.

A German friend of mine once told me: "When I am in international company, and everyone presents themselves, I am always jealous of the proud way they mention their fatherland. I am from Norway! I am British! I am from the Netherlands! I can almost hear them cheer. And when my turn comes, I have to say: I am German. And I feel this unbearable weight on my shoulders and a shame to express my country's name. It's awful. Yet I had not even been born! I have nothing to do with that time; I loathe the war and any war forever. But there it is: my shame at being German."

Dorothy Mandy could have been one of Sabine Bode's interviewed subjects. Exactly like the others, as a child in the Third Reich, Dorothy had played no active part in Nazism and the Holocaust, yet she also feels the weight of guilt and shame described in Sabine Bode's writing. And in the same way, Dorothy did not feel free to tell her family's story until she grasped the reality of civilians having to deal with being the perpetrators, but also victims.

Dorothy realised there are many of The Forgotten Generation whose parents immigrated to Canada after the war. Over the years she has met several of them, and found that they welcomed her stories. These descendants of German immigrants began to talk about the difficulty of having only small glimpses into their parents' experiences. Understandably, because their parents were of the post-war generation that looked forward rather than back and felt shame and fear about their stories not being welcomed by their new fellow country folk.

Dorothy is fully aware that her family's story is not nearly as horrendous as that of countless others. In no way does she want to deny or excuse the horror of the victims of the Nazi regime by acknowledging the suffering of German citizens of World War II. But people from all walks of life are searching for their backgrounds. Grief and the experience of loss is not a competition, but a reality in every family that has lived through any war. All deserve compassion and their own understanding of their part in the greater puzzle.

Dorothy's wish for this book is that it may help others of her generation find their story, answer some of their grown children's questions, and preserve some history for grandchildren before it is forgotten.

Sieneke de Rooij, Amsterdam, the Netherlands
October 2023

Preface

My grandfather, Jacob Ulmer, saved over a hundred letters written by my mother to members of her family during our time in Germany.

On our return to Canada, when he offered to give them to her, she accepted reluctantly because the memories were still too fresh. Many years later, when she wondered what would happen to the letters after she died, I told her I would take care of them.

My younger sister, Helga, had only sketchy memories of our experiences in Germany and expressed an interest in the letters. She could no longer read German and that prompted me to begin translating them. In doing so, I have attempted to preserve my mother's voice in words and expressions she would have used. I feel I have succeeded because—in rereading them—I cannot always distinguish between the ones she wrote in English and the ones I translated from German.

In 2007, my oldest brother Walter died. For his celebration of life, his partner, Helen, asked me to talk about his early years. With the help of our brother, Carl, I came up with some stories, mostly light and funny, to keep me from being overcome by the memories. I was surprised when a number of their friends asked if they could have a copy of my notes. They wanted to know if I was planning to write the whole story, possibly as a book.

When they were young, my children enjoyed stories about my

family's experiences in Germany; as adults, they also expressed interest in the letters.

When Carl died, I did not know how much he had talked to his children about our childhood, and I regretted that they had never known the boy who was my friend and protector in good times and bad as we were growing up.

I wanted them to know the family story, so I sent digital copies of the letters to my sisters, my children and my nieces and nephews. Helga read all the letters in one sitting; several others said they also had trouble putting them down and were enthralled by the content.

Their reaction prompted me to reread the letters. I was surprised by the flood of memories of the many happy and crazy times of my childhood. I immediately started writing those stories, and I had no trouble putting them on the page. The dangerous and frightening times were more difficult. I was reluctant to delve into them, but reading my mother's words and being reminded of her courage made it possible to write the hard stories as well.

For inclusion in this book, I have shortened my mother's letters and have removed many repetitions. Not all the gaps in her letters have been marked with ellipses.

A minister at Hope Lutheran Church in Nanaimo, Pastor Richard Dixon, asked my parents to talk about their lives in a videotaped interview in 1989. I only heard of the existence of the tape after both my parents had died, and I was reluctant to look at it. I was well into writing our story before I worked up the courage to watch the tape. I am grateful that I was able to tell some of our story in their voices.

The Longing

My father, Werner Rudeloff, settled in northern Alberta after emigrating to Canada from Germany in 1927. He took on a homestead about six miles west of Wembley, where my mother, Elisabeth Ulmer (most often Betty), lived with her family. He had proved up the homestead and was building a log house when they met.

This small community was largely German-speaking, and the Lutheran church was the hub of all social activities. My mother's family was very much part of that community. My father's family, in Germany, tended to be baptized, confirmed and married in the Lutheran church, but they rarely attended. He would have found the church very modest compared to what he was used to, but he counted himself a Lutheran and found a welcome gathering place where his lack of English was not a barrier.

In the 1989 interview with Pastor Dixon, Dad was often overcome by emotion. At one such moment, he said, "Well, I should let my wife tell you about our life on the farm."

Pastor Dixon turned to her and asked, "Betty, how did you and Werner meet?"

"Well, Werner came to our church, and my parents lived kitty-corner to the church, and after every service my little mother (she was just over five feet tall) would stretch her neck and look around to see who needed to be invited to dinner." As she spoke, my mother stretched out her own neck, looking here and there, to demonstrate. "And so Werner became one of those who was often invited to dinner. He even came sometimes when he wasn't invited."

They both laughed and Dad said, "It looked like a wedding table every Sunday, and she still had to invite somebody."

"Oh, yes. My mother was the most hospitable person I have ever known."

"A small person with a big heart," Dad agreed.

"There was no fancy food or special trimmings," Mom continued. "Just good, solid food and plenty of it. My parents weren't well-to-do. They struggled along. With a family of twelve, of course, they would have.

"In 1928 my mother and I went to Vancouver for my oldest brother Jack's wedding. After the wedding, Mother went home, but I stayed. I stayed for a year, and then I went back home to Wembley."

Many years before this interview, my mother told the story of their encounter when she returned from Vancouver.

Dad had never paid her much attention, and he did not know she was back when he arrived at her parents' place. She may have appeared somewhat more sophisticated than when she had left, and she enjoyed the pleasure and surprise with which he greeted her.

She liked to tell of another sweet moment when the two of them were riding on the gliders at the back of a horse-drawn sleigh. I'm pretty sure there was a kiss involved, but she never quite admitted that.

The interview continued with my mother still speaking. "Then we kind of got together and in December 1930 we were married.

"So then we lived on the farm in our little log house. It was all one room to start with, but eventually Werner put up some partitions. Our four children were born during that time."

In rural communities, where farms were somewhat isolated, women often stayed with family in a town with access to a doctor or medical facility.

This was the case with Walter and Carl, who were born in the hospital in Grand Prairie. Heidi was born at our grandparents' home in Wembley, and I have always been rather pleased to know that I was born in the log house my father built.

"So how did you decide to go to Germany?" Pastor Dixon asked.

"In 1938 Werner's mother wrote and said she would like to meet the children," Mom said. "Our children were her first grandchildren. We knew she had the money, so Werner replied, inviting her to come to Canada for a visit.

"Oh, no, she couldn't do that. She was too old." Mom smiled and shook her head. "She was sixty-three, but that was too old to take a trip like that. So she said we should come over there."

"Had you been to Germany before?"

"Oh, no, but Werner had been back."

Dad nodded and explained, "I went over in 1937 to check things out. I had an inheritance from a wealthy uncle and the money would have been helpful, but there was no way to get it out of the country. So we decided to go for a visit."

My mother also answered the question Richard had asked. "I don't know why we did it; we were so naive. People asked us, *Why do you want to go now? There is going to be a war.* We didn't want to believe that. I don't really know how we felt anymore."

Our first stop after leaving our home in Wembley was Edmonton, with a side-trip to Stony Plain. In 1939, it was still very much a rural village and involved something of a journey from Edmonton, but none of Mother's family members could have gone to Edmonton without visiting Stony Plain. Her father's family had settled there in about 1890 after emigrating from Galicia, and this is where Mother and most of her siblings were born. They moved to Wembley in the Peace River area in 1927.

While we were visiting in Stony Plain, my mother wrote to her parents.

> *Everyone is asking about you and is surprised that we are going away. The hatred against the Germans does not seem as strong here and there are people here, also British, who think well of Germany and Hitler ....*

This is the only comment of this kind, but I know Dad had sensed resentment against him in some parts of the community. During the First World War, Germans in Canada had been interned or required to report to a government office regularly.

In July 1939, my parents got ready to go. They had an auction sale, they rented the farm to my Uncle Georg and embarked on an adventure nobody could have anticipated.

The Longing 4

Leaving Canada

In her first letter from Germany, Mother tells the story of our voyage on the ship *Hansa* from New York in August 1939.

Dear Parents and Siblings,
    Although I am very tired I will finally write a little. I know you must be anxiously awaiting word of our arrival.
    The voyage was very nice. The weather was wonderful, except for Sunday. It was cloudy and cold and the sea was a bit rough. Seasickness is not nice, but it was not too bad. One day we saw an iceberg. It got so cold that we froze even with our coats on.

> *Hapag (Hamburg America Line) had promised us a good cabin in third class but because so many people checked in ahead of us they stuck us in the worst part of the ship. The air was very bad, especially the first night. Then we had to climb so many steep stairs and there was no toilet on our deck. Werner complained to the purser and we were given two cabins in the tourist class. They were also well below deck but much better than the third class. All the stewards were very kind.*
>
> *We could participate in everything in the tourist class except for the main meals which we had to take in the third class because of the difference in price. In the morning, as the children were still sleeping we ordered buns and coffee in the cabin from the deck steward. The stewardess also brought milk for the children, morning and evening. To go for our meals we had to walk the length of the ship and saw much more of it than we might have done. We did not make many acquaintances. With the children we did not have much time for socializing.*

At the time of this voyage, I was just a baby. I have no memory of the ship, but we all remembered the story of a special dinner on the final evening on board the ship.

There were four of us children: Walter was six years old, Carl not yet five, Heidi three and I, nineteen months old. Mother likely had me on her lap, feeding me while her meal got cold; Dad was probably helping the older ones with their meals.

The dessert was ice cream. Mother loved ice cream and would have happily accepted a serving but by the time she finished her meal, it was almost certainly completely melted. The crew must have been anxiously waiting for this moment and may even have been watching her as she was likely the last one to eat her dessert.

She was spooning up the last drops when, to her surprise, she found a small silver charm in the bottom of her dish. It was in the shape of a horse and she learned later that it represented *Das Weiße Rössel* (The White Horse).

She was even more surprised when she found that this was a token for a much more impressive prize—a big beautifully dressed doll, *Die Wirtin des Weißen Rössels,* (the hostess of the White Horse Inn). The horse and the hostess were made famous in an operetta called *Das Weiße Rössl am Wolfgangsee,* a real place in Bavaria.

The doll had a lovely porcelain face and an elaborate hairdo of black curls. Her wide-brimmed hat matched her dress, which had a hoop skirt covered in layers and layers of satin and lace ruffles.

Heidi and I were enchanted with her but we were not actually allowed to play with her, and she was never on display. We had to ask to see her, and any time she was taken out of Mother's bedroom wardrobe we gently touched her clothing and admired her beautiful face and hair.

When we examined her more closely, we discovered her hoop skirt was actually a wire structure that made her stand, and we were a little disconcerted when we found there were no legs under there.

The beautiful hostess of the White Horse Inn is no more, but the small silver horse is entrusted to my grandson, Spenser Mandy.

Arriving in Hamburg

The return address of my mother's first letter after our arrival is my German grandmother's: Hamburg, Hochallee 117. Both the name and the place hold many fond memories and some of us have visited the street in later years just to see the building again.

Mother's letter resumes.

> *We arrived on Friday forenoon, about eleven thirty in Cuxhaven, but could not leave the ship until the clearance of approximately 560 passengers was complete.*
>
> *That happened about two o'clock in the afternoon. After waiting a long time at customs our hand luggage was never thoroughly checked ...*
>
> *We were some of the first of the third class passengers through customs, and Werner ran to arrange for us to get on the first train. We were five minutes late. We eventually left Cuxhaven on a poky little train and arrived here just before seven in the evening.*
>
> *We had our noon meal on the ship and our very friendly steward gave each of the three children a package with a bun and sausage and an apple, which we ate in the waiting room at the station.*
>
> *And now finally the most important part. We are actually at the end of our long journey and have arrived at Grandmamma's*

> in Germany. She and Werner's brother Hasso picked us up at the train station. When we arrived here there was a small table, set with dishes that she bought for the children, and four small chairs all of which they are to take with them later. The beds were all made and above the boys' beds was a long shelf full of toys. The bed folds up against the wall in the daytime and becomes a play area. A door leads from the room to a balcony where they play most of the time. The little group did not want to go to bed.
>
> They all love the Grandmamma but when something goes wrong, Walter says sadly, "We want to go back to Canada to Opa's." After the long trip and the interaction with so many people, the children are not at all shy and are feeling quite at home. Luischen does not yet trust everyone.

Mutti refers to me as *Luischen* (diminutive of Luise). I was rarely called Luischen; I was called *Baby*. That originated in Canada when my godmother, Aunt Margaret, called me *Baby Lou*. That was cute in Canada, but not something known in Germany, where the *Lou* was dropped and I was simply Baby.

> The relatives are all very friendly and don't treat me like a foreigner. I would not let myself be treated that way either. I belong to this family with all the rights and responsibilities and that's that. Werner's mother is pretty much as I had pictured her and yet not quite. She is so good and kind that one has to overlook the idiosyncrasies that one does not like ....

Mother was being tactful. In some ways she and our *Omchen*, as she liked to be called, respected each other, but they were never close. I know that Omchen, while very generous and kind in many ways, could be harshly critical. Mother, who was painfully honest, had trouble tolerating the half-truths and manipulations her mother-in-law used to get along in life. Omchen, in turn, was completely intolerant of Mother's way of thinking and coping.

Mother's defensiveness about being treated as a foreigner indicates that she had already had a sense of it, and she was somewhat bitter about that all her life. She was a country girl from Canada, unused to city life and city ways.

Dad was critical of her as well, and I imagine he saw her through his family's eyes once they were away from the log house on the prairies. She was never very well organized and did not fit into the mould of the *"energische Hausfrau"* (enthusiastic housewife) much praised and admired in Germany.

She was a truly devoted mother to us, and while the German family eventually acknowledged this, they also felt it was at the expense of her husband and a well-run household. It was quite true that she often lost track of time while teaching, singing or simply playing with us, and meals would be late or poorly organized.

For our part, my siblings and I treasure the many times her devotion got us through frightening, desperate times, and I regret that her so-called failings made life difficult for her.

> *Friday evening*
>
> *I have to look after the children, keep our room in order and it is fairly easy. I don't need to concern myself about the kitchen and that suits me. The big laundry is also not my problem. Twice a week a woman comes in to do the heavy work. I iron our clothes and sometimes wash a few of our things.*
>
> *In the afternoon I take the children to the park. There are many lovely parks here where mothers can take their children to play. Most people live upstairs and do not have a yard. The houses are built so close together that one cannot see between them. It looks like one big house from one corner of the street to the other.*
>
> *I cannot say anything definite about our future, but we are anxious to be independent. Werner is in school. He wants to learn to drive a car and here one has to take a big exam to get a driver's licence. There is a big fuss here about every little thing. I guess it has to be like that ....*

War was still only a rumour and Mother was concerned.

> *There is great excitement here. If England really loses its power, what will become of Canada? Will it be worse or is it possible it will be a change for better?*

In her next letter on September 7, Mother reported some good news but also new concerns.

> *We are well in spite of the gloomy times. We hope that Werner can begin earning money soon so that we can have our own home. The children are fine here, but we do not feel free to care for them or raise them as we would like.*

Yesterday, on my return from the park with the children, a woman from downstairs approached me and asked if I would appreciate having a young girl to take my children for a couple of hours each morning. The German Frauenschaft (Women's Ministry) ensures that mothers with small children have one of these young girls every morning for a couple of hours. This does not cost anything as the girls are members of the "Hitler Youth."

Naturally, I was very happy about this, and this morning two very nice young girls arrived. The three children went off quite happily with the girls and wondered why the "Fräulein" would not come again in the afternoon. So now I can do my work in the mornings and can still take the children out in the afternoon. I take hand sewing or some socks to darn and enjoy the fresh air.

Werner's mother does not agree with our ways of feeding or treating our children. The doctors here say you should feed the children more, give them only very little milk and hardly any water to drink....

We would like to have our own home as soon as possible.

                Again, greetings to all from your children...

War is Declared

On 1 September, 1939 Germany invaded Poland, initiating WWII.

Mother does not mention the war, but when it was suddenly a reality, my father realized his mistake in coming to Germany, and he explored the possibility of returning to Canada. When he visited the office of a steamship company, or perhaps a travel agency to make inquiries, he received a very cool reception, and no useful information was forthcoming. After leaving the office, one of the employees followed him outside and warned him against making any efforts to leave the country. If word of these kinds of questions reached the wrong people, there could be serious consequences for him and his family.

I don't know how information was relayed but there must have been other warnings regarding our connection with Canada. In one of her unique post scripts in the margin of her letter, Mother instructs the family to send letters through the United States, *the way she had done.*

She was making it clear that she sent her letter via the United States for a reason, and they must do the same. She may have been warned that letters could also be censored or her instructions to address mail to her sister Helen in the USA would have been more direct. From that time until the USA entered the war, all correspondence was sent via American relatives and faithfully circulated to all members of the family in Canada.

It was fortunate that Mother was fluently bilingual with no accent in either language. She was raised in a German community in Stony Plain, Alberta, where she attended a German-speaking parochial school until it was closed by the government during WWI. She went on to English schools, but all church services and activities were held in High German.

At home, the family spoke *Schwäbisch*, a dialect originating mainly in southern Germany and Bavaria, a region historically known as *Schwabenland*, or Swabia.

In the history of his family, my grandfather Ulmer described the migration of his ancestors from this region of Germany to Galicia sometime between 1780 and 1790. Not feeling free to practise their Lutheran faith without restrictions led to their immigrating to Canada: "*On April 6, 1889, our entire family, consisting of my parents, my grandmother, my brother Josef, and myself, left the homeland, Galicia, to settle in the new world of Canada.*" My grandmother's family came from the same region.

Mother's younger siblings attended only English-speaking schools and their high German was not as fluent as hers.

My siblings—Walter, Carl and Heidi—had learned to speak in both languages before leaving Canada, but when I learned to talk, I had my own peculiar *Kauderwelsch* or gibberish. *"Kappy coady an, komm gehen down."* (Hat and coat on, come, let's go down) was my way of asking to go outside while we were staying with our grandmother in her third-floor apartment.

As far back as I remember, our father was Papa, and our mother was Mutti. In writing about events from our childhood I usually use Mutti and Papa, more formally Mother and Father. I now think of them as Mom and Dad.

The Longing 12

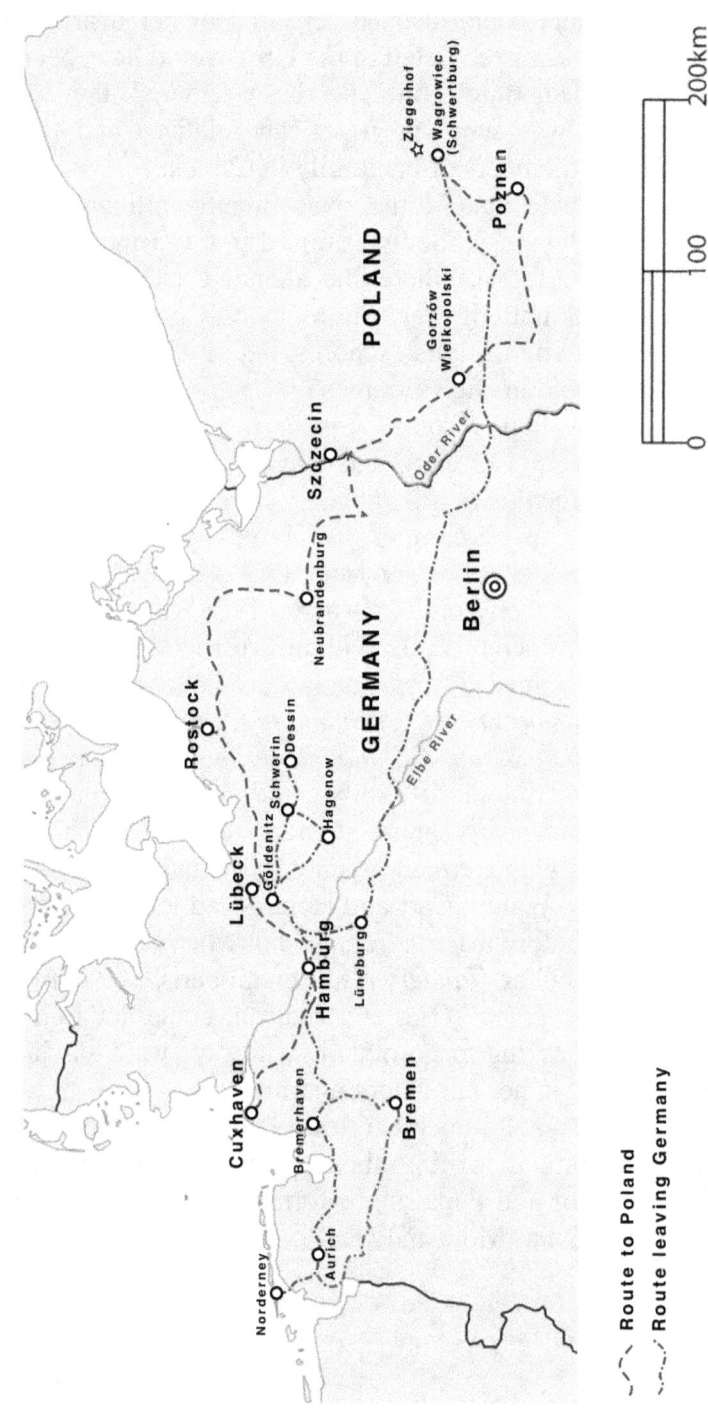

Rostock

In November 1939, Mother wrote in English to her Uncle Louis Hennig in Chicago. We had left some of our things behind when we visited them before sailing for Germany.

After receiving the parcel you sent and two letters from Helen we know that there is a chance of at least some mail getting across. Thank you very much, it was good of you to send it.

Helen has probably told you that we arrived safely, etc. Due to conditions in general, things didn't turn out the way we had expected. We still haven't a home of our own and Werner just started working today. He's back on a farm as an inspector like he used to be before he went to Canada. It was pretty hard for him to get a job like that and he doesn't earn very much to start with, but after being away for so long he has to work his way into it again. Things have changed quite a lot while he was away.

Thanks to Werner's kind relatives we've been well taken care of but have had to live apart. Werner and the boys stayed with his mother, and the girls and I have been with his aunt here in Rostock for about two months now. Werner's mother is sixty-six and not at all used to children so it was too much of a strain to have us all there.

This afternoon I finally got word that I can have a flat that I have been after for about two weeks. It is a very nice little place in a new part of the city. It has a nice bright living room facing southwest and a good size, a bedroom, and a kitchen. Also a toilet but no bathroom. The rent is low and Werner only being here occasionally on weekends I guess we will manage.

I'm so happy to think that I'll soon have all my children

together again. We're making our home in Rostock instead of Hamburg mainly because it is much closer to where Werner works & he can come home oftener. Besides, this isn't such a big city and I like it better. I've met some very nice people here too.

My earliest memories, few and vague, are of the streets and sidewalks of Rostock. I have none of the inside of the apartment Mother describes.

There were many children in our building and on our street, and I believe we were quite happy playing outside much of the time.

Some of the girls skipped rope, the boys played marbles, and others rolled their hoops along the street or rode scooters. The streets were narrow and paved with cobblestones; the vehicles were all horse-drawn carriages, wagons and buses.

The sidewalks were paved, and I remember that is where my longing for roller skates began. I was fascinated. I imagined having little wheels on my shoes, and the idea of gliding along the sidewalk was pure magic.

I remember some big wooden boxes under all the windows on the main floor on which the bigger children, my siblings included, climbed and played. The boxes were the width of the window, from the ground to the window sill, about a foot wide out from the wall, with a slanted wooden cover on the top. The boxes contained sand that could be accessed from inside the apartment and was intended to be used to control or put out fires.

It is possible my brothers and sister had friends among the children on our street, but I only remember the name of one of the boys because it continued to come up in a family story. Even after so many years, I am aware of an instinctive bias when I first meet someone named Heinz.

The story goes that Heinz was a nasty boy, but his unforgivable offence was his torturing of an earthworm. He held the worm, one end in each hand and kept pulling in both directions while snarling, *"Regenwurm kannst du noch aushalten?"* (Earthworm, can you still stand it?) until he tore it in half.

Mutti did not try to hide her contempt for him and impressed on us, at each telling of the story, how wrong it is to abuse any of God's creatures.

Mother goes on to describe Rostock.

How do I like Germany? I've seen so very little of it that I really can't judge but what little I have seen, and lived in, I like very well and have a very good impression of it generally. I didn't see much of Hamburg but saw some real pretty places there. Rostock is an old city of some over 100,000 inhabitants. It's really interesting to see the old buildings, some of them built five and six hundred years ago. The churches are outstanding among them. There is still part of the old city wall standing with its gates and towers. The city has, naturally, grown far beyond the part that was once enclosed by the wall. Some of the streets in these old parts are so narrow that people can almost shake hands across the street. The modern streets, of course, are much wider, more like the American and Canadian cities.

To you all I send my most heartfelt greetings & all good wishes for good health and God's blessings for a happy Christmas season and a prosperous New Year. With love to you all also from Werner.

Your niece & cousin Elisabeth

The following note, addressed to Aunt Helen in Wisconsin, was enclosed with a letter to the family in Canada.

I hope you won't mind that I don't write more to you personally, my letter would be too bulky & I've written about everything of interest in the one to the folks. It is useless to try to send cards or letters so they will get there in time for the birthdays. I hope & pray that when our birthdays roll around again, world conditions will have changed & peace will be restored. Why can't we two "exiles" live in the same town. I don't believe that about being the makers of our destiny or how that goes, but life is short & then we'll part no more.

My best love to you & yours, Betty

Helen in turn enclosed a note, written to the family on Boxing Day 1939, with Mother's letter:

Dear Parents,
I would have liked to have written a letter also but did not wish to delay Betty's letter. Perhaps you will have it before New Years ....

We join our prayers with all of Christendom so that peace will reign again on earth.

Your Lene

Mother's next letter is the first one from the address of our own home in Rostock.

Königsberger Straße 43

Dear Parents, brothers and sisters,

I don't imagine this will reach you for Christmas, and I am sorry about that. Werner was here two weeks ago and brought your letters from Hamburg. You can imagine how pleased we were to finally receive something from you ...

Everyone here who hears is amazed that I found us a place to live so quickly. They say I have my 4 children to thank for that. Then I say to them "yes my children are my luck." All vacant residences must be reported to a department of the police who give preference to "Kinderreiche" (child-rich) families. (Kinderreiche families have 3 children or more). You are then on record and you have to go twice a day and if anything suitable comes up (number of rooms, cost of rent etc. is shown) you run there immediately ...

Now it depends on when we can get our furniture shipped from Hamburg. I hope it will be before Christmas because it would be too hard if we could not all be together. I haven't seen the boys since 20 September and miss them terribly. They are still with their grandmother in Hamburg. Werner says she takes good care of them and does not want to think about giving them up. She had hoped we would be living in Hamburg.

I am beginning to feel less strange here as I learn my way around and it is not as big cityish as Hamburg although Hamburg is prettier in some ways.

Now I have wandered way off the subject of my new home, as I am wont to do. Our flat is in a small apartment building (family houses exist only for the rich) in a new part of town fairly far from the shopping area of the old city. (I will write more about the town later). It is in a long row of attached houses, each one separated from the next by a common wall. There are three storeys in this building, two flats on each floor, right and left, also completely separated. It is not very big but very pleasant and affordable.

Most importantly we finally have a home .... Everyone praises the boys. They are well behaved and nice. They don't appear to be harmed by the situation.

Heidi would be better off if she did not have to be with strange *people so much of the time. She has had to endure too much schoolmarm-upbringing from the elderly maiden aunts. She misses the boys and has little contact with other children. Now she goes to Kindergarten. She enjoys it so much it has really cheered her up.*

She speaks only German now. All four of them have learned to shake hands and say "guten Tag" and "auf wiedersehen" and Heidi adds a little curtsy. Tante Drefall, the landlady here and Tante Hete, where they both like to play, taught her to do that.

Baby is a little imp. She gets to be more and more like Carl in her personality. She is everyone's sweetheart. She has grown a lot and is much less babyish. She speaks much more since she only hears German and learns very quickly. She calls Tante Hete and her friend Tante Trude simply Tete and Tude. Her hands get "muckig", Tante Hete cooks "Suppfsen" (soup) *and a "Picke-Nade (Nadel) macht au, dann Baby tot"* (loosely translated: poke-needle makes ow, then baby dead) *With any thought and every mood she has a special expression. Yes, Esther, I think she is still so "cute."* (Esther was one of my mother's younger sisters.)

Tante Hete was my father's aunt, our great aunt, and the living situation must have been very difficult for everyone.

The only other time I met Tante Hete, some years later, I had the impression of a straight-laced, rather rigid, imposing figure and Mutti's comment about *too much schoolmarm-upbringing from the elderly maiden aunts*—seemed like an apt description. On the other hand, it was very generous of her to put up with a stranger and her small children for what appears to have been several months.

Tante Hete and Tante Trude were retired schoolteachers and lifelong friends, and their names are inextricably linked in my memory. Tante Trude was not actually our relative, but since we were never allowed to call adults by their first name she was also a *Tante*.

Tante Trude lived in a second-floor, corner apartment with a bay window protruding over the sidewalk like a large nose. The boys referred to this as *TanteTrudes Nase* (Aunt Trude's nose) and I have the impression that she also had a somewhat prominent nose.

We heard later that Tante Trudes Nase was knocked off during an air raid. We never learned the details but she was not at home and was not hurt.

> *My letter is getting very thick and I could still write so much more, sense and nonsense ....*
> *I can't think of anything to ask. When the letter is gone, the questions will come to mind. You will surely write everything of interest anyway. Our thoughts and prayers are with you for Christmas, and you are here in spirit with us.*

Kindergarten would have suited Heidi very well. She was always very socially adept and made friends easily. Mutti sometimes regretted that Heidi did not have more time as the baby of the family before I was born. Having to be a big sister and holding her own with two older brothers may have been the cause of so much contrariness. Heidi was very proud of the fact that she remembered Oma and Opa and some of the aunts and uncles in Canada and, of course, I did not. The following note included at the end of this letter would have been Mutti's way of devoting time to Heidi and distracting her.

> *Liebe Oma & Opa and all, all you others.*
> *Thank you for the little letter. The boys are with Grandmamma. We are still with Tante Hete. Soon we will have a new home and then the boys will come and sometimes Daddy. Then we will be very happy. I am going to school. It is very nice and there are many boys and girls that play with me. Yesterday it snowed and Mamma took us for a walk.*
> *Pretty wishes and much from Santa Claus. Your Heidi.*

In 1940, Mutti either did not write regularly, or the letters were lost. A postcard addressed to Mr & Mrs M.A. Mundt in Sheboygan, Wis. USA (Helen and husband Marvin) was sent on Easter Monday. It is a picture of a part of our street.

Written on the front is the description:

Königsberger Straße: An extension of our street. We live two blocks along. Here is the bus line to downtown.

On the back:

Dear Parents and Siblings.
I hope you had a happy Easter celebration. Werner was here for 3 days, the first time since Christmas and left again at noon today. He is a bit chubby and healthy. The children are all happy. In spite of wartime conditions, we had a lovely Bescherung (gift-giving). *Mother-in-law was here for a week and a half, she stayed at Tante Hete's. She's very good, especially with the children. She brought presents and hid the Easter sweets and everyone had fun. Yesterday, Werner, the boys and I went to church. We thought of all of you. Today is Werner's Birthday* (March 25).
Much love and many blessings. Walter starts school next week. I have a little "Pflichtjarsmädel." Your Christmas parcel arrived shortly before Easter. Thank you so very much. Many good wishes to all.

Pflichtjarsmädel were the young girls in the Hitler Youth who were required to spend a year, after completing grade eight, working in a household and assisting mothers with children. I remember Mother telling stories of the various levels of competence of these girls and one in particular who stood in the centre of the room with the broom and swept only as far as she could reach in each direction.

I don't know how much Mother contributed to their *Hausfrau* skills, but there were no round corners in her house and they would have been taught how to clean properly. The girls were a big help with us children.

In October, Mother wrote again.

> *My dear Parents,*
> *We received your loving letter of 19 August on 20 October. This has been the shortest time that a letter was underway to us. You can imagine how happy I was to get news that was not months old. I have worried so much about the boys and wondered where they are and how they are. It was a great relief to hear that at least so far everything is fine and hope it continues that way ....*

The *boys* Mother mentions are her six brothers, all but one of an age to be drafted. This continued to worry her for the duration of the war and the long periods between news from home. Aside from this concern, she does not express her feelings about the war. Perhaps because letters were being censored and it was not safe to do so.

> *A short time before we received this letter we had one sent in February from Helen with one from Elsa K. to her. It seemed funny to read a letter in October that was written in February, but I enjoyed it anyway.*
> *I must sadly confess that I have not been as good about writing as I would like to be. The news that we have a new little niece interests me greatly. We wish much luck and many blessings to Georg & Elsa! No doubt their little daughter already makes them very happy. Bobby must be quite a little man already, the children talk of him often as well as the rest of you.*
> *Luischen does not remember but chatters along when she hears the rest of them. When asked who else is where Opa is, she always mentions Hans first. Then Etti (Esther) & Dudie (Ruth) & Marik (Margaret). Then it's Onkel Carl, "he carried me on his shoulders in the picture" and Willie, who is nice. About Oma & Opa she says they are over the big water and they should come here. Then there are the questions "Where is Amerika?" and others.*
> *Heidi is a real little mother. They tend to play in pairs—*

> *Walter & Heidi, Carl & Baby (that is what we mostly still call her). Sometimes there is a bit of jealousy "ours is better than yours" etc. but for the most part, they get along pretty well. Walter is very interested in school and is happy doing his homework. Heidi often sits at the table with him and very importantly also does her homework. She already copies the numbers and letters. Carl tries it too, but he often gets it backwards or upside down.*

Much later in life, Carl felt that he was dyslexic and suffered from attention deficit disorder. He struggled with his schoolwork but was always the most patient and kind with me.

There is a family story about a time when his patience was seriously tried. Mutti had to go out, and Carl was left in charge of me. No doubt a neighbour was alerted, and he could go to her if there was a problem. I don't know where Walter and Heidi were. It is possible that we were confined indoors because I was not feeling well or I was just miserable, but it seems I cried and grizzled the whole time, and he could do nothing to stop me.

Finally, in desperation, he dragged me down the hall, knocked on the neighbour's apartment and when she opened the door, gave me a little shove, saying, *"Nehmen Sie die bitte. Ich kann nicht mehr."* (Please take her. I can't take any more.)

> *The big ones have not changed so very much but through life in the city something is lost and I regret that. They no longer show an interest in nature or animals etc. but that could also be because of the war which seems to fascinate them. They talk about soldiers, aeroplanes, flak, u-boats and whatever else goes along with that. Sometimes when the soldiers march past, they march along and sing the marching songs. That amuses the soldiers ….*

War Time Impressions

The boys would have seen themselves on the same side as the German soldiers. They would not have understood that their Canadian family was not. We all learned to identify the markings on the aeroplanes flying overhead; the ones with a cross that showed them to be German were the *good* ones, and we cheered them on.

The soldiers singing as they marched was a typical sight. Everybody seemed to sing at every opportunity. German folk songs are generally ideal for marching. Most of the lyrics, while patriotic, might not have been alarming until their intent became clear in the years to come. We learned them all.

As an adult, I once found myself absentmindedly singing one of the songs from that time. I was unsure of the words, and their message escaped me. I was shocked when I found the lyrics in German and English and understood their sinister meaning for the first time. It was the *Horst Wessel Lied,* a song praising the SA *(Storm Division)* for its resolve and determination to banish perceived oppressors of the German people. The song, a co-national anthem at the time, has been banned in Germany since the end of WWII.

I can't be sure which impressions of this particular time were my own and which are based on stories told to me later.

I don't believe I was ever fully awake when the siren was sounded and we rushed to the air raid shelter. I have only the vaguest memory of being taken out of my bed, bundled up and carried down some dark stairs. In a later letter, Mutti wrote that we had only four or five of these alarms, over a period of several months.

When both boys were in school and Heidi started kindergarten, I was very often alone with Mutti, and she took me with her wherever she went. I remember walking with her, holding her hand, skipping along when she did her shopping or went to visit the aunts. She was always courteous and considerate of others and often stopped to greet acquaintances.

I don't know how the instructions to discriminate against Jewish people were communicated, but I know my mother was outraged at the very suggestion. I was only four years old at the end of our stay in Rostock, but I know her indignation was evident at the very thought of forcing another person into the gutter from the sidewalk. I hope she was never faced with that situation.

> As usual, I have wandered way off topic and have only told about us but I hope that will be of interest to you. After all, you know much better than I what is happening there.

Tante Hete and I visited a friend of hers in the Markgrafen Heide (heath), which is actually a big forest and not a heath at all. The woods were lovely in all their autumn splendour. The fruit harvest is not very good, as many of the best fruit trees froze last winter. Werner has managed to put together some winter supplies for us in spite of this.

Werner has been in West Galicien, in Mielec über Krakau for about three weeks. He is employed by the "Reichsumsiedlung als Taxator." There are several men there, also from Rostock, that work together in the same area. Each day they are assigned to a location, given a car and then drive to farms, assess the land etc. and estimate the value. Werner writes that the work is pleasant and not difficult, and he is making approximately double what he was making previously.

I don't know exactly where your homeland was, but believe it is further east near Lemberg. Is that correct? Werner does not speak well of the region nor the people. He is trying to find a more permanent position in Posen and if he succeeds we will join him there ...

Werner has changed quite a lot. I can hardly believe that he is the same man. Physically he is much improved. He feels well and has gained a lot of weight, but his personality has also changed. Whenever I wonder if we should have stayed in Canada or that I would rather be there, I think of Werner and it is alright. So much depends on whether you feel satisfied with your surroundings ....

Mother writes that we all took cod liver oil but that isn't quite true. They tried to give it to me more than once but I was not able to keep it down. I threw up, not only the oil, but whatever else I had eaten that day.

The others did not let me forget that I was a spoiled baby because I was given some yummy-tasting orange vitamin tonic instead.

Several years later, when food was scarce and we were given some cod liver oil, I wanted to be a *big girl* and take it like the others but my gag reflexes again betrayed and humiliated me.

> *I am also well again after a sinus infection which made me miserable for some time. My lungs were also checked out and found to be healthy. I also had some teeth filled. I seemed to be running from one doctor to another. Heidi had ten ultraviolet treatments to which she had to be taken. It was supposed to improve her appetite and even though she is very delicate the doctor says she is healthy. Today she received a new doll from Tante Hete for eating so well.*
>
> *It is a shame that Jacob has to do all this heavy work while his spiritual talents lie dormant. Both he and Marvin should be here where teachers are much in demand. Here they would not have to fear, or hope, that they had to leave their teaching positions before their 65th birthdays. Teachers here have between 50 and 100 students in a class, at least now during war time, but there is a shortage of teachers even in peacetime. The people, work and worldly goods are not evenly divided in this world ....*

Jacob, Mother's oldest brother, was educated as a Lutheran parochial schoolteacher, and the Marvin she refers to also trained as a Lutheran teacher. Marvin married Mother's sister, Helen, and they moved to the US. Neither of the uncles ever returned to teaching.

My mother would have made much better use of an education as she preferred reading a book or teaching her children over housework. Although she excelled at school, she only received a very basic education. As the oldest girl in a family of twelve children, she was expected to stay home and help with the farm work and the care of her younger siblings.

In another letter from 1940, Mother enquires after everyone in the family and adds her concern for her sister in the US.

> *Helen will also reply to your letter, Father. She complains that you write to her so seldom and in fact everyone writes only rarely. She is all alone over there and feels quite lonely. When one is at home with brothers and sisters and a circle of friends, one does not feel lonely but to be alone is not always easy. Please try to make it a bit easier and more pleasant for her with your letters. Even a short letter is a ray of sunshine in the grey days.*
>
> *To all of you, our nearest and dearest family, we wish you all the best, also from Werner, who always enjoys your letters, and of course from the children. I think of you constantly ...*

Margin note: *When the post improves, I will send pictures.*

On December 2nd, Mother follows up with two small note cards written during a stay in the hospital. The gynaecological procedure she underwent is now far less invasive and would require a hospital stay of only one or two days. She seems to have endured the major surgery of the time without pain medication. I am grateful that it was successful and she did not have to endure this again.

> *Hello everybody,*
> *Just a card written in bed. Am in the hospital & this is the 6th day after my operation. Don't be frightened, it isn't anything so tragic & I'm getting along quite well. When you get this, I'll be quite well again & stronger than I was before. The first days were terrible & I am still suffering some but am getting better from day to day.*
> *Werner's mother is keeping house. Walter had the measles last week and the other three have them now, but she says she manages very well & the children are very good..*
> *Werner is at his third place in Poland now, changed again a few days ago but I don't know any more than that. He's in the Warthegau which used to belong to Germany. Hope we'll find a home there at last. He's coming for Christmas. Hope this will find you all well & that you can read it, I'm still on my back. Don't worry, I'll write soon again.*

In a second note, in German, she described the length of time her recovery may require. I am not sure that she would have been able to follow current advice not to return to normal activities for about 6 weeks, and get more rest, and avoid heavy lifting or long periods of standing, for another 3 months.

> *Since no one came to mail this for me I will add a bit more today. Sunday, after twelve days I was allowed to get up. I am supposed to spend several more days at Tante Hete's until I am stronger. This is a private clinic near her home.*
> *The children are well. They are already looking forward to Christmas and are making mangers and nativity figures. They love to make little surprises. Yes, Christmas, the celebration of*

love and peace, when "Peace on Earth" rings everywhere on earth but still there is no peace. But our inner peace, that the Christ child brings, cannot be taken from us by the war.

With happy greetings for Christmas and many blessings for the new year ....

As the war dragged on, Mother expressed her worries in a letter to her sister Helen in English.

Rostock, 3.2.1941

Dear Helen and family,

Your letter was, as always, a happy event, even though its contents were, of necessity, rather disturbing. The news about Willie was the greatest shock of all, even if I had been half expecting it and should have been prepared. Even if it doesn't mean much for the present, it was, no doubt, a shock to you all, but, being on the "other side," I think it is even more so for me. And that it just had to be Willie, shy, quiet, modest, backward little Willie. The training was, no doubt, just what he needed to shake him up a bit, but I can only pray to God to protect him from the rest.

Isn't it a crazy world! Why must there be war at all and why does Fate arrange it so that people are forced to be the enemies of not only people of their own nationality but even members of their own families. As what was Willie trained and where? There must have been several boys from home about the same age. Wonder how he took it ....

Willie was one of Mother's younger brothers, and she repeated the concern for him and the worry about her other brothers. Eventually, my grandfather managed to have Willie exempted from military service as he was needed at home on the farm. Some of his siblings felt he would have benefited from more time away from home.

Another thing that made me feel pretty bad was that the folks are having such a hard time and have to work so hard. And it doesn't help either to realize that when we were all there and could help we didn't do nearly as well as we could have, and now that we have more sense—or is it only because we can't be there to help that makes us think we'd like to? Parents like ours, who did so much all their lives, not only for their enormous families, but thereby also in other ways for a country, ought to have some kind of a reward ....

Werner wasn't here for our 10th anniversary so we couldn't celebrate that. Christmas holidays were nice tho. Werner came on the 22nd and his mother was here until the 28th. First Christmas Day we were all invited to dinner at Aunt Hete's and on the second day we had her here for ours. We all had lots of presents, lots of eats and also took in several good movies. I go once in a while even when he isn't here, sometimes with Aunt Hete and her friends, sometimes alone. Werner had two weeks vacation and then was sick for nearly another week so we had him here for three weeks. That was the longest time we've spent together since I left Hamburg in Sept. 1939. After those three weeks, he won't get off so soon again. Ordinarily he is to have a week every two months and three weeks summer vacation, again with fare paid.

I'm quite proud of my old man, he earns about M.400.00 a month besides "Tagesgeld" (daily stipend) for room and board. His superiors are well satisfied and he's well liked among his fellow workers.

As for our health, outside of a few severe and some slight colds, we're all well. I still can't work so hard and tire quite easily but otherwise my operation seems to have been successful.

When you write home, tell them what I wrote and send our love, or send this if you like.

Your sister Betty

My mother's memory for the birthdays in her family was remarkable. In the following letter, she sent wishes of *good luck and God's blessing* to nine family members, including her father.

Dear Parents, Brothers and Sisters,

We received your loving letter of 6th January about 12th February. Since airmail is significantly faster I will use it, at least this time. If one writes frequently it is too expensive but now and then I will allow myself the luxury so that you have news of us more quickly. I know from your letters that you worry about us, which we know anyway, but when you receive a letter you should be reassured. It's the same with me. When I don't hear for a while I worry, especially about the boys but so far everything seems to be fine. Pray God that it continues that way ....

It has been very quiet here all winter, no air raid alarm to *disturb our sleep and we know nothing of bombs and such here. If it gets bad later, which we hope not, I will go to Werner with the children as he is further from the danger zone.*

Margin note: Please excuse this cut off page. I made some mistakes and as this paper is hard to come by I did not want to throw it out.

Margin notes were my mother's way of adding a PS. The shortage of paper was constant and she always wrote very small, from the very top of the page to the last fraction of an inch at the bottom. Consequently there was no room for a PS. She managed to add these notes by turning the page sideways and writing in whatever tiny margin she had allowed herself.

Another family habit, which my mother used all her life, was to refer to a couple or family, by the husband's name in the plural. In her letter Jack and Millie became Jacks, Helen and Marvin became Marvins with no apostrophe, simply the plural for the couple and their children.

I am happy to hear that you are all well. I read all the news with a great deal of interest. Now I think of all the birthdays coming up in the next few weeks ,...

Our most sincere thanks for all of your good wishes to us. Carl's birthday was very nice. There were several presents and cake. Tante Hete, Tante Gitta and little Dirk, who live in Hamburg, came for coffee in the afternoon. Gitta is Hasso's wife. Hasso is Carl's godfather. Dirk is their 1 1/2 year old son whom we had not seen before. The children were delighted with him, and all of them played very nicely together. Carl was sorry that Daddy and Opas were not here.

Werner is still in Pleschen, in the Warthegau. At Easter he will likely come again for about two weeks. He has not been drafted into the military yet, but it remains a possibility. Hasso is in or near Paris and Hans-Jürgen is in Poland.

Aside from the odd cold, we are all in good health as well.

Margin note: *Mother, you should write again sometime. When I get a letter and there is nothing in it from you, it feels as though I have come to visit and you are not at home.*

A short, undated letter came from Father to Carl for his sixth birthday. This is all I can make out of Father's handwriting. He wrote in German but referred to himself as "Daddy." I imagine this was because we had not stopped speaking English very long before.

> *My dear Carlchen!*
> *So now I must belatedly congratulate you on your birthday ... stay healthy and happy. Your Daddy wishes for you whatever you wish for as you blow out your birthday candles. You will soon start school, so study well and always be good and listen to your mother. Since I can't be there you all have to show Mutti much love and spoil her a little.*
> *When Mutti talks to you about things it is because she loves you, so you must always do as she says. If you are not sure if you should do something, ask your Mutti.*
> *Tell Mutti that I am very happy that she bought herself a dress that pleases her. I already urged her to do that in my last letter. Give Mutti a kiss for me.*
> *Well Carlchen, I am sending you and your brother and sisters a box of bon bons. I hope they taste good and you enjoy them. When I come home we will go to town and buy ourselves something else, that will be fun. Give my love to your Mutti and your siblings.*
>
> *Your Daddy*

Mother's next letter is dated June 26, 1941, four months after the previous one, and I assume some had gone astray.

> *I received your lovely April letter on June 4. On April 30 I received one from Helen sent on April 10. Airmail is so much faster but, of course, I am happy to receive any news from home. I hope you have already received my reply to Lene's letter. I wonder how you are, dear Mother? You have had such an ordeal. Nobody wrote that you have had a "Wild Fever" since Christmas. I hope you have completely recovered by now. Also your poor arm, how on earth are you coping?*
> *How did you spend your 40th Wedding Anniversary, did you celebrate or do you also not feel like celebrating? I thought of you on your day and wanted to write but I was waiting for news from Werner. Since there is nothing from him I don't want to wait any*

longer. Who knows how much longer it will be possible to get mail to you. If the mail does not work anymore, I will try to send news through the Red Cross.

I wish you God's blessings and may he grant you many more happy and peaceful years together. For your golden anniversary we must all try to be with you again. It seems a long way off but ten years passes quickly and it would be so nice and it is something wonderful to look forward to.

Oh, that this were all at an end already! And yet, we can't complain. We, at least personally, are still fine. Things are still fairly quiet here and in the last six months we have had maybe 4 or 5 air raid alarms, but things stayed quiet.

I worry about Werner. If the work he is involved in the East comes to an end, it is not out of the question that he could end up in the armed forces. Both his brothers are enlisted but in administrative duties.

The children are well again after a bout of mumps which was not very serious. They spend much time outside and are getting quite brown. We finally have some nice weather now after a cold, late spring. I don't see any fields here but am told the crops look good.

Another day has passed and my letter is still here. I received a card from Werner. He is fine but is working very hard, mostly office work.

Pentecost Monday we drove to Müritz with the boys and Tante Hete. It is a summer resort on the Baltic Sea where we visited Werner's sister-in-law and little Dirk. The two sisters-in-law have rented rooms in a comfortable, very old farmhouse and will spend the summer there. It is a beautiful spot, but the weather was not good. This past Monday we went to Warnemünde where it was nice and warm and we swam in the sea and sunned ourselves on the beach. Yesterday Tante Hete took the girls there again. They really enjoy swimming and playing in the sand.

The children have all grown so much. Walter is getting along well in school. Carl starts school after the summer holidays, it is high time! Heidi is our wild child, but that is likely because her only playmates are boys, except for Luischen.

We have exchanged our Luischen for a Dorle. At Easter there was a young girl visiting with Tante Hete whose name was Dorle. She liked that name so much that she now wants to be called Dorle or Dorli.

It suits her better as Luise seems so stern for such a sunny little creature. She says when she goes back to Opa's, she will be *his Luischen again. If she tells a story and the others don't believe her or disagree, she says: "That was in Amerika and you don't remember that."*

No Longer Baby

In June of 1941, I was three and a half years old and still being called Baby. I have to rely on family stories for some of this as I don't remember it, but the *Big Ones* admitted that they had taunted me for being a baby. Then they thought it was funny that I chose my own name and laughed at me again. I don't know if I knew that my name was Luise. It seems I thought it was alright to choose a name for myself since I did not have one. I do remember having to assert myself when one or the other of my siblings or the adults continued to call me Baby.

My new name caused some consternation among the Canadian family. They would not have remembered this little news item and some of the aunts asked from time to time who Dorli was and did my family not have a girl named Luise?

I was called Luise in school in Germany, and I was never comfortable with that. The German spelling of Luise is also surprisingly awkward in Canada. When I give my name verbally, I have to spell it; in written form, the pronunciation causes confusion.

My middle name is Dorothea and at age three and a half I chose to be called Dorle, this became Dorli, or Dorchen, all diminutives of Dorothea. It was usually Dorli, and I liked it well enough until our return to Canada. My cousins, who didn't speak German, couldn't pronounce Dorli and called me Doily. I was dismayed to learn it was a crocheted thing on furniture.

I was given another chance to choose my own name, back in Canada, when my Aunt Margaret asked me what I wanted to be called. I was somewhat surprised, but I didn't hesitate to choose Dorothy. Except for the odd awkwardness of using my middle name, I have been happy with my choices.

Mother's next letter, dated July 20, was an unusually prompt reply to a letter received just two days earlier.

> *Your kind letter of 19 June arrived on 18 July. I also had one a few days ago from Helen & Elsa, also sent on 19 June.*
>
> *I am so pleased that your arm and shoulder are improving, even if slowly. It has certainly taken long enough. It is a shame about your back. Can the girls not help you in the garden? All that bending is too hard for you and it would be good for the girls to learn ....*

She goes on to speculate about her sister, Margaret, working in Edmonton.

> *She should at least be home for the harvest and then she could go to town for the winter. There she can also meet up with Hans now and then which would be nice for him. Walter and Elsa are also there and she should be able to meet nice friends in Youth Group ....*

Elsa is another of Mother's sisters. She married Walter Kastner and was usually called Kass by everyone except our grandparents. My mother's youngest brother, Hans, also known as Johnny, was attending Concordia Lutheran College in Edmonton at the time.

> *I imagine Hans came home for the holidays. He wrote to me but his letter did not reach me for which I am sorry. What did you write, Hans, that I was not allowed to have the letter?*

She seems to be suggesting that the letter from Hans was censored and did not reach her because of something he wrote. Interesting that she would ask, "What did you write ..." perhaps not realizing that If he told her it would likely be censored again.

> *Try again, please. I am pleased to hear that you are getting good marks in school. Your poem in the college newspaper was also very good. I always knew that my "Hänschen" would do well. I don't imagine I should be calling you that now that you are a grown man.*
>
> *Is Esther still in school? Is she learning something in particular or just getting a general education? Do you have a teacher or were the parochial schools closed in this war as well?*
>
> *I could ask so many questions but one should not write very long letters just now. The postage here is usually the same on airmail letters. It goes by weight and is expensive if I write too much or use heavy paper. It seems that short letters arrive more safely.*
>
> *Now it is 28 July. Last Sunday Werner surprised us with a 5 day visit. We spent 2 days at the seashore with the children, went to town a couple of times and so it goes. The holidays are always too short. Werner is fine and healthy. He is still involved in the relocation but will soon be doing farm management and then we will join him. It is all going too slowly.*
>
> *We do not feel we have anything to fear from the East and we are fine here. The children are happy and brown. We go to the beach now and then which is a bit awkward but nice. They would like to be in the country where there is more room to play. Carl would like a "real" dog that can pull a sleigh. Dorle seems most keen on horses but likes all animals. Walter received a violin for his birthday and will have lessons after the holidays. He is very enthusiastic but will that still apply to practising? His report card was very good. One can't really tell what interests Heidi except she would like to go to school. When we have a bigger home she wants a piano, "a thing to play like Opa has."*

The family piano was bought for my mother, and she had lessons when she was a young girl. All her sisters played but we were given the piano when we returned to Canada, and it eventually went to my Aunt Ruth's son, Kenneth, who excelled in music.

> *I must close for now. I will reply to the girls' letters soon. Werner sends love and good wishes. He finds your letters very interesting. Walter should write a thank you letter for your lovely letter to him which he enjoyed very much. He is not here at the moment, must be playing somewhere. He'll have to do it next time. We send our wishes for all that is good and also greetings to all the relatives and others that ask about us. I hope the harvest has turned out as you hoped and that the boys are there to help with it. The harvest here seems to be very good overall.*
>
> Your Lisbet & and little "Wildfängen"

A month later, on August 23, Mother wrote to her sisters in English.

> *I must at last answer your letters or you'll get discouraged and write no more and I was so glad to get them. You had a birthday yesterday Ell, (Elsa) I thought of you all day and wanted to write but didn't get time. I sent my love and good wishes "by wireless." I forgot to send them in my last letter; it was so long before your birthday but would probably have got there in time.*
>
> *Did you take your trip home, Helen? If so, be sure to tell me all about it real soon. I'm eagerly awaiting a letter, am always anxious about Willie and news in general from you all. Was glad to hear that you are all well and getting along not too badly. I found all the news very interesting.*
>
> *Did you get your sewing machine, Helen? It must be grand to have a washer. The only kind I have is a washboard and one of those plungers, a good one and it helps quite a lot. They have different methods of washing here, overnight soaking in softened water, in a boiler in the laundry much like the feed cookers some people have. These hold a lot at a time and we put the boilable clothes right from the soaking water into the boiler. That removes nearly all the dirt and that part of the washing is quite easy. The worst is the coloured things and I have quite a lot of them. They only wash every 4 to 6 weeks here, but I can't make it do that long and wash about every 3 weeks.*
>
> *Now I'd better write about us a little. Things are slowly developing in the direction of a new home for us, at least a temporary one. Werner is taking over a Gutsverwaltung, I don't*

know what one would say in English (Management of an Agricultural Estate), on the 1st of September. The family can join him 6 weeks later so we hope to be moving about the middle of Oct. Are we glad?!! Even if it is only for an indefinite time, we'll be together at last. We'll have our living free and a good salary. A lot of work and responsibility too but that's a part of life I guess, and it's work that Werner enjoys and I think I do too ....

Gutsverwaltung

In the 1989 recording by Pastor Dixon, my father described the training he had as a youth that prepared him for the work of a *Gutsverwalter* or *Agricultural Estate Manager*.

"As a boy I didn't have a choice. I had to go to military school and I hated it. I only lasted one year and was glad to get out of there. I was never a good scholar and when I left there I had to attend a private school to catch up on my French and Latin.

"We lived on a large farm with my grandparents and I just wanted to work with the horses. Agriculture was my life. When I finished grade eight I went to agricultural college where I began my career in farming on a large estate."

He goes on to explain the work at what he calls an *Apprentice Training Station* which follows agricultural college. He does not make it clear if all the practical experience occurred at the training station or if he went on to apprentice on an estate. This lasted for three years and he is very clear about the long hours and the extent of the work involved.

"We worked with the men in the fields, we worked with the cows and in the dairy. There were over 400 sheep and we worked with the shepherd.

"We had to learn how to turn potatoes into alcohol in the distillery, and we spent time in the machine shop and the carpentry shop. After all of that, there was office work where we learned to keep the farm records and the registration of the breeds of animals.

"Our days began at five in the morning and ended at ten at night. We were lucky to get a good night's sleep. A night watchman kept an eye on all the stock. If an animal got sick or needed help at calving or lambing times, we had to get up and look after them.

"After my apprenticeship, I became the assistant on a large

estate. We kept the same hours, but after a long day of hard work you could sleep well.

"Some of the workers had Sunday off, but for us there was no weekend. In addition to all the usual work, it was up to the assistant to ensure the feed was correct for all the animals on the estate. The proportions of protein, starch, calcium and whatever else had to be measured for horses, cows, sheep and even poultry."

It was customary for workers on farms in Germany to have a first breakfast of porridge before attending to the animals. A second breakfast of hardier fare followed, and the main meal was generally served at noon.

"Occasionally we could have an afternoon nap followed by *Kaffeetrinken* (a coffee break) before returning to work."

My father remembered the work was hard, but he appreciated the intensive training that qualified him for the *Gutsverwaltung* (Management) of Ziegelhof and the two adjacent agricultural estates in Poland he was managing.

As she continues, Mutti refers to our German grand-mother as Oma, but she always insisted on being called Omchen.

> *Oma has been here for 2 weeks and is staying till Sept. 1. She and Heidi are going to Schlesien to her sister-in-law for three weeks. They wanted to go to the coast, the place where Gitta is staying but that didn't work out and the warmer weather is past anyway so they'll enjoy the country more I think. Mother has the idea that Heidi is most in need of Erholung (rest, relaxation or more accurately, recovering good health or benefiting from the country air, etc.).*
>
> *I have a lot to do before we move and with less family I can do more work. I'm knitting a sweater for Heidi, it's nearly finished and I made her a dress. She should have more to take along on the trip but I don't know if I can manage it.*
>
> *I'm certainly enjoying Schwiegermutter's (mother-in-law's) stay here, more than she is, I think. It's been awful to be alone all the time. She's a very lively old dame and quite nice once you've learned to understand her. Once or twice I flew off the handle because she, like Tante Hete, is always telling me I can't manage the children and all the virtues and good training they possess is due to other influences.*

In spite of the differences of opinion there was a degree of acceptance and respect between Mutti and Omchen.

Monday P.M.

Didn't get this done before the post office closed on Saturday. It's a lovely sunny day for a change, it's been cool and rained a lot lately. We did a big washing, in the forenoon and we had it nearly done by dinnertime. Omchen cooked, she's good at it. Now the children are out with Omchen, as usual on nice days. I want to go and mail this yet, so I must hurry ....

Heidi is happily looking forward to her trip, but you'd hardly notice it. She doesn't get excited about anything the way most children do. Even if she—or more often, other kids—breaks a treasured toy or she loses something, she only looks surprised and a little disappointed for a moment and then forgets it. In a way it's alright but she's so careless with her things. Dorchen is still the little sunshine she was but a little hot-head and often cries a lot, guess she doesn't sleep enough, I can seldom get her to sleep in the aft. anymore.

The children here go out with lanterns in the evening, Japanese lanterns with candles inside. They walk and sing. Last nite ours went out too, and had me making lanterns half the afternoon. It doesn't get dark early enough yet tho and I won't let them stay up so late, so we came in and darkened the room. It was pretty and they had a lot of fun.

Now I must close and run. You can send this on to the rest. Oh yes, nearly forgot again. Do any of you know what became of Knut Patze? If you know where he is, please tell me about him. His mother hasn't heard from him for a long time and believes him dead.

With heartfelt greetings to everyone from us all, Werner is always interested in your letters and has often said he'd write but has never carried it out so far. Someday he'll surprise you all and write.

Love to all, your sister Betty

More good news of Papa preparing for our impending move to the country in another letter.

These lines should be directed particularly to the September birthday children. For various reasons it is now too late. Since I wrote not long ago, it is not so bad. For the beginning of your new year we wish you, Mother, Jacob and my little Dickie who is going to be 9 already, all the best.. I would have loved to have sent you a little package but sadly we have to leave that for other birthdays. I am so grateful that I am still able to write to you.

How quickly time flies! And yet it seems a long time ago since we were all on our farms and so much has happened ...

I have not heard from Werner in a week as he is very busy getting things ready for our move. Finally, the time is coming when we will all live together again as a family. Werner is managing 3 estates and we will live on one of them. The house is in bad repair and needs a lot of work but will be all nice and new and clean. The farm is also in a very bad state but it is a beautiful and fertile area, and it will be rewarding to see it thrive. Werner will have a secure position with the family's living expenses included and paid workers on the farm. It is located northeast of the city of Posen.

Carl started school a week ago already. He likes it well enough only "the Ulmenstrasse (Ulmenstreet) is so very long," he says. They have about a twenty-minute walk. Heidi is in Schlesien with Omchen and is enjoying life in the country. We are all looking forward to life in the country. I am sure I will have a lot to learn. The pictures are old, but I don't have any recent good ones, maybe later.

Heartfelt greetings to all from your
Werner, Elisabeth and Children.

Margin note: *Our new address is: Gut Ziegelhof bei Schwertburg, Kreis Eichenbrück, Warthegau. Write to us there!*

Sunday 19. October 1941

Dear Parents and Siblings,

I must finally answer your latest letter. I also did not write in time for Ruth's birthday. Our Dudi is already 14, and it seems like such a short time. Her baby time is the clearest in my memory. Also when the two little girls played "Mottel" (Mother), and when Esther started school and Dudi (Ruth) stood at the fence in the corner and watched longingly as the children played in the schoolyard. And now she must be about finished with school. I will think of you on your birthday, my "Schwesterchen" (little sister) and will pray that God will continue to grant you a happy and carefree youth.

If you have my last letter, you will imagine that we are all together out in the country by now but it still has not gone so quickly. Werner's "Chef" (that is what the person in charge is generally called even a doctor in a hospital is called der Chef by the nurses, etc.) feels it is better if the family does not come immediately. As I have said, Werner is working very hard and it is better if he can get organized and get used to the situation before he faces the demands of the family. We were all disappointed, but it is probably better this way. I am hoping it will not be more than a couple of months.

In about 2 weeks, I will visit him and will have a chance to have a look around. That will be a nice holiday for me. It is Werner's wish that Dorchen come along. She was to go to Tante Hete while Oma stays here with the others, then she told Tante Hete, in a very serious expression: "Tante Hete, I can't possibly come to stay with you, I have to go with Mutti to visit Papa, he wrote and said so." She is really looking forward to this. Werner is having the house prepared for us and in the meantime is organizing a household for himself. The wife of his Polish worker is keeping house for him. I am looking forward to the big house. It has 9 rooms, one of which will be a playroom for the children. We likely won't need to use them all, but after this tiny place it will be nice to have so much room.

Tante Hete, Walter, Carl, Heidi

A New Home in Ziegelhof

Monday afternoon. (20, October 1941)

Last night I stopped writing because my finger was very painful. Today it is worse. It seems to have something to do with circulation and, of course, it is the right index finger. It is very inconvenient and hurts a lot, which you, Mother, know all about. Carl has had open sores on his feet for seven weeks. He has to go to the doctor every day for Hohensonnen Bestrahlung (ultraviolet treatments). His wounds are also treated and they seem to finally be healing. The doctor says it is very much like impetigo. Walter's healed quickly and was not so bad.

Heidi has punctured her knee and although it is healing it also looks like impetigo. Other than that, our health is good. I too am feeling much better and stronger. Walter is still quite a nervous child which makes him restless at night and he has nightmares. It is fortunate that he likes to draw. He is quite good at it and amuses himself very well. I haven't been pursuing his violin lessons as we felt we would not be here long.

Carl is very conscientious about his schoolwork. If he hasn't finished his homework in the evening he can't sleep in for fear he will forget to finish it. He is often awake at 6 o'clock and asks: "Mutti, do I have to go to school at 8 today, is it time?" They go to school at 8 on 3 days a week and the other 3 at 10 and ten thirty. Even though they are in the same school, they don't always go at the same time and don't have the same teacher.

On Sunday, all 3 go to Sunday school and do so very happily. Sunday school is pretty much like at home. Dorchen feels left out but is too young to go and sometimes she goes to the "big" church with me.

Heidi had much to tell when she came back from 'Schlesien' (where she went for a visit with Omchen). She saw and experienced a lot on the big estate. Tante Katel, Werner's cousin, organized a Kindergarten in the village and Heidi went a couple of times but didn't like it because the other children stared at her and called her the "Fräulein vom Schloss" (the little lady from the castle).

When Oma comes she has to do "magic." She makes a coin or a button disappear up a sleeve or other part of her dress. It was fun but they didn't get it at first. Then one day Carl said, "Hey Walter, she can actually do magic." One evening she said she wasn't "aufgelegt" (in the proper frame of mind) and then the magic can't happen. Now they always ask "Omchen are you "aufgeregt" (agitated, excited) can you do magic?"

She plays with them a good deal of the time, reads to them or goes for walks.

Omchen

While many of the events in this story did not take place until we were living in Ziegelhof, Mutti's description of Omchen's magic evoked so many memories of her, I had to tell her story here.

Omchen's magic tricks were particularly exciting because we played a part in them. When she made a button disappear up her sleeve, she sent us off to look for it, hinting that we were getting warmer or colder as we searched the room until one of us found it. We learned eventually that if she was not *aufgelegt* (in the mood), it meant that she had not had a chance to prepare for the magic by hiding an identical button for us to find.

She was a remarkable character, and her visits caused great excitement. We were jumping with anticipation as we watched her alight from the carriage that had picked her up from the train station, and her many bulging bags were brought into the house. We wanted to say:

"Omchen, was hast du uns gebracht?" (... what have you brought us?) We learned quickly that this was not acceptable and we knew we would get the *look* from Papa.

Those many bags contained wonderfully interesting food, which we realized later must have been bought on the black market. Omchen introduced us to caviar, capers, smoked fish and many different kinds of sausage and cheese.

Walter told the story of her sucking the eyeballs from fish heads. Carl was skeptical; he remembers her sucking the open part at the back of the kipper heads, as that was the most succulent bit. They may both have been correct, but I'm inclined to trust Carl's memory as Walter loved to enhance a good story, a skill he likely learned from Omchen.

As we gathered around Omchen's chair to witness her magic or listen to stories, we noticed what looked like a cloth under her hair. Heidi, the impulsive one, asked, *"Omchen, was ist das auf deinem Kopf?"* (... what is that on your head?)

"It's a bandage. When I was a girl, I injured my head and they put this bandage on it," she explained.

"Did they have to pull each hair through the holes in the bandage?" Walter asked.

"Yes, and it took a very long time," she answered solemnly.

I did not realize for many years that her red hair, the same colour as mine and Carl's, was actually a wig.

Omchen's parcels at Christmas and for birthdays were always a great source of excitement. The presents were unique and interesting and whether they were useful or just for fun, we loved them.

The boys once received a Meccano set. They built marvellous structures, providing them with much entertainment. One year, Carl received a harmonica which he learned to play very well. Heidi and I were given paper cut-out dolls and their wardrobes, as well as hair ribbons and barrettes. Walter was very good at drawing and was the beneficiary of her art instructions and art supplies.

The parcels from Omchen usually contained a board game, some unique, others traditional. I learned to play the games, but *die Grossen* (the big ones) were already going to school, so they knew how to outsmart me. The idea of playing Parcheesi, called *Mensch Ärgere Dich Nicht* (Man, Don't Get Angry), can still send me into a panic. I was constantly being sent back home while the others never seemed to hesitate on their way around the board.

We played a card game called *Schwarzer Peter* (Black Peter) which I always lost. That made me Black Peter, and they smudged grey ashes on my nose and forehead to mock me.

Omchen was an artist and supplemented her income by painting. Visiting her in Hamburg years later, I admired her paintings of a series of Hummel images on small white tiles. The paintings were as beautiful as the Hummel figurines. Sometime before Helga was born, Omchen sent four small tiles with a picture of an animal representing each of us children. Walter, serious and sensitive, was a fawn, Carl the redheaded mischievous one, was a little red fox. Heidi, long-legged and always running and jumping, was depicted as a hare and I—another redhead—was a little red squirrel.

There is a much-told tale of a beautiful birthday *Torte* (cake) arriving in sad shape after its box had been turned upside down accidentally and Omchen exclaiming, *"Ach, wie schade."* (Oh, what a shame.) to which we, even as adults, always chorused her next words after sampling the cake: *"Aber Kinder, das ist die reinste Butter!"* (But children, that is the purest butter!)

Mother's letter continues.

> *Now it is Friday evening the 24th and my letter is still not done. My finger still looks bad but doesn't hurt so much anymore. This afternoon I went to Tante Claring for coffee with Tante Hete and Gitta, Hasso's wife. Hasso and Hans-Jürgen are both in the East in administration for the military close behind the front line. The stories that came out of Russia from the Mennonites and other Germans are being confirmed by the German soldiers.*
>
> *Tomorrow Tante Hete, Gitta and I are driving to the forest. The fall colours are beautiful. Sunday they are coming to us for coffee ....*
>
> *So now I have told you all kinds of things about our days here. I hope I have not neglected to answer any of your questions. I am happy to hear that you are getting slightly better prices for your grain, that wages are increasing and that you all seem to be well. Mother, you should have some treatments so that you don't have so much pain. All the news and for that matter everything in your letters is of interest to us. I might be able to make my letters more interesting if you were to ask questions so I would know what you would like to know.*
>
>   *With all our best wishes ...*

The Longing 44

The US entered the war against Germany in December of 1941 and correspondence with American relatives came to a halt in 1942. The following is part of a cover letter from Mother's sister Helen sending the last news from Germany to the family in Canada.

Sheboygan, Wis.
Sunday the 17 August, 1942

Dear Parents,
I want to add a quick note before I mail Betty's letter. Her letter arrived on Thursday but I could not find time before this ... Betty's letter was mailed July 28 and got here already on August 14. Airmail is sent according to weight from here too. We are always surprised, but pleasantly, when another letter gets here from them. Am thinking they will soon stop, now that the US has taken a more definite stand in regard to the war ....

All my heartfelt greetings from Marvin and the children and from your,

Helen

The opening of Mother's letter seems to indicate that any letters that may have been sent in the previous months did not reach us.

>   *Ziegelhof*
>   *14.5.1942*
>
> My Dear All.
>   We have not heard from each other for a long time so I will finally write. I wonder how everyone is, how did you come through the winter? The long cold winter has to finally make way for spring even here.
>   We have been with Werner in the country since before Christmas. Once we were here, Werner would not let us leave and that naturally suited all of us. In Rostock, the landlady's daughter, husband and small child are living in our apartment because of the shortage of housing, we cannot let it remain empty ....
>   There is nothing like country living. Since our furniture and household items are still in Rostock I travelled to the city to check things out. Everything was in order but I don't want to live there anymore. I brought our clothes, bedding and my sewing machine back with me ....

The House

Mother mentions in one of her letters that the house was run down. That did not mean anything to me, but I do remember some of the work being done on the house. It seems strange now that there would not have been indoor plumbing when we arrived. Papa had a toilet installed, and it was a big improvement over visiting the outhouse.

The kitchen was moved into the basement and this required a new staircase. My mother liked to tell the story of her part in the installation.

She was in the room as the men heaved the massive staircase into place. They went back and forth, debating whether it was properly aligned. When the discussion became heated and they saw her watching, one of them asked her opinion. She said it needed to go about a centimeter in one direction and some of the men agreed; others were skeptical. They found a level to settle the matter and there was high praise for *die gnädige Frau,* (the gracious lady) as she had been completely accurate.

Mother was looking forward to a more spacious home after our small apartment in Rostock. I remember a big front hall, a living room with space for the dining table near the door and the grand piano in the far corner. The floor-to-ceiling tile stoves in each room did not begin to warm a space of that size, and it was often uninhabitable in winter.

Papa had an office across the hall and there was another small sitting room which was always nice and warm. Further down the hall were the stairs down to the kitchen, the bathroom, our parents' and the children's bedrooms and our playroom.

We had four wonderful years there, and many fond memories of the house and the farm remain.

My partner, Larry, arranged a three-week home exchange for us in *Köln* (Cologne), Germany in 2018. We considered including a trip to Poland during our stay, but the likelihood of finding Ziegelhof after seventy-three years seemed remote. The farm (like all the towns and cities)—had been given a German name during the occupation, but the Polish names had long since been restored.

I enlisted the help of my daughter, Carla. I could only give her the German names I remembered, but with skill and persistence she not only ferreted out the location of the nearest town to Ziegelhof but found an English-speaking guide who could take us to what Carla was fairly certain was our farm. With this prospect in mind, and knowing we had the use of a large house in Germany, it seemed only right that I invite my younger sister, Helga, to join us. We grew to a group of six when her daughter, Kristin, Larry's daughter, Krista, and Carla joined us in Cologne for the trip to Poland.

In Poznan we connected with Anna—our guide and interpreter—and we set out in a rental van.

Not surprisingly, none of the surrounding countryside looked familiar, but I hoped I would recognize the house and perhaps some outbuildings.

We found a house, red brick as I remembered, but any similarity ended there. I was not convinced that this was the right place.

The house was derelict. The front porch was gone, replaced by concrete steps that faced the wrong way, and the spreading chestnut trees and tall poplars were no longer there; fields surrounded the house where the garden and fruit trees had been.

In front of the house there was no trace of the circular driveway I remembered, where the buggies and sleighs drove to the front door to take us to school and for outings. The grassy circle in the centre, the site of our birthday parties and Easter egg hunts, was gone, as was the stately linden tree. Several barns, as old and worn as the house, evoked no memories.

I hesitated to go around to the side of the house, afraid of what I would or would not find.

But there it was. Cement steps led up to a porch and the main floor of the house, and at ground level stood an arched doorway with a heavy wooden door. There was no mistaking that door into what used to be the kitchen. It didn't matter that the house was in bad repair, and the basement a black cavern; I had found my precious place, and I was awestruck.

So many happy memories of treats from that kitchen and games on the porch came flooding back; I was rooted to the spot.

A farm worker who questioned our trespassing called the owner, who agreed to talk to Anna on the phone. After hearing my story he gave the farm worker permission to let us into the house.

I was overcome to see it so changed and yet delighted to be there.

Helga had been born here, but we had left before she was old enough to remember the house. I showed her the room where I thought she was born, but it was such a tiny room, I may have been mistaken. It is also possible that the rooms were altered. There was evidence of doors being bricked up and others opened. The famous staircase was gone, but markings on the wall reassured me that it had been where I remembered it.

The owner stayed on the phone with Anna and when I mentioned the linden tree at the front of the house, the backdrop of family photos taken on special occasions, she asked him about it. He knew of the tree, but it had been struck by lightning and had to come down.

We lingered for a while and took pictures but once more, as I said goodbye, all I had to take with me were bittersweet memories.

Mother's letter continues on a hopeful note.

> *Werner has put much in order here and has received a very good offer which he will likely accept. Until summer we will certainly be here ....*

Managing Three Estates

In the 1989 interview, my father relates his responsibilities at Ziegelhof.

"I was fortunate that I was assigned the position of *Gutsverwalter* (Estate Manager) of three large mixed-farming estates. Each estate was about 4,000 to 6,000 hectares and most of the land was worked with horses. I had over a hundred workers on each of the estates and hundreds of horses to do the sowing, harvesting and hauling of grains, potatoes, turnips and sugar beets. We also had a large herd of cows, and milk products were sent from our dairy to the nearby villages. We raised pigs, sheep and poultry.

"My agricultural training was paying off. I worked day and night. Strict quotas had to be met but I was able to stay out of the military. To begin with, these positions were only available to men past the age of military service. I was lucky because this position became vacant at the perfect time for me."

Pastor Dixon turns to Mother and asks, "And Betty, how did you feel about life in Germany, coming from a farm in Alberta?"

"There were hard times for me too. Werner was not with us most of the time we were over there. The children and I always stayed together but we could not always live where he found work.

"We were able to join him when he took over the management of Ziegelhof and those were the best years we had over there. We had enough good food and the children were in the country and they felt free. There was a church but it was difficult and we didn't go."

Father picks up the story. "My mother insisted on sending our furniture to Poland and that meant we were quite comfortable."

Life in Ziegelhof

Ziegelhof was a wonderful place; life was good and the war was far away.

Mother describes our reaction to our new home.

> The children all seem much more healthy and don't want to hear about the city at all. They are outside all the time and get excited about each animal and the new spring awakening of nature. They are especially enchanted by five new foals and calves ....

In addition to the large barns for horses, cows and pigs, there was a carpenter shop, a blacksmith shop, farm workers outside, servants in the house and always good things to eat from the farm or the garden. We ran barefoot and wild and loved it all.

I am sure we were a nuisance to the Polish workers, who were always kind and patient and likely not in a position to complain.

One of our favourite haunts was the blacksmith shop. The blacksmith was a big man who always wore his leather apron and allowed us to watch him work from a safe distance. Sometimes he let the boys pull the rope that pumped the big bellows to make the fire flare up and send sparks flying.

We saw him shape the red hot iron rods into horseshoes, his big hammer ringing out on the anvil. There was a great hiss as the steam rose each time he plunged the hot metal into the water bucket to temper it. I asked him if it hurt the horses to have the horseshoes fitted to their hoofs and fastened with nails. In his halting German, he reassured me that it did not.

The carpenter had a small pot-bellied stove in his shop and, summer and winter, we visited him and watched as he hammered and sawed, planed and sanded, many large and small projects. We were fascinated to see handles for farm implements emerge from rough pieces of wood. Much of the work in the fields was done by hand, and the scythes, pitchforks, rakes and shovels all needed handles. I am reminded of those happy times when I get a whiff of freshly planed wood and see curly wood shavings on a rough wooden floor.

I know Mutti tried to keep us from watching the animals breeding, giving birth, or being butchered, but we managed to see it all. The animals were well taken care of and that was a good part of our education. I believe Carl's longing to be a farmer came from this time in our childhood.

Animals

We never tired of spending time with the animals on the farm. Every spring, dozens of day-old chicks arrived from a nearby hatchery and they were great fun. We attempted to teach the fluffy yellow chicks to swim, thinking if we caught them early enough they could learn. We gave no thought to their anatomical limitations but we always had to rescue them so they wouldn't drown.

In one batch, one of the chicks arrived with a broken leg. Mutti would not hear of it being put down. She wrapped a soft bandage around its middle, tucking the tiny leg up against its body. It seemed unconcerned as it hopped around on one foot. It would have been only a few days later that she felt the break was healed, and she removed the bandage. We watched as it hopped on one leg a few more times before running off among the rest of the chicks.

Dorothy with kittens

I fancied I had a pet goose for a while and for the most part the geese were friendly, unless the gander was among them. Then the whole flock seemed to become fierce, making a horrendous racket with their cackling and hissing, necks outstretched. We were warned that the gander was dangerous and we gave him a wide berth.

We were given a small white horse called Prinz but he was a big disappointment. He had been a circus horse, and if anyone tried to ride him he reared up and pranced in circles. This was way beyond even the boys' level of confidence, so we could only take pride in the ownership of a beautiful animal.

I was too small to groom a horse although we moved freely among them. We learned how to feed them a piece of carrot or an apple, and I remember those soft, velvety muzzles. As an adult, on the rare occasion I allowed myself to be persuaded to ride one, being on a horse filled me with sheer terror.

It was scary to walk very close to the bull when dared, as he snorted and pawed the ground in his pen when anyone approached. The cows were big and warm, and I was comfortable among them in the big barn where they waited to be milked. I always wanted to try milking but it was not allowed. We were told that the cows might not give up their milk if we fumbled it.

Carl loved all the animals but he really wanted a dog. One day Papa brought him a little fox terrier. Carl named him Phipps. He was mostly white with light brown eye patches and ears. He was friendly and playful, endlessly entertaining, and he and Carl were inseparable.

The piano once again came into play when Carl discovered that any kind of playing, or simply banging, on the piano made Phipps sing along. Carl laughed until the tears streamed down his face as Phipps pointed his snout to the ceiling and howled like a wolf. When Omchen gave Carl a harmonica, he learned to play it and that had the same effect on Phipps. He could never play for long if the dog was in the house because he simply dissolved into puddles of laughter when Phipps chimed in.

We hoped that Phipps howled with pleasure rather than pain.

> *The boys are in school here. It is about 3 kilometers. In the morning they are driven to school. In the afternoon they walk home now that it is warmer. After the summer holidays Heidi will also start school. She was 6 last Sunday. Soon we will no longer have any small children, but they bring us great joy ....*

Carriages and Sleighs

I also started school eventually. I don't remember much about the school but I have some recollection of the walk to or from the village where the school was located.

Mother writes in her letter that it was about three kilometers and the boys were driven in the morning but usually walked home when the weather was fine.

We often walked along the country road, where the fields on either side were sometimes broken up by small groves of trees or a long row of very tall poplars that served as windbreaks. Telephone poles lined one side of the road, and we delighted in putting an ear to a pole and listening to the hum. We imagined what we heard were conversations travelling along the wire and down the pole, but more likely it was the breeze making the wires sing.

If it was raining or cold, but we did not yet have snowy conditions, we were driven both ways in a closed *Kutsche* (carriage). The carriage was usually pulled by a matched team of horses and always driven by the *Kutscher* (chauffeur). Others could drive the one-horse buggy and, of course, there were many horse-drawn farm wagons and machinery.

Both summer and winter, the boys were sometimes allowed to sit up front with the Kutscher, and Carl was particularly interested in learning to manage the horses; this turned out to be a great help during the difficult times to come.

When Omchen was visiting and the whole family travelled in the carriage, the boys had to sit up front with the driver to accommodate us all. It was not unusual for us to sing at these times.

On one occasion, the boys began to sing a song they had learned in the schoolyard which was in questionable taste. It was also a song that had to be belted out, particularly the chorus.

When they began singing the song with great enthusiasm, Mutti was horrified, but she was helpless to stop them from her position in the back of the carriage.

The offensive line in the song goes something like this: *Enjoy life, Grandmother will be shaved with a scythe, but it is all for nothing because her face has not been lathered.*

Mutti's embarrassment was obvious but Omchen just laughed. She also knew the song and did not take offence.

One day, Papa had to go to a meeting in Schwertburg and I begged to go along with him since I was always bored while the others were in school. I was warned that it would be a long time for me to wait outside the meeting hall, but I was determined. Papa was always agitated and distracted when he had to attend these meetings but he agreed I could come along.

In Schwertburg, I amused myself as best I could, poking

around with pebbles and sticks and likely getting quite filthy. No doubt the Kutscher lost track of me as I wandered a little further away. After a very long time, Papa came rushing out of the meeting, strode over to the carriage and jumped in, the Kutscher flicked the reins and away they went. I ran after them and screamed but they did not hear me over the noise of the horses and wheels on the paving stones, and I was soon left far behind. I panicked. I did not remember the way, and I didn't know how to find the school where my siblings were either.

A friend of the family saw me running down the street crying and took charge of me. We had recently had a telephone installed, and she was able to call for help. The carriage was sent back to get me.

On cold, dark winter days, after the morning ritual of dressing warmly enough to please Mutti, we were driven to school in the *Schlitten* (sleigh) and collected at the end of the day.

Riding in the sleigh was particularly exciting when we went visiting as a family in the evening and came home after dark. We children were wrapped in blankets in the bottom of the sleigh where we could look up at the stars in the cold, dark sky, the only sound the muffled *clip-clop* of the horses' hooves on the snowy road.

Mutti often started us singing, especially around Christmas, and that added to the magic. She had the same experience when, as a child, she and her many siblings were bundled up in the hay on the bottom of a big sleigh on northern Alberta roads.

> *Now it is your turn to write. Even a brief note now and then, just a sign of life and to let us know if you are well. How are all the other siblings?*
>
> *I will close for today. Werner and the children send greetings. Please don't worry about us, we are all fine which we also wish for all of you with all our hearts.*
>
> *Love and greetings, Your Elisabeth, I almost forgot that!*

I don't know if Mother was dissuaded from continuing to write to the US or if letters were intercepted. None of the letters from the family in Canada survived our travels.

We did not move again after joining Papa in the Warthegau (the Polish territory annexed by Germany in 1939) as our address continued to be Ziegelhof for the remainder of the war.

Christmas in Ziegelhof

Mutti wrote

> *We have been with Werner in the country since before Christmas. Once we were here, Werner would not let us leave and that naturally suited all of us.*

We celebrated four Christmases in Ziegelhof, and I am sure I don't remember any one in particular, but I cherish the memories of the festivities that were so much a part of our childhood.

During Advent, the time leading up to Christmas, there was much whispering and planning, and Mutti helped us make little presents for each other; the older ones made cards and gifts for the parents. I don't recall what we might have created with our limited resources, but I remember I was terribly nosy and wanted to snoop and had trouble keeping even my own secrets.

While we were *basteling*, as Mutti called our crafting efforts, we learned and sang many of the Christmas songs we have never forgotten. When we lit the candles on our *Advents Kranz*, (Advent Wreath) on each of the four Sundays leading up to Christmas, Mutti taught us to sing *Macht hoch die Tür, das Tor macht weit* (Make High the Door, the Gate Make Wide) in preparation for the coming of our Saviour.

We might have sung other songs when we were allowed to help in the kitchen, which was filled with the aroma of the season's baking. We cut out and decorated cookies and gingerbread people and argued over who got to scrape the bowl and lick the wooden spoon.

Parcels arrived from Omchen in Hamburg and were shaken and smelled, poked and prodded to try and discern the secrets inside. Her parcels were the most welcome. She sent interesting, unique board games, art materials, books and goodies, never socks or underwear.

On December 23, we had our one chance to sing *Morgen Kinder wirt's was geben* (Tomorrow will bring something special).

When Christmas Eve finally arrived, the suspense built as the door to the living room was closed to us and only our parents and some of the house staff went in and out. I don't remember if we had to sit down to have dinner first or if that came later, but I do know we were dressed in our best clothes. For this important event, our clothes may even have been new, sewn by Mother with the help of the Polish women, often made from the best parts of worn adult garments as it was rarely possible to buy new fabric. Heidi and I wore dresses, and had ribbons in our hair, Walter and Carl were in smart short pants, knee socks, white shirts and possibly ties. Everyone's shoes would have been polished to perfection.

As we anxiously waited in the big front hall, we tried to look in the keyhole, jumping with excitement and anticipation, until a little bell rang and the doors were opened and the magic was revealed. We were filled with awe and wonder by our first view of the splendid Christmas tree.

Floor to ceiling, the big tree sparkled with silver decorations, reflecting the light from many small white candles on its branches and casting lacy shadows on the walls and ceiling.

We admired the tree as we each recited a little verse or poem we had memorized. These were poems about shepherds keeping watch, the singing of the host of angels, the bright star of the East, and, of course, the baby Jesus, Mary and Joseph. I stood on tiptoe as I tried to see what was on the table and which presents were for whom and what the goodies on each of our plates were.

Finally we could sing *Stille Nacht* as the Silent Night had arrived, and the moment for the *Bescherung* (the presentation of gifts) arrived. We could receive our gifts and nibble our goodies.

One year we each received a spade, the blades made by the blacksmith and the handles fashioned by the carpenter, just the right size for each of us to dig in the garden or the big sandpit nearby. Another year there was furniture for the playroom built by the carpenter, cupboards to hold our books and games, and tables and chairs to play on. Heidi and I were thrilled to find our old dolls newly dressed in lovely clothes with new hair made of sheep's wool curled with a curling iron. The clothes were beautifully put together out of tiny scraps of cloth. The dolls wore dresses, underwear, coats trimmed with velvet and hats to match. I still have some of those clothes. Our precious dolls were made brand new again. I don't remember the small trinkets and toys that were surely also there for each of us.

Every day, the candles on the tree were lit for a while and we sang as we watched them flicker and shine. *Kling Glöckchen* (Ring Little Bells) or *Ihr Kinderlein kommet* (Come Little Children) were some of our favourites.

None of our trees ever caught fire from the candles, and we left them up until at least January 6th, often later, as we were always reluctant to take them down.

Music in the Attic

My older brothers never had any trouble finding interesting diversions even when we were confined to the house in bad weather, and I was always happy to be included.

The attic in our house in Ziegelhof was not a low, dark, dusty room filled with old trunks and other junk. It was a large, airy space with a high ceiling running the full length of the house under the peaked roof. It was a great place to play on a rainy day. We did not have electricity, but the windows in the gables at both ends let in plenty of light. I think the staircase and the wooden floor must have been newly installed as the bare boards were smooth and light in colour.

The room was not entirely empty. The most intriguing find was a large wind-up, disc-playing music box. When it was closed, it was a beautifully finished, cube-shaped wooden box with an ornate metal wind-up handle on one side. Inside the box was a mechanism not unlike a large version of a traditional music box, but instead of a cylinder it played metal discs. It was bigger than the standard square record player I owned in the sixties and the metal discs were larger than 33 rpm records, possibly as big as eighteen inches across.

I was delighted to find I remembered it accurately when I saw it described online as an *automatic musical instrument in a box that produces musical notes by using a set of pins to pluck the tuned teeth on a revolving disc.* There were several such discs with the music box, and we never tired of listening to them.

Another machine that had been relegated to the attic was a wind-up gramophone, complete with the big horn and the picture of the dog listening to its master's voice. It was smaller than the music box and played 78 rpm records. We played them over and over. Walter had us in stitches, practically rolling around on the floor laughing, when he let the machine slow down as the music growled ever more slowly, in a lower and deeper voice before it died away.

The attic was eventually converted into a bedroom with several beds, complete with sheets, blankets and pillows, in anticipation of the arrival of children being evacuated from cities threatened by air raids. The children never actually arrived, and we only had one privately evacuated boy.

Papa's secretary, Fräulein Klemm, was from Dresden and when we heard how severely that city was being bombed, it was agreed that she should bring her brother, Wilfred, close in age to Carl and Walter, to stay with us. Immediately on his arrival, we noticed his Dresden accent. I am ashamed to say we mimicked and teased him mercilessly.

With Fräulein Janke at the pond

House Staff and Fräulein Janke

We were very fond of the Polish people who worked on the farm and in the house. Only a few names remain in my memory.

The cook—a lovely round, red-cheeked woman—was Hanna, and Irene was our favourite maid. She always seemed to have time for us and went along with all our crazy schemes.

Then there was Fräulein Janke. It was not clear what her role in the household was, but she frequently attempted to organize us, and Walter scoffed, "She thinks she is some sort of governess and we certainly don't need one of those."

We secretly referred to her as Yanktzip. This came about after we overheard Papa say, *"Die ist so eine Xanthippe"* (She is a Xanthippe), and Walter learned that it was not a term of admiration but likened her to a proverbial shrewish woman.

I don't imagine the rest of us really grasped what that meant, but we followed his lead and behaved badly. In the summer, we frequently managed to evade her and ran wild. Forced to spend time with her when confined to the house, we complained and were less than cooperative.

She tolerated much of Walter's bad behaviour, but eventually she complained to Mutti that he had insulted her when he said she was stupid. Mutti was really upset and told him to apologize. We got the idea that she also had some sharp words for Papa. This would have been in English which they spoke when they did not want us to overhear their conversation, but names were mentioned within our hearing.

It would not have occurred to Mutti to be present when Walter made his apology and she would have been shocked to hear him say, "Fräulein Janke, I am very sorry that you are stupid."

As an adult, he admitted that his arrogant behaviour and backhanded apology were unacceptable. "The Yanktzip wasn't as bad as I made her out to be. I was surprised she did not rat me out more often."

A Kiss for Maria

I sometimes forgot that I was not supposed to like Fräulein Janke, and I was probably more cooperative with her than the others. One Sunday, she invited me along on an outing with friends of hers. I am not sure why she chose to take me along. I imagine the other Polish people working for us would have said she wanted to show off to her friends that she was trusted to take the child of the *Deutschen Gutverwalter* (German Farm Manager) for an outing. I was proud to be the only one asked, and I accepted.

She had permission to use a small, one-horse, two-wheeled buggy for our outing. I had to be helped into the buggy over the big wooden wheel and someone shouted, *"gut anhalten"* (hold on tight), as we rattled around the circular driveway and out the gate.

At Fräulein's friends' house, we picked up a girl about my age, Maria, and her younger brother whose name I don't remember. There was only one rather narrow seat in the buggy with the tiniest armrest, but we all squeezed in. Maria was on one side, I sat next to her, with the boy and Fräulein Janke on the other side, holding the reins and driving the buggy.

We spent some time at a lake. We could not actually speak to each other. I was not encouraged to learn Polish, and these children did not speak German. As it was too early in the year to take off our shoes and socks to go wading, we had to find other ways to amuse ourselves. We started throwing pebbles into the water and setting small sticks afloat, and soon we were smiling and laughing. With much pointing and hand waving we improvised some sort of game where running around in circles seemed to be the main object.

When it was time to start for home, we were not as shy with each other. Back in the buggy, we exchanged smiles, pointing out animals in the fields and naming them in our own language. The road was not paved, but it was in good condition and the buggy rattled along, not bouncing us around too badly on the hard little bench.

I saw a big rock ahead on the road, and I remember thinking it looked like a very large turnip. Fräulein Janke did not seem to see it as she did nothing to avoid it.

Maria was laughing at my attempt to pronounce a Polish word

when the wheel on the other side of the buggy went over the rock. As the buggy tipped down on our side, it jolted us and knocked Maria forward. I watched in horror as she slid from the seat, off the side of the buggy and fell onto the road in front of the steel-rimmed wheel.

Fräulein Janke reined in the horse and stopped the buggy. She rushed around our side and with some difficulty picked Maria up and hoisted her onto the seat beside me. Maria wasn't crying and didn't speak. Her eyes were closed, her head hanging down, chin resting on her chest. I thought I should help her as she slumped on the seat, but I didn't know what to do. After a while, she vomited down the front of her pink dress. I felt terrible for her.

On our arrival at the children's home, Fräulein rushed into the house. Others came out and gently took Maria from the buggy. Everyone spoke in hushed voices and two older girls helped me down and led me into the garden where they played with me and picked flowers for me.

After a while, Fräulein Janke came outside and took me into the house. There were a number of adults standing around a bed on which Maria was lying, now in a white dress, her hands folded on her chest. She looked very pretty and peaceful. I knew she was dead, but I had never even lost a beloved pet and did not realize what a terrible loss this was.

Looking back on this, I admire the quiet calm the girl's family maintained around me. I did not hear or see any of the shock and grief they must have felt.

Fräulein was very quiet on the drive home. When we arrived I felt I had something important to tell. My older siblings were going to school and often had stories to tell and when I wanted to participate and made things up, they laughed at me. This story was real, and I blurted out, "The buggy went over a rock and the girl fell out and the wheel went over her stomach and—"

"No, no, hush, that is not what happened."

I was stunned. Why was Fräulein Janke saying that? Her explanation was wrong. She denied that Maria had fallen under the wheel and instead rambled on about the road being rough, and Maria not holding on, and falling over the side of the buggy. I imagine she did not want my parents to believe she had been careless and I had been in danger.

I was frustrated and angry because I knew *die Grossen* (the big ones) would once again not believe me even though they did not like or trust Fräulein Janke.

After a while, Mutti took me into another room, helped me change my clothes and washed my face and hands. For the rest of the day, I felt the adults and the siblings watching me, but no one encouraged me to talk about what had happened.

The only criticism of Fräulein Janke I heard came from my mother when at bedtime I told her that she made me kiss the girl when she was laid out on the bed. I didn't want to do it, but she had picked me up and held me over the bed, and I had no choice. Mutti said that was wrong and she shouldn't have done that. "We don't kiss our dead."

The Piano and Music Lessons

In my father's privileged position as the Estate Manager, he was able to obtain a piano. A beautiful shiny black grand piano was delivered with considerable fanfare. It turned out to be a source of a great deal of entertainment.

When I visited the house in 2018, I marvelled at how they might have managed to get the piano into the house. The doorways were not as large as I remembered, but perhaps, neither was the piano.

The boys, no doubt needing to find entertainment on rainy days, came up with the idea of positioning the four of us under the piano, our backs against the underside and on the count of three we all heaved and lifted the piano a few inches off the floor. I can't imagine that this manoeuvre would have been allowed if our parents had been aware of it.

The piano was always dressed in a silk scarf and displayed a beautifully ornate porcelain vase. It was something of a miracle that the vase never came to any harm. It is a unique hand-painted, gilded antique, much admired in our family. The names of the virtues represented by the two women, pictured one on either side, are inscribed on the bottom. One, in rose tones, is called *Schönheit* (Beauty) while the one in filmy blue on the other side is *Demütigkeit* (Humility). This family heirloom survived all our travels and travails and now belongs to my sister Heidi.

In a letter written from Rostock, Mutti mentioned violin lessons for Walter. I don't know if those ever became a reality. However, there was an attempt made to provide him with piano lessons.

One of the Polish staff members, frequently in the house, was a man known to us as the *Organist*. He sometimes worked in Papa's office, and he may have been the interpreter for the Polish workers on the farm, many of whom did not speak German. He seemed always to be involved when the men came to the house for their pay packets.

Mutti had taken lessons as a child and tried out the piano when it first arrived but I don't remember her playing it very often. The Organist played the organ in the Polish church, and he too was persuaded to try the new piano. He was likely the closest that they could come to having a piano teacher, and he was asked to give Walter piano lessons in addition to his other duties.

One day Mutti was in the room when Walter was practising scales. I remember the Organist as a quiet, somewhat shy man and the presence of the *Gnädige Frau* in the room was almost certainly intimidating. The poor man may not have had the courage to correct Walter in her presence when he played nine notes to a scale instead of eight. Mutti took pity on him and released him from that particular ordeal.

With an experienced teacher, Walter would likely have done well. He took up some musical instruments in his teens, but he never learned to play the piano nor the violin.

A Visit From the Stork

Helga, my youngest sister, was born in Ziegelhof in 1943. I was the only one not yet in school, and I was often bored.

I don't know who told me about asking the storks to bring me a baby brother or sister but I did so, frequently and with great enthusiasm. Storks were in abundance in the area. Papa had the men put old wagon wheels up in some of the tall trees, and the storks built their nests of sticks and twigs on them. We heard the whoosh of their wings when they swooped down into the grain stubble to catch mice or landed near the pond to hunt for frogs. Seeing them close up in the yard, I was in awe of them and truly believed one of them could bring a baby, and I called out, *"Lieber Storch, du bester, bring mir eine Schwester. Lieber Storch, du guter, bring mir einen Bruder."* (Dear stork, you're the best, bring me a sister. Dear stork, you're so good, bring me a brother.)

When there was actually going to be a little brother or sister coming, I was told it was growing in Mutti's tummy, but somehow a stork continued to be involved.

Omchen came for a visit and we met Frau Birnbaum, the midwife, who came to call a few times. One morning Frau Birnbaum arrived quite early and went right into the bedroom where Mutti was still in bed. I remember Papa was pacing around, Mutti seemed to be crying in the next room, and Omchen was fussing and taking a very long time to find some pencil crayons and paper to entertain me. Later, Mutti scolded them both for letting me hear what was going on, but I don't recall being upset by it.

When I was led into the bedroom, there was the new baby. It felt as though I was in a fairy tale. This tiny little baby had appeared like magic. I thought she was the most beautiful thing I had ever seen. She was born prematurely; she was very tiny, and she had a full head of dark hair.

Since the others were in school, I was thrilled to be the first one to see her. That made her pretty much my baby, and I was proud to be sent up to the attic room to get a pillow off one of the beds for the bassinet.

It was with some dismay that I found out fairly quickly, not only did she replace me as the baby of the family and demanded far too much attention, but I couldn't play with her. She was not the source of entertainment I felt I had been promised. Still, I did not like to hear her crying so much. It gave me stomach aches.

In her letter of June 26, 1941, Mother writes: *Who knows how much longer it will be possible to get mail to you. If the mail does not work anymore, I will try to send news through the Red Cross.* None of the earlier telegrams was among the letters and messages. The first one of September 1943, mentioned in my Father's message, would have been the announcement of Helga's birth on August 16, 1943.

| REPLY | RÉPONSE | ANTWORT |

Message to be returned to enquirer—Message à renvoyer au demandeur—Mitteilung an den Anfragesteller zurückzusenden—

(Not over 25 words family news of strictly personal character) (25 mots au maximum, nouvelles de caractère strictement personnel et familial) (Nicht über 25 Worte, nur persönliche Familiennachrichten)

EXAMINED BY D. B/

Ziegelhof, den 26,5,1944

Message at last! Have sent four, first in September, 1943. We are all well and together. Helga healthy. Don't worry, quiet here.

Greetings to all,

DATE:
DATUM:

Please write very clearly — Prière d'écrire très lisiblement — Bitte sehr deutlich schreiben.

2 8 JUIN 1944

It is interesting that both telegrams bear a signature. I believe the custom was to deliver the telegraph message promptly, followed by a mailed copy.

Deutsches Rotes Kreuz
Präsidium / Auslandsdienst
Berlin SW 61, Blücherplatz 2

21. NOV. 1944 * 726753

ANTRAG
an die *Agence Centrale des Prisonniers de Guerre, Genf*
— Internationales Komitee vom Roten Kreuz —
auf Nachrichtenvermittlung

REQUÊTE
de la Croix-Rouge Allemande, Présidence, Service Etranger
à l'Agence Centrale des Prisonniers de Guerre, Genève
— Comité International de la Croix-Rouge —
concernant la correspondance

1. Absender   Elisabeth Rudeloff, Gut Ziegelhof,
   Expéditeur Kr. Eichenbrück, Post Schwertburg.

bittet, an
prie de bien vouloir faire parvenir à

Verwandtschaftsgrad: Tochter.

2. Empfänger   Mr. Jacob Ulmer.
   Destinataire
                Hudllen, Alberta. Canada.

folgendes zu übermitteln / ce qui suit:

(Höchstzahl 25 Worte!)
(25 mots au plus!)   All well. No disturbance, don't worry. Grandma here. Walter attending school at Kolmar nearby, home weekends. Werner home. Crops good. Anxious about brothers.

Greetings.

11.10.44.
(Datum / date)

Elisabeth
(Unterschrift / Signature)

3. Empfänger antwortet umseitig
   Destinataire répond au verso

Faith, Secrets and Trouble at the Pump

My maternal grandfather's family story provides the background for my mother's Christian faith. It begins in 1780 when his great-grandfather accepted the invitation to immigrate from Germany to an area of Austria known as Galicia. When the Hapsburgs took over the reign of the area, Lutherans were persecuted. This continued under the Empress Maria Theresia and while her son and successor, Joseph II, allowed some religious freedom, more than one hundred years later Protestants were still not permitted to build churches.

They also suffered poverty and hard times. Hoping for a better life, the entire family left the homeland to settle in Alberta, Canada in 1889, when my grandfather was nine years old. The prevailing theme throughout his story is clear.

A colony of about sixty Lutheran families from Galicia set up camp, building soddies and houses in a number of locations before eventually settling in Stony Plain. In each new place, my Opa's family home was used for school and church services until a house was built that served as the church and the pastor's residence.

When the family moved to the Peace River country in northern Alberta, the church was again the centre of their community. The practice of their faith was foremost in their lives to the point that my mother was not allowed to marry an English-speaking man she fell in love with because he could not participate in the German-speaking church.

This was my mother's background and she never wavered in her faith.

My father's family in Germany was also Lutheran but with a much more casual approach. While in Germany, attending church regularly or becoming part of a church community was not made easy for Mother. She was rarely assertive, but she simply and quietly persisted in attending church whenever possible, and she taught us the songs and prayers of her upbringing.

Being relocated to occupied Poland in 1941 meant we were safely in the country, away from crowded cities and the threat of air raids. Food rations were not an issue. There was as much fresh food as we wanted. We were free to roam and explore, and life was good. This was not entirely so for my mother.

Under the Nazis, churches were not actually closed in our area, but regular attendance was not popular with the people in charge. Germany was at war with Canada, and having recently arrived from Canada, we were cautioned not to draw attention to ourselves.

One Christian sacrament Mother would not forgo was the baptism of her baby. She arranged for a Lutheran minister to come to Ziegelhof, and Helga was baptized at home, somewhat in secret.

Omchen rose to the occasion and set the stage. She arranged a small table with a white lace tablecloth and a crystal bowl of water for the baptism. Everyone was dressed in their finest clothes, the boys very likely in matching suits, the girls in matching dresses. The minister wore his black robe, and it was a solemn occasion as we gathered around the improvised baptismal font.

Proxy godparents were Papa's secretary, Fräulein Klemm, and the assistant manager, Herr Hase.

The official ceremony for newborn children by the government was called a *Namenstag*, (name day) whereby the children were recognized and the mothers honoured in a ceremony.

She continued to suffer from being unable to attend church and could not let Sundays pass without honouring the day in some way.

One Sunday morning, she had the four of us dressed in our Sunday best and told us to stay clean and out of trouble while she got herself and the baby ready. I don't remember her saying what was planned.

We wandered outside and, being bored, were drawn to the old pump in the yard. Someone, probably Carl, told us that when one person pumps the big handle and another one holds a hand firmly pressed under the spout, water erupts out of the top of the pump. Of course, we had to see for ourselves. It was a successful manoeuvre. When Mutti called us to come inside we were in a deplorable state. Our clothes were wet and muddy right down to our socks and shoes.

We trooped into the house, and it strikes me that we presented ourselves to Mutti, thinking we were very funny. When she saw us, she snapped. As she turned to leave the room she said, *"Jetzt kriegt ihr es alle durch die Bank."* (You are all going to get it.)

I don't think we believed she would carry out her threat. I certainly did not think that she would spank poor little me. When she came back with Papa's riding crop, we knew how serious this was. She simply started with the oldest and even though I was crying pathetically by the time she came to me, I got it too.

Afterward, she cried as hard as the rest of us.

I was only six years old but I remember we were all very subdued when we realized how important Sundays were to my mother and how badly we had disappointed her. That was the only time I remember my mother ever hitting any one of us with more than a swat with her hand.

Mother received the *Mutterkreuz* (Mother Cross) and wore it in a number of family pictures.

The Pond

The pond was one of our best-loved places in Ziegelhof. Undisturbed on a warm summer day, the water surrounding the small island in its centre sparkled in the sunshine. Dragonflies flitted among the reeds and bulrushes at the far end. Trees and shrubs grew all around, and on one side—close to the house—was a large acacia bush. Whenever I encounter that fragrance, I visualize this scene from my childhood. Every spring, we saw flowers on the island and were convinced they were more beautiful and rare than anything we had on dry land, and so we made many attempts to reach them.

Heidi, Helga, Carl and Phipps

None of us could swim, but we had great fun trying to get there in an old horse trough. We carefully caulked all the cracks with mud before pushing it into the water. Then three of us scrambled into the trough while Walter, the tallest, struggled to push us out as far as possible before also jumping in. Our hopes of paddling to the island were dashed as water poured in.

We never tired of this exercise, and the trough sank every time, leaving us scrambling for shore in the muddy water. Our *swim* usually ended with all of us hurling clots of mud at each other until we were completely covered in black muck.

We reminisced about this many times over the years. When Carl and I visited Walter at St. Paul's Hospital in Vancouver, where he was in palliative care in 2007, he reminded us of the time we had guests and were reprimanded. Some of the visiting girls were horrified by the black mud and slimy water and had to be rescued from our mud fest.

We had no garden hoses and we all had to be washed off under the pump or in an old wash tub before being allowed in the house.

The pond was also home to many ducks and geese which gathered with the chickens to be fed. On the day I was finally allowed to take their food to them, I carefully carried the dish of scraps in front of me. They must have recognized the enamel dish that held the food because I was suddenly surrounded by a mob of quacking, cackling and hissing fowl. In my terror, I held the dish as high over my head as possible and screamed for help. I could not be heard over the racket, and it seemed forever before someone came to my rescue. When asked why I didn't just drop the food, I replied, "I was afraid they would chase me." It had not occurred to me that they would be far too busy scrambling for the food.

One year, Mutti set a broody hen on some duck eggs to hatch. In her experience, ducks were not as reliable as chickens when it comes to hatching their eggs and the hen dutifully hatched the duck eggs. She could not understand the behaviour of her babies when they encountered the water and swam away. She frantically paced back and forth at the edge of the pond, going into the water as far as she dared, clucking desperately as the ducklings swam out of her reach.

In the winter we were able to cross to the island on the ice but, of course, there were no flowers.

Skates could not be bought at any price, but Papa asked the carpenter and blacksmith to make little sleighs, just big enough for us to stand on. They came with a pole, like a small broomstick, with a spike in one end. With the pole between our legs, we jabbed the spike into the ice behind us and propelled ourselves across the pond. The surface was like glass and if there was a wind, the boys held their coats wide open and sailed across the pond on their little sleighs.

We found another use for our spiked poles. One day in late summer we spotted some apples through the partly open window of the cool room. We knew the apples were being stored for the winter and there was still other fruit available in the garden, but we could not resist.

Suddenly, when we had successfully speared a couple of apples, an arm reached out and snatched our stick from inside the room. We recognized our friendly maid Irene's sleeve and—as this was not a very serious crime—our only punishment was having to admit our guilt by asking her for our stick.

Propaganda, Partisans and Hitler Youth

It was quiet where we lived and our parents assured us that we were safe from the war. While that was mostly true, we were not spared some of the conflict's ugly aspects.

There were rumours of horrors inflicted on the German people by the enemy. We were told that in addition to bombing our cities, their planes were dropping booby-trapped dolls and other toys or household items. These were said to detonate when children picked them up, killing or maiming them.

There were suggestions that you should throw stones at such found objects from a distance to ensure that they did no harm if they exploded. Heidi and I worked ourselves up into quite a panic when we saw an enamelled pot at the edge of our pond, and we proceeded to throw stones at it to see if it would blow up. We must have scored some hits, as Mutti was not pleased with having a perfectly good pot chipped by our rock throwing.

In spite of our parents' efforts to spare us, there were other frightening incidents. From adult conversations we picked up enough to know when partisan activity was reported, and the men in the area sometimes met at our place to hunt down the perpetrators. I remember the fear I sensed in my mother when this was happening. She and Father whispered, and spoke in English, so we should not hear.

Papa was not in the military, but he had a uniform which he only wore for certain public functions. He also had guns for the annual hunt for rabbits and venison.

I didn't know what exactly partisans were, but when he put on his uniform, took out one of his guns and joined the other men to go after them, I was frightened. I don't know if any partisans were ever found nor, if they were, what their fate may have been.

For the most part, our lives were carefree and great fun, but Walter did not entirely escape the effects of the Nazi regime. When he reached a certain age, he was expected to attend boarding school to prepare him for further education beyond what the local school could provide.

In the video interview with Pastor Dixon, Father relates that he felt pressured to enrol Walter in a Hitler Youth school. Mother hated the idea, and Walter, a sensitive, gentle boy, was understandably unhappy. At the school, he witnessed bedwetters being humiliated, and he knew that there was punishment for any sign of fear or weakness.

On one occasion, a group of perhaps twenty boys from the school travelled to Ziegelhof on a field trip to experience farm life. They had their meals outside at long tables and benches and that night, slept in the hayloft. Some of the older boys demonstrated the rigorous training they were receiving, such as running in circles while carrying several bricks, squatting, hitting the ground and jumping up on command. They seemed proud of their strength and endurance.

When they discovered the pond, they became just a bunch of kids and had a great time as the mud really flew. We girls were not allowed to participate on that day.

Later in life, Walter acknowledged that the conditioning in the Hitler Youth was extremely effective as, in spite of his distaste for the discipline, he confessed to feeling some ambivalence on being removed from the school at Mother's insistence.

She writes that Walter's first school was in Kolmar, a town near us, and after leaving there, he was enrolled in a private school and boarded with a family in Posen, the nearest city of any size, where he stayed until we left Ziegelhof.

Spades and Caves

The spades described in *Christmas in Ziegelhof* were prized possessions and when you have a shovel you have to have somewhere to dig. We found the perfect spot within easy walking distance of our place.

Ziegelhof is German for brickyard and while bricks were no longer being produced during our stay, an old ruin of the brickyard still stood, a landmark where our long driveway turned off the road. I was always under the impression that the sand to make bricks came from the sandpit where we loved to hang out.

But research tells me red bricks are made from clay, and the giant sandpit was unrelated. The sand must have been carved away for some purpose as the walls of a large open-ended oval were approximately the height of our two-storey house. They appeared to be solid, and we made many attempts at carving out caves with our spades.

I remember one day in particular when Walter and I were doing really well and our cave was deep enough for both of us to stand inside when suddenly, he threw himself backward dragging me with him as our cave collapsed. Flat on our backs, buried up to our armpits we had quite a time digging ourselves out. He was very quiet as we walked home. He knew better than I did that we could have ended up where my spade was, irretrievably buried.

When I mentioned this particular close call to Carl years later, he told me there were many such cave-ins and the danger to ourselves was very real.

Foraging on the Farm

We children were not usually expected to do any farm work and were discouraged from getting in the way of the workers. Potato harvest was the exception. We were eager to help, and we worked hard to fill the buckets as the men and women dug potatoes out of the ground. When the end of the field was reached and the last wagon was loaded, we helped to gather the dry tops into a huge pile. The farm workers set this on fire, added some brush, and it made perfect glowing coals for roasting potatoes.

Some of the men and women sat on the backs of the wagons or on gunny sacks on the grounds, and we kids arranged ourselves in a circle, sitting on the upside-down buckets. This was one time Mutti also appeared on the field with one of the kitchen workers, bringing butter, salt and a few implements.

The potatoes came out of the fire black and crispy. We opened them, slathered them with butter and feasted until we could eat no more. We happily went home to clean up our black faces and hands.

There was another occasion when huge quantities of potatoes were steamed and buried in big pits for silage. If we were lucky, the butter and salt would also appear at these times and everyone stood around and ate a lovely snack before the pit of potatoes was covered and preserved for winter feed.

We frequently raided the garden for gooseberries, red or black currants, and strawberries, as well as apples, pears and cherries. We pulled the young carrots, wiped them on our shorts or shirts and ate them right down to the greens. I don't think we should have eaten the small cucumbers but it seemed to us there were many more.

When the garden had been harvested, the boys had us trekking out to the turnip field. They usually managed to smuggle a knife from the kitchen out to the field and there they peeled one of the big rutabagas.

One day Heidi and I had to amuse ourselves without the boys and we decided to get our own *Wruke,* as we called the rutabagas. We found the field and picked out a nice big one which we took turns attacking with a table knife. That was almost impossible and it took a long time before we could actually hack off a piece to try. This turned out to be a huge disappointment. We had gone to the wrong field and were attempting to eat a sugar beet. They are sweet but not tasty.

While Walter was away at school, the three of us left at home managed to get ourselves into a unique kind of trouble.

Much of the work on the farm was done manually and with the help of horses, but there was at least one incident when one of our ripe grain fields was set on fire by a spark from a tractor. A considerable area burned.

I know that there were large fields of wheat, rye and oats, but this may have been barley as it was decided that the kernels of grain could be salvaged to make *Kaffee Ersatz* (coffee substitute).

To accomplish this, several of the older classes in the school my siblings attended were transported to the field to pick the scorched grains from between the rows of burnt stubble. A group of Polish children was also brought to the field to help with the salvage operation.

This turned out to be a field trip for the German kids and the progress along the rows was slow and sporadic. This being our place, Carl, Heidi and I behaved more badly than the rest and did not accomplish much.

The Polish children stayed on their knees with heads down and moved well ahead of our noisy group, filling many more baskets. I am sure the adults with them discouraged any kibitzing or slacking off to avoid trouble. I think I knew even at that time that this was not right. Any grain recovered, as was the case with all harvests, went to feed German people but the Polish people did the hard work.

Papa was always very busy and absent for long hours as he managed the three estates. I am sure he had German assistant managers at each of the farms; the one at our place was *Herr Hase* (Mr Rabbit). He was a young man and often joked with us, even about his own name. At other times, when he did not approve of our behaviour he was bossy and officious.

Our performance at the scorched kernel harvest did not go unnoticed. A few days later, Herr Hase spoke to us very seriously. He said that we had not done our part and Hitler would be very disappointed if he heard of our poor performance.

Reluctantly, the three of us trudged back to the field with our baskets. It was a long walk and without adult supervision or encouragement, we failed miserably. After some half-hearted attempts at picking up tiny scorched grains, we returned with our baskets looking much as they had when we left and nothing more was said about it.

Harvest Festival

My mother found many aspects of our years in Ziegelhof troubling. For her, it was not the carefree time it was for us children. I don't know just when we found out that she did not feel the propaganda spouted by the Nazi regime was necessarily the real story and secretly listened to the BBC on the radio in her bedroom for news of the war. That was a dangerous practice and Father warned her to be careful never to express her views to anyone.

In spite of her many misgivings, she enjoyed the good times and some truly memorable occasions. One annual event she found profoundly moving was the harvest festival known in Poland as *dożynki*.

We were the enemy, the occupation, and the Polish people had many reasons to hate us. The Germans had confiscated their land and their houses and those who had not been sent to a camp, or worse, worked for the Germans as labourers and servants. In spite of that, they honoured my father, *den Deutschen Gutsverwalter* (German farm manager) and his family as they would have done the former landowner.

Harvest festivals in European countries are usually celebrated on one of the Sundays following the end of the harvest season and so it was by us, in spite of the war.

I don't know how our parents were alerted to the festivities but on the appointed morning we presented ourselves on the front porch overlooking the gate and circular driveway in our best Sunday attire.

We could hear the sounds of a horse-drawn wagon approaching before the procession came into view.

It was a colourful sight with young men and women dressed in their traditional clothing, some leading the team of horses, bridles adorned with flowers and ribbons. Others walked beside the wagon carrying the tools of their work, scythes, pitchforks and wooden rakes, bedecked with ribbons.

Young women in embroidered dresses, floral wreaths in their hair, rode high on a load of golden straw from the grain harvest.

When the wagon came to a stop, two young men came forward, walked up the steps of the porch, bowed formally and presented a large harvest wreath of intricately woven straw, adorned with gilded ears of grain, poppies and cornflowers, to our parents, *der Gnädiger Herr und die Gnädige Frau* (the gracious gentleman and gracious lady).

They were followed by several young women who presented each of us children with a corsage, also fashioned of wheat, barley and flowers. Long ribbons trailed almost to the floor from where they were pinned to our Sunday best. My younger sister also received a corsage, ribbons fluttering from where she was held in Mutti's arms.

The colours of these gifts, enhanced by red, blue and white ribbons, perfectly reflected the view of the grain fields before the harvest, which Mutti so admired. Papa said the flowers were weeds, but we didn't believe him.

Mutti marvelled that—at a time when so many things were unavailable—they managed to obtain the colourful ribbons to decorate the horses, the wagon and our wreath and corsages. I know that when our corsages faded, she made sure the ribbons were returned to be used another year.

After the presentation, it was incumbent on the landed gentry to provide a meal to honour the reapers and their families for their work during the harvest and the past year. This duty now fell to the Gutsverwalter.

Harvest festivals are also celebrated in Germany, and Father would have been aware of his role in the celebration.

He was a good manager and he would have ensured that the kitchen staff hired what extra help they needed. The carpenter and helpers provided long trestle tables and set them up on the front lawn before they too joined the festivities.

When all was ready, large bowls heaped high with new potatoes and fresh produce from the garden, and platters of meat and sausage from butchering and hunting were carried to the tables where the guests were assembling.

When all were seated at the tables, our parents and we children helped the house and kitchen staff to serve the guests. It was a grand and cheerful feast with everyone still dressed in their traditional folk costumes.

Whatever else the Polish people thought of us or feared from us, they honoured us on this day. I like to think that my parents treated them fairly and that this was a sign of affection. None of us ever heard or saw anything to contradict that.

Omchen with Helga

Leaving Ziegelhof

Mother's first letter to our Canadian grandparents after a long silence was enclosed with a note from our Aunt Milly when she passed on the *grand news* that our family is intact, and we are safe.

I am inserting parts of Mother's letter where I feel it provides the best information of our journey.

The Trek

When Pastor Dixon had heard some of our parents' stories, he asked them to tell him about leaving Ziegelhof. Father started off.

"We got the word to leave. That meant take what you can and get out of there."

"Could you have stayed?"

"No. The Russians were coming. Sometimes very close behind us and in some places we could hear the cannons."

"So that was the Eastern front. What year was that?"

After some hesitation, with Mother trying to help, they decided it was the winter of 1944-45.

"So, January '45?"

"Yes, and it was cold."

Father described the wagons he had constructed for our travel in the middle of winter. The men must have worked through the night to build a wooden cover over our wagon, somewhat like a horse-drawn motorhome. The door was at the back, and wooden benches inside ran along the sides. Near the front, a little pot-bellied stove struggled to keep us warm. The front of the wagon was partly closed in, but there was an opening where our Polish driver sat. He had some benefit of the warmth from the stove on his back.

Two other wagons carried our belongings, food supplies, and feed for the horses. These were fitted with canvas covers.

We children were not told anything until we got up in the morning to find our things were being packed. We were not allowed to bring more than one or two toys. Heidi and I asked about the big beautiful doll Mutti had won on our voyage, but we had to leave her behind. Our Christmas tree was still up, and I don't believe we knew how final this departure was.

When I saw our little house on wheels I was excited about going on a trip, but I did not like to see our lovely companion Irene crying as she bustled around making sure we were warmly dressed and packing our things. We found out later that she was supposed to come with us to help with us children, but she pleaded with Mutti to let her stay because she and the Organist wanted to get married.

Seeing some of the other women helpers whispering among themselves and wiping away tears made me uneasy. Helga was only a year and a half old, and one of our helpers in particular did not want to let her go. She was afraid that the *kleine bobby* (little baby) would not survive the bitter cold.

After starting out, we had to make one stop to pick up Walter before we joined a long trek of horse-drawn wagons.

Walter had returned to his school in Posen after the Christmas holidays, and word was sent for him to come home immediately. He liked to tell the story of his trip on the train from Posen.

"Over the Christmas holidays, I had started to build a structure with our Meccano set and when it was time to go back to school I took it with me. I was convinced I had figured out how to build a perpetual motion machine, and I put an elastic band around the mechanism to keep it from starting up before it was quite ready. It was pretty big. When I held it on my lap the top of it was just above my head.

"When I was told I had to get home, there wasn't time to dismantle my machine, and I refused to abandon it. My hosts got me and my suitcase to the train station and then it was up to me. I struggled through the crowd holding onto my Meccano project, and when I got to the train it was packed.

"I don't think I understood or appreciated at the time how helpful everyone was. People squeezed together and found a spot for me, and no one even suggested I should leave my apparatus behind."

He was very fortunate indeed. Later we heard many stories of children who were unable to get home in time and became separated from their families.

The Kutscher had been sent to meet Walter at the train station and we picked him up before we joined *The Trek*, a wagon train which stretched as far ahead and behind as we could see.

My Ride of Terror

For us children, the Trek began as a great adventure. Days were cold but sunny, and we had brief rest stops and periods of play. We knew nothing of the danger that prompted the evacuation. While we were in farm country, all those who joined us had wagons, most of them covered and well-equipped. The Trek was orderly and no one was on foot.

Caring for and entertaining Helga kept Mutti confined to our wagon most of the time. The boys were occasionally allowed to ride on one of the other wagons while Heidi and I stayed cozy in the big one and played with our dolls. We learned later that Papa played a role in the organizing of this migration, and he was seldom with us during the day.

Whenever there was a stop, we escaped outside to run around and explore the area or simply play in the snow. Walter and Carl were charged with looking after Heidi and me and keeping all of us safe. For the most part, we stayed together and kept the wagons in sight.

When a rest stop was ending and the call came to move on, there could be no hesitation. The long string of horses and wagons was set in motion, and it became a wagon train. Like any train, every part of it had to move.

There was a day when Walter was not with us as we clambered into the wagon. Mutti anxiously looked around, but the door had to be closed as the driver released the brake and flicked the reins to urge the horses on. We could not wait. It was an anxious time until we reached the next stop, and a great relief when he was found. He had hitched a ride on another wagon.

The wooden cover on our horse-drawn camper was built onto a farm wagon commonly in use at the time to gather and transport crops such as potatoes or turnips. Solid wooden sides sloped outward from the floor and protruded out over the wheels. The front was closed in by sturdy boards which also added support to the wooden bench where the driver sat.

Normally, at harvest time, the unhinged tailgate at the back end was removed for loading and unloading of cargo and slid back in place to secure the load. It was left behind for our journey and the door, which reached from the floor to just under the roof of our camper, was installed in its place.

To prevent the sloping sides of the farm wagon from spreading when it carried a full load, a heavy chain was attached to either side at the back to be connected in the centre with a large hook and ring when needed.

This chain was still in place on either side of our door but I don't remember when, if ever, it was secured. As a rule, the two ends dangled within easy reach and whoever was the first to arrive used the long hook attached to one end of the chain to bang on the door for Mutti to let us in. The way the door was constructed, we were unable to open it from the outside.

I don't know how it happened that one day, when the signal came to move on, I found I was alone as I ran for our wagon. I grabbed both ends of the chain, but before I could bang on the door to be let in, the horses began to move. All I could do was to hang on.

We started to go downhill, and my screams could not be heard over the rattling and creaking of the wooden wheels. I was running as fast as I could, but as the wagon picked up speed, my stride lengthened and eventually I only occasionally touched the ground with one foot or the other. My hands were burning inside my mittens. I could feel the breath of the team of horses behind me and I knew if I let go I would be trampled and run over. It seemed to go on forever, and I was terrified that I could not hold on much longer.

Eventually we slowed, and I was able to take some of the weight off my aching arms as my feet hit the packed snow on the road more firmly. Before we came to a complete stop, I heard our Polish driver on the wagon behind me shout something. I needed help badly and glanced back to see him wave me over to my left. I was scared to let go and I don't remember exactly how I managed to jump to one side. When I did, and he came alongside, I raised my arms as high as I could and he reached down and pulled me onto the seat beside him. He held onto me with one arm until we came to a complete stop.

Between us, my rescuer in broken German and I—still sobbing and gasping—were able to convey my close call to Mutti. I'm sure she had tears in her eyes as she thanked him and held me rather tightly for a long while.

I don't know if I ever found out where the others were during my ride of terror, but I can't imagine that I was able to describe it well enough to impress them.

The Trek Goes On

> *We left Ziegelhof Jan 21 in covered wagons. The first week it was very cold and most people in the many miles-long treks suffered and many even froze to death. We had a stove in ours, so it wasn't so bad. I'll write more about that later ....*

The first time we pulled into a large town, or perhaps a city, Papa and the boys went in search of fresh supplies while Mutti and we girls stayed in the wagon. We had no windows, so I begged to sit at the front with the driver while we were stopped.

The scene was very different from any of the villages we had visited in the past few days. The streets were crowded with wagons; many piled high with crates and bags and household items, some covered in canvas. Children and adults rode along among their belongings. The sidewalks were also busy. I had never seen so many people in one place before.

We hadn't waited long when a loud bang made me jump. The driver was startled too, but he smiled and nodded to reassure me. As the big bangs kept coming, I pictured big boards being dropped off a roof. I don't know why that image came to mind, but perhaps I had heard a similar sound when a roof was being repaired.

Suddenly, Papa and the boys came running and jumped in the wagon. I scrambled inside and we sped off. We did not slow down until we had put some considerable distance between us and the city. When we finally slowed down, the relief among the adults was palpable. The *boards being dropped off a roof* were in fact the Russian tanks and cannons advancing and firing on the city.

As we travelled on, we noticed changes in the landscape. There were many more houses, often surrounded by trees and everything felt more crowded than it had been among the big open fields and meadows of the Ziegelhof area.

The Trek also changed. The wagons from the city joined us; some were old and shabby; occasionally we saw one broken down at the side of the road. There were people on foot with push carts, bicycles and even baby buggies loaded with what little they could carry.

The city people who joined the Trek did not have access to the sturdy farm equipment we travelled in. We were the privileged ones. Papa contributed some of the supplies and feed and gave up one of our wagons to assist others. I don't remember any comments my mother may have made about those poor people, but I can imagine her feeling of helplessness. She often says in her letters that there were people much worse off than us, and the story that follows is one of those times.

During the video interview, Pastor Dixon asked, "Betty, you had a story of two girls during this time."

"Oh my, yes. It was very sad. That was when we were on the Trek along with miles and miles of wagons moving west, heading for Germany.

"On one of the wagons, there were two girls and their mother travelling with some other people when their mother died. The girls were just in their teens and they didn't know what to do. One of the leaders of the Trek, the director or whatever he was, told them they had to just lay their mother down and leave her.

"They did not want to do that but there was no other way. There were some trees off to the side and they were told to leave her there. They cried as she was laid among the trees. Some of us said a prayer with them and then they had to move on.

"Oh, there were many stories but also some good ones. At the beginning of the trek we stopped in a village along the way every evening and people put us up for the night. That was always very nice. In the morning, they hitched up their wagon and joined us."

I remember some of the village homes fondly. The situation must have been very difficult for others. The Trek was growing and changing. More and more people joined from further east and north than we had come. On one occasion, we were among a number of families directed to a castle where we were put up for the night. It was not a fairytale castle with red-roofed, round spires but rather a big square, grey stone building with crenellated roof lines and one tower.

While the adults were making preparations for meals and sleeping quarters, we took advantage of the rare chance of being with other children and running around inside a building. There were interesting nooks and crannies to explore and stairs to climb. The boys in the group found small doors which led into passages in the outside walls. The space inside was wide and high enough for easy access and seemed to go on for a long way. I was not brave enough to join them, convinced I would get lost in there, never to be found.

After we finally settled for the night and all was quiet, everyone woke with a start when there was a loud boom and the building shook. A bomb, possibly intended for the castle, exploded very close by. We saw the crater it left behind as we drove away the next morning.

It was still very cold when we reached our first goal, the Oder River, hoping safety lay on the other side. When we arrived, the river was covered in ice and there was no bridge in sight. The route across the ice was marked and several men, stationed on the river bank, indicated when the next wagon was to cross.

I have a strong impression of a stillness surrounding the operation, as though we were all holding our breath. It was good to hear that everyone crossed safely.

The Trek Disbands

In mid-February 1945 we had officially reached the end of the Trek but that was by no means the end of our Gypsy travels.

> *All of Kreis Eichenbrück was sent to Kreis Lüneburg.*
>
> *We reached our destination, a friendly Bauerndorf (farm village), after twenty-two days on the road. It was a hard trip although we spent all but three nights in houses and had hot food for supper and coffee in the morning. Helga had a severe cold which later developed into a severe "flu." She was in the hospital for nine days, is quite well again and eats like a man ....*

Our destination lay west of the Elbe River and we were happy to see that there was a bridge and we did not have to face another risky crossing on an icy surface.

At this point, many of the wagons dropped out of the Trek and life became much more complicated. Throughout our adult lives, my siblings and I reminisced about this time and tried to recall the names of places. We could picture and describe many of them and we had good times looking back at the crazy scrapes we got into, but we could never quite work out the correct sequence of events or locations where our travels took us.

There are also inconsistencies between what Mutti wrote, what both parents related on the videotapes, and my recollections.

When we reached the *farm village* Mutti mentioned in her letter, we were finally out of our wagon for a time. I don't remember the people nor what the arrangements were for our meals, and it seems to me we were very much at loose ends still.

We were given only one room in the attic of a house. What made it memorable was a small door that led to the space under the eaves, where we found an old cradle which became Helga's bed. We could not stand up in the space, but in the evenings, Heidi and I took turns sitting on a little stool and rocking Helga to sleep. We weren't always happy to do this chore because it meant missing Mutti's reading aloud by the coal oil lamp or leading us in singing until we all went to bed. It was also Helga's lot to be left out of the evening *Gemütlichkeit* (socializing) in the next room.

It was here that Helga, aged two, became very ill. She was diagnosed with a serious flu and was confined to a hospital for nine days. Mutti was not allowed to visit as the doctors and nurses considered it too disruptive to their routine and disturbing for Helga each time Mutti had to leave again.

This was a traumatic experience for both of them. At home, Mutti choked back tears every time she talked about seeing Helga from a distance, sitting forlornly on a potty in her crib. Helga recently told me, "I have this vague and unsettling memory of looking at a window and not seeing Mutti there, and I have wondered if that was from that time"

After our confinement in the travel wagon and now in one small attic room, the rest of us went a little wild as we explored the farm and roamed the countryside. We were accustomed to always being together with no other playmates, and I think we had become a bit of a gang. The local children mocked us for arriving in a *Ziegeuner Wagen* (gypsy wagon). They called any newcomers *Fremtscheit* (foreign shit). Mutti would have been shocked if she had heard us taunting them back, but she quite approved of our singing *Lustig ist das Ziegeuner Leben* (Happy is the Gypsy Life) whenever we rolled into a new village or town on our travels.

This was also the place where we lost Carl's beloved little dog, Phipps. He was very ill, but the farmer would not allow us to bring him into the house. Papa helped Carl make a comfortable warm spot in the barn for him, and he still sometimes came with us on our jaunts.

One morning, Papa told us Phipps had died. Carl was devastated. He said later that he believed Dad shot him. Phipps had distemper, and he wasn't going to get better.

I find it impossible to know how long we stayed in that village and I also don't know if this is the time to which my father referred in the video interview. The situation would have felt confining and hopeless, and this may well have been when he made a bad decision.

"I couldn't stand it anymore and I knew that my (late) Uncle Charlie had a hunting lodge, in Volsrade, on the east side. So I went east and back over the (Elbe) river."

Mother interjects. "I did not want to do that, and I fought against that." She was right to object, but he rarely listened to her once his mind was made up.

"I still had my two horses. I drove to the estate, which I knew quite well. It was my uncle's hunting ground, adjacent to Goldenitz.

"Anyway, we lived in the hunting lodge and were quite happy for a while, but there was a large ammunition camp nearby. I was afraid that it might explode, so we moved out and for a while we slept in our covered wagon.

"We threw our guns into the water and destroyed our documents because we never knew what was going to happen."

Mutti adds, "I threw my *Mutterkreuz* into the pond." (The mother cross she received when Helga was born).

Richard asks, "Why did you do that?"

"We did not want to get caught by the Americans and the Brits with those things on us; they might have thought we were Nazis."

Mutti describes some of this adventure in her letter:

> *Early in April, we moved back across the Elbe into Uncle Willie's Jagdhaus (hunting lodge) in Volzrade, a big "Gut" (estate), a pretty little place. When we feared the Russians were coming we trekked once more, tried to get up to Holstein to Hans-Jürgen's wife. We didn't get far, just escaped some heavy artillery shots and were cut off by the American troops. We went back to Volzrade and found all the houses full of Americans, so we drove back again and tried to get across the Elbe and back to our former Dorf (village) ....*

I don't know when or where our Polish drivers left us. We all remembered how kind and patient they had been, and we often wondered how they felt, being taken so far from home. I hope they made it safely back to Poland if that was their wish.

We still had two wagons and, from my recollections, I can only conclude that our parents were attempting to carry on without drivers. Mutti grew up on a farm with horses, buggies and farm implements, so she would have been capable of driving one of the wagons and agreed to do so. It's very likely that what happened next changed her mind about carrying on that way.

I am sure when Papa and Walter left us at the side of a country road one day, possibly to scout out a safe route, they thought we would be safe. Carl, who loved working with horses and had frequently been allowed to handle a team, was left in charge of one wagon. Mutti and we girls were in the bigger wagon.

Suddenly a loud whistle screamed across the sky, followed by a big boom. The horses tensed, restlessly stepping in place, tossing their manes. Mutti pulled the reins tight and called, "Whoa, whoa, whoa."

We saw Carl struggling to control his team. He was strong and tall for his age but he was just eleven years old. The brakes on the wagon would have been set, but that was not enough to hold the wagon if the horses bolted.

I remember how scared I was for him as Mutti called out, "Carl, hold on, keep calm. You can do it. Talk to them."

I don't know if he could hear her over the clattering of hooves. A second scream ripped through the sky and a third, each one followed by a crash. It was eerie not knowing where the screech began and where it ended. I don't think it went on for very long, but we were all badly shaken and so grateful when it stopped.

Years later, a military officer told me that under that sort of artillery fire, you only hear the whistle when the shell is directly overhead and you are safe as long as you can hear the screams. "It's the ones you don't hear that will get you."

I don't know where in our travels this took place, but I know we carried on with only one wagon and with Papa driving.

Places I Remember

The snow and ice were gone by the time we had our first encounter with the Russian occupation. Considering the great lengths to which we had gone to evade them, their actual takeover must have been uneventful; I have no memory of anything dramatic occurring to mark the takeover. We shared a small house with another family on the grounds of a *Schloss* (a small castle) where some Russian soldiers were in residence.

As always, we spent a great deal of our time outdoors. There was nothing threatening about the soldiers, but we were told to keep our distance and not stray too far from our house. Heidi and I were often expected to look after Helga while Mutti was busy.

We were horrified one day when we looked up from some game and saw Helga with a couple of the soldiers just as they took her by the hand and led her into the Schloss.

There was nothing we could do. We hung around the gate, anxiously watching the door and windows. What if they didn't bring her back? Finally, a whistle made us look up and to our utter relief, we saw her waving to us from an upstairs window, a soldier on either side of her. A little later a whole troupe of them, laughing and chatting, brought her back outside. She slowly walked toward us, smiling proudly and very carefully carrying an egg in both hands.

That was a welcome treat. Food was in short supply and it was in this place where Mutti carefully picked the leaves off stinging nettles as a substitute for spinach. We didn't think too much of it or the dandelion leaves in our salad.

The Russians also found a way to subsidize their diet. Every now and then, one of them threw a grenade into the pond causing a great plume of water and dead fish to erupt. Papa was dismayed as these ponds were traditionally stocked with trout and—at this rate—the fish would not last long. One day, he was invited into the rowboat to help pick up the fish floating on the surface. We ate very well that day.

Papa found us better accommodations as, once again, we travelled on, still under Russian occupation, but in a village where we had a rowhouse all to ourself. Mutti unpacked some household items for the first time, and Papa found a few pieces of furniture. I remember Mutti's dismay as she found several plates of a dinner set had broken during our travels.

We always referred to this village as *the place where Heidi had her wedding*.

We finally had a chance to play with other children in the neighbourhood. Heidi, not quite ten years old and always very sociable, became friends with a boy about the same age and they decided to get married. An elaborate celebration was planned.

Somehow she managed to acquire a white dress and a lace curtain for a veil, and there was to be a true German wedding procession. I don't remember who married them or if there was food and drink involved, but I am sure Mutti got into the spirit of things.

Heidi told me this part of the story many years later.

"I was having a good time planning my wedding, but it was taking too long. I think the boy actually wanted to back out, but I made him go through with it. It was great fun."

Helga heard the story many times. "I don't remember there being a wedding, but I have this image of girls in white dresses on a grassy slope." That may well have been the celebration.

To Walter's delight, the village where Heidi had her wedding was also one of the few places where we had electricity. A skill he had to acquire rather quickly was fixing the fuses, which blew frequently and could not be bought. They were the kind he could safely repair with some very fine copper wire.

I can't imagine how Walter came by his expertise in electrical gadgetry but even at that time he already owned a soldering iron. I was intrigued, and begged to be allowed to try it. After much nagging, he relented and helped me solder together two small pieces of wire. I was thrilled. I was wondering what to do with my little creation when I spotted the perfect thing. There on the wall was a white porcelain thing with two round openings. I stuck the two ends into the holes and came to, halfway across the room—a painful lesson at 220 volts.

It may seem strange under the circumstances, but it was a time when appearance was important. We had an electric iron, and Mutti ironed Papa's shirts and kept us all looking our best. Nothing else was normal or in good order. For some reason—likely the lack of an ironing board—the iron ended up on the floor on a trivet of some kind, still plugged in. Helga, just a toddler, played quietly amongst the clutter and confusion when suddenly we heard her scream throughout the house. Poor girl had shuffled her little bottom right onto the hot iron and suffered a very bad burn, right through her panties. She had a paisley-shaped scar for many years.

Carl and Walter were lucky not to suffer more serious damage when they found some small rail cars on narrow tracks going down a steep slope. Each tub-like car was only big enough to hold a couple of kids or maybe one adult. Carl thought they were likely used to get some kind of cargo up a rather steep hill where there was no road. The winch at the top was not operational. They manoeuvred one of the carts to the top of the hill where they jumped in and careened down the track, going much faster than was safe, with absolutely no way to slow down or stop.

Carl could never suppress a sheepish grin when he told this

story. "Some of the local boys joined us and helped get the cars to the top. We thought they were a little stupid not to have thought of it themselves. When I think of what could have happened, I guess I know we were the stupid ones. It was a lot of fun though."

Another well-worn tale of our stay in the rowhouse was of the Russians marching past every evening, singing the same song with a chorus that we interpreted as, *Leberwurst, Leberwurst* (liver sausage), *da dum di, dum dum dum*. We never forgot the tune and we burst forth with our version whenever something brought it to mind.

The story of this part of our travels is much abbreviated in Mother's letter. There were several stops between the ones she mentions.

A Refugee Camp

Once again, I have no idea why we left. We may have been told to move on because our destination was to be Kreis Lünenburg and we had gone back east after arriving there. It is also possible that Father found that we could move to an area occupied by the American armed forces which was preferable to remaining under Russian occupation.

That would seem to fit with his comment in the 1989 video interview.

"We were rounded up by the Americans first in a field and then in a refugee camp where we stayed for a few days."

Mother interjects vehemently. "Weeks!"

The camp was housed in what seemed like a large warehouse. Rows and rows of burlap ticks filled with straw lined the floor where we slept.

The excitement of being allowed to sleep in the hayloft in Ziegelhof for a special treat was now a distant memory. This was not fragrant hay but old, dusty straw. Neither hot water nor bathing facilities were provided, and I am sure Mother struggled to keep us clean.

Dad was not with us much of the time. He may have had to stay with the wagon and horses wherever they were put up. He came during the day and usually brought some kind of food to supplement the daily rations of soup and bread that the camp provided.

My memories of this place are vague, but I remember clearly one day when Mutti asked Carl to comb and braid my hair. Heidi and I always had pigtails and I was still too young to manage mine by myself. He was being very gentle, but suddenly he flung the comb away and shouted."There are bugs crawling on her head!"

I was devastated. My brother was disgusted with me, and I couldn't stop crying. I don't remember how the head lice were dealt with, but it turned out that just about everybody had them.

News From Germany

On May 8, 1945 WWII officially ended in Europe. I don't remember being told that the war was over but it was Spring when we reached the next village and Mother wrote just ten days later.

During the post-war confusion there was no mail service of any kind. After three years of silence, Mother's first letter was entrusted to an American soldier to be mailed to her sister Helen in the US and did not reach our grandparents until early August 1945.

May 18, 1945

My dear Helen & family,

As our American boys are moving on today (they've been in the house here about a week), and one of them hopes to go home soon, he promised to send this to you when he gets there. I certainly hope it reaches you soon. I imagine you are all wondering what became of us in this awful turmoil things have turned into. I hope we'll soon get mail across directly as we are anxious to hear from you all. The last Red Cross message I received was dated Jan 30, '44 ....

We were on the road and in a camp for about a week, slept in our wagon and cooked in the open air. The camp was near Niendorf, a pretty little Bauerndorf (farm village), so we simply drove into the village and found a small room in the house of a very plain but very nice family. We can cook in their kitchen. So far, we still have a little to cook and we hope that we shan't have to suffer too much. Food is scarce enough but we hope to get along ...

> We can't go back to Ziegelhof of course, that's Polish again now, and we don't know yet what will become of us. The Yankees aren't treating us badly but are guarding us quite strictly. When we get out of here again, Werner wants to try to find work similar to that back East here, then we'll at least have a home again. It's a hard life when you have no place you can call home, but millions are worse off than we are. I wish we could go back to Canada, but that's a dream.
> As these boys are leaving any minute I must close for now, hope I can write soon again. Don't worry about us.
> Love to everyone from Werner, Betty and family.

Margin notes: *You'll send this on home I imagine. As soon as possible I'll send an address so you can <u>all</u> write as soon as mail goes. We took all our clothes, bedding, linens, and most of our dishes along on all our trips, all furniture is lost.*

My memories of the village of Niendorf are made up of small incidents. I remember only warm, sunny weather during this time and our first encounter with U.S. Army personnel.

We enjoyed a brief time of relative peace and safety under the American occupation and even shared a house with a number of U.S. soldiers. Mutti was thrilled to visit and chat with the *American boys*. I imagine they also enjoyed her visits, since they were so far away from home and many of them were truly just boys.

They spent evenings in the large living room. There was no electricity in the house. Instead of using coal oil lamps, they lit candles on every available surface all over the room. These were similar to what we now call tea lights.

Helga was just a toddler and she loved the little lights. The boys made a fuss over her until, after a while, she happily went to each one as they invited her to sit on a lap or share a chair or a treat. They were good to the rest of us as well.

Working for the occupation as an interpreter, Papa had certain benefits. He sometimes came home with chocolate and other treats from the army canteen. We had our first taste of peanut butter when he was given a large tin with quite a bit left in the bottom. It was a new experience at the time, but I have never developed a taste for it.

When they were leaving, one of the young men promised to mail a letter to Mutti's sister in Wisconsin as the mail was still not moving and the family had not heard from us for some time. The letter reached my Aunt Helen in the US, who sent it to the Canadian family.

Later, I heard Mutti deplore the fact that some of these boys were not necessarily going home but were being redeployed to Korea.

There was a family of several children from Berlin living next door. The woman—very likely a widow—had a hard time, especially with the oldest boy already in his teens. He was called *Hansien* (pronounced Hanzine) which may have been a variation of *Hans* but we had never heard it before and thought it strange. I remember his and the baby's names only because their mother was often heard to shout, *"Hansien, Berndt's Milch!"* (Hansien, that's Berndt's milk) when he drank what little milk there was available for the baby.

Hansien persisted in telling his younger sister that the large dog on the property, possibly a Rottweiler, was a calf until she finally believed him and repeated it to someone else. She was ridiculed, of course, and he found it very funny. For many years afterward, one of us was prompted to shout *"Hansien, Berndt's Milch!"* and we recalled his behaviour with much disdain and laughter.

I don't believe the house was on a farm, but there was a barn on the same property and some people were put up in the hayloft. Heidi remembered something about Mutti being involved with a couple living in the loft.

"I think the couple was Latvian. They were quite young and the woman was pregnant. You know there were no doctors available and when the baby was coming, Mutti went to help.

"I remember how moved she was by the experience. She shared that with me again when I had my first baby. She felt she had participated in a miracle by helping to deliver that baby."

When the Americans left, the British army moved in. There was little change in our circumstances as Father again worked as an interpreter.

Flags of Surrender

When the map of the occupied sectors of Germany was redrawn and the British were moving out, they agreed to take us with them. Papa had acquired a Volkswagen Beetle, and it was packed full of our belongings. The VW was to be loaded onto a truck, and we were to travel with them to the new western zone the next day.

In the morning, we found the British were gone. We and our loaded car were left behind. I remember my father's bitter disappointment. Our previous experience with the Russians was uneventful, but we had heard stories, and we did not know what would happen to us this time.

That day we awaited the arrival of the Russians.

We children were all outside playing, but we were also waiting and watching. The parents—no doubt worried and not knowing what to expect—stayed inside. Berndt's mother had washed diapers and they were hanging on the line, waving gently in the sunshine. One of the men came outside and said the diapers looked like white flags of surrender and demanded she take them down.

We heard the rumble before we saw the Russian army arriving in a great convoy of trucks with many soldiers on board. They came peacefully and were billeted much as the British had been before them.

There were questions about the loaded car. We were allowed to keep our belongings, but the car was confiscated. We had to leave the house where we were living and were sent to a potato farm owned by the Habermanns.

Life at the Habermann's

We felt at home on the farm to begin with and had some good times. We met Herr and Frau Habermann and the two hired men, Fritz and Franz, and at least one other woman. I don't know if she was hired help or a relative.

We were there during the potato harvest, which we had experienced in Ziegelhof. We worked just as hard on this field and were rewarded with the same baked potato feast when the harvest was complete and the piles of dry potato tops were lit to create a bonfire.

We had a room at the front of the house but spent evenings and very cold days in the large farm kitchen. We were allotted a certain amount of food and ate our meals after the farm folk had finished theirs.

Helga was only two years old, but she spoke well and enunciated all her words very clearly, having only a small problem with the letter R. When the farmers were having their dinner, Fritz or Franz often shared some of their meal with her. Fried potatoes were a staple at every meal and she liked the brown crispy bits. She would point and say, *"Die bwownen, bitte?"* (The brown ones, please?)

Butter was not part of our meagre rations in spite of the fact that it was made on the farm. It was kept in large, shallow wooden troughs in the cool room in the cellar. One day, when Mutti had been to the cellar for potatoes, she came into our room with a tea towel draped over one hand and a sheepish grin on her face. We gaped in amazement when she showed us the handful of butter she had scooped out of the trough in the cellar. I think I was as thrilled to be part of her secret as I was at the prospect of having butter on my food. We were taught that it was wrong to steal, and even then I realized how remarkable this small act of rebellion was for my mother.

We had to do our cooking and eating in the kitchen where the women of the house could see what she was doing, and the stolen butter could only be used on the sandwiches we sometimes ate in our room.

The boys roamed the countryside looking for adventures. Carl told this story of one that could have gone very badly. Near a pond, not far from the farm, they had seen an abandoned anti-aircraft gun and ammunition which they had to investigate. Carl describes what they did.

"We set the anti-aircraft munitions container afloat on the pond and used the live shells like huge darts in an attempt to detonate them when connecting with the container. Luckily they didn't.

"We were actively involved in opening large, live cannon shells when a man came by, telling us to stop because two boys had just been blown up doing the same thing. We went with him to find them. They were badly disfigured and burned. A very scary experience at our age."

Heidi and I stayed close to home most of the time. We were happy to entertain ourselves around the farmyard and in an empty woodshed where we played house. We had been warned to come in at dusk but often pushed it well past that, which resulted in our own scare.

One evening we had just decided it was time to go in and were leaving our wood shed when two Russian soldiers suddenly appeared in front of us. One had a gun slung over his shoulder by a strap; the other carried his in front of him. We froze. They did not say anything, and—in a few minutes—moved on as quietly as they had come.

We ran to the house and told what had happened. I could sense the adults' fear. By this time we had overheard many horror stories, and Mutti again warned us never to stay outside after dark by ourselves.

Mother's Angel

Papa was able to secure the position of manager of a collective farm established by the Russian occupation, but the rest of the family could not join him immediately. We remained on the potato farm for a time.

Our room was not heated, but we spent evenings in the big warm kitchen each day until bedtime.

Our belongings were piled in trunks and boxes in the big front hall of the farmhouse. Late one night, we were awakened by a horrendous, wood-splintering crash, followed by shouts and the sound of boots trampling on wooden floors and fists pounding on doors. A shot was fired somewhere in the house. It was terrifying. I know I was crying and clinging to Heidi, with whom I shared a bed. Mutti whispered, "Girls, be very quiet. Boys, stay in your bed," as she hushed the baby.

We all froze each time our door handle was rattled. It seemed like hours before the intruders left. They were Russian soldiers on a rampage. They had ransacked our belongings, but we were not harmed. We were safe because Mutti had listened to her angel.

There was a big key in the lock of our door but we had never used it. The evening before the break-in, when we went to our room, Mutti turned around and locked the door. She often told the story and believed with all her heart that an angel had told her to turn the key in the lock.

Shortly after that, we were able to join Papa in Goldenitz. We had to share a house with some other people, but we were finally a little more settled. We attended school and had some good times, but we were always on guard, always a little afraid.

Sgt. Hennig's Airmail

Goldenitz

After the first news from us in early August 1945, our grandparents heard nothing further until January 1946 when a nephew in the RCAF, stationed in Germany, sent news from our German grandmother.

Sgt. Hennig was in the RCAF overseas and his letter, sent by Armed Force Airmail, was addressed to my grandfather, Jacob Ulmer, in Walnut Grove, BC. My Canadian grandmother's maiden name was Hennig, so this was her nephew.

Jan. 29, 1946

Dear Uncle and Auntie,

Sorry I can't tell you as much as I'd like to but maybe with a start now I hope to be able to pick up added pieces of news and send them on to you. Managed my last trip to Hamburg to dig up Werner's brother. From him I got the following information:

Werner, it seems, was in the British occupied area after the capitulation. He got a job with the Mil. Gov. as interpreter and had things fairly good. When the occupation zones were reshuffled, he got caught in the Russian zone.

The brother has not yet received any word directly from Werner but letters from acquaintances from the same place as Werner say that he is doing quite well. He has been given the job of running some large estate, Agricultural Inspector. This is at a place called Goldenitz. Betty and the children are living in the village of Niendorf ....

Don't know what the papers are telling you about how things are in the Russian Zone but the people who have come from there say that except for the food shortage conditions now are fairly good. Should actually be better than here. We have the food shortage here as well and on top of that we have overcrowding due to so many refugees fleeing from the battle areas. Will write again as soon as I get any more news.

Sincerely, Henry.

Sgt. Hennig did not realize that many of the people causing the west to be overcrowded were, in fact, fleeing the Russian zone because there were many serious problems in addition to the food shortage.

There was a second letter from Henry in mid-April.

Dear Uncle and Auntie,
    This will be my last letter for I'm about to start for home. Have very little news for you tho. Mrs Rudeloff and her son still live at the same address you gave me (Hamburg Hochallee 117) and are getting along ok. Of Werner and Bettie I have very little news .... The young Mrs. Rudeloff told me Bettie had written ... that they were still getting along comparatively well ....
With the mail service open now I imagine Bettie will be writing you direct since she has your address.

Respectfully,
Your Nephew, Henry

Finally, the first letter from Mother since May 18, 1945, reached the family in Canada. She begins with a PS at the top of the first page, in German:

Brothers and Sisters, please write! We are as hungry for news and updates as we are for chocolate!

Goldenitz, the 10. 5.1946

Dear Parents,
    At day's end on Heidi's birthday, which was very nicely celebrated with 8 girls from our village, many beautiful flowers, some small presents, and even some cake, I will at last write to you. I hope Helen forwarded my letter to you so that you have had some news of us. Onkel Philip's Heinrich (that would be Sgt. Henry) wrote me a short note on April 13. He was in Hamburg a couple of times but did not write before April 13. I wasn't sure

which of my cousins he was, but when he visited the mother-in-law, I was very happy to hear that you are all alive and well. I have worried so much about the brothers. Did none of them have to be soldiers?

Ach, I have a thousand questions to which I want answers, but I will try to have patience a little longer. Heinrich wrote that he leaves Easter week for home and will write to you right away. Too bad that he could not visit us.

We are particularly pleased with the news that you have moved to BC. When you know how beautiful it is, one has to be happy about that. Have you bought land? I wish that we could join you there, but at the moment we can't even think about that. Since the breakdown here, it is not nice anymore and the future looks dark for us. I often think we could care for the children better over there.

Where are all the siblings now? You must all write soon, the last news we had from you was 30. January 1944. Is Walnut Grove far from Vernon?

Under the circumstances, we are doing well, much, much better than many thousand others. The refugees as well as the people in the cities have a very meagre living. We live very simply and frugally, but we still manage to have adequate meals. Soon there should be fresh vegetables. Potatoes and bread are adequate, meat and fat is in very short supply. Things that are taken very much for granted over there, like rolled oats, cream of wheat, rice, cocoa, barley, etc. have not been available here for some time. Since Easter, we actually have a couple of eggs. Since we left Ziegelhof, we have hardly ever had any. Now we have 6 chickens of our own. We also have a pregnant sow and 2 horses. Now all we need is a cow. For weeks now we have only had 1/4 liter (1/2 pint) of milk for Helga from a neighbour, now we get 4 liters from the farm workers. That is not enough to make butter, but at least the children have milk to drink.

We still have adequate clothing. I have to sew a lot and make things over and better for which there is never enough thread, but one just has to manage.

It might interest you to know how we live here. To tell you everything, also about our flight from Ziegelhof until now, I would have to write a book. For that I am not nearly clever enough.

From January until December 1945 we had no home. We lived sometimes here, sometimes there, mostly by farmers and travelled around like gypsies.

In October, Werner had the good luck to take over the management of Goldenitz, even though it is all very difficult and hard on Werner. In Kreis (county) Hagenow, there are only 3 of these state-run estates. To begin with, they were managed, or mismanaged, by the Russians. They took the whole harvest, all the cattle, pigs, sheep and the best horses. All but 8 were starved or worked to death. Spring cultivation was done with 3 to 6 tractors. We are supposed to have milk cows and horses in the next few weeks that are coming from Thueringen and Sachsen. A hundred sheep are already here.

The estate is about 3,000 Morgen (Morgen = one quarter of a hectare) in size. It belongs to two neighbouring farms that used to be owned by an aristocratic family who left the estates prior to the breakup. Most of the big estates were divided into settlements. The rest belong to the state.

Werner's Onkel Willie had a 1,000 Morgen forest bordering on Goldenitz and a hunting ground not far from here, both of which he has lost. We were able to get some of the furniture from the hunting lodge where we lived for a time before the occupation. We have made our home here, four rooms and a kitchen, quite comfortable. Our furniture we had to leave in Ziegelhof. We were able to bring linen, bedding, clothing and dishes. Since we are a "big family" we may eventually live in the Schloss. At the moment a couple of Russians live there. We have the Secretary and an apprentice as boarders and also a woman and her 20-year-old daughter, refugees, who help me out in the house.

The children's health is for the most part good. So far we have survived all the upheaval very well. We can only hope that we will be able to stay here so that we are finally able to feel at home again.

The children have all shot up. The boys are always estimated to be 2 years older than they are and frequently seen as twins although there is little resemblance, neither in appearance nor in personality. They are the same height, Carl the stronger, Walter the cleverer. Carl is a born farmer, Walter does not yet know what he wants to be. For the time being, he is going to a higher school in Hagenow (children must start this in Grade 5 or they will not be accepted). He is learning English and Russian but not much else.

The other three are in the Volksschule (regular school). A whole year was lost to them and even now everything is still unsettled. Heidi is my wild child and a bit difficult to keep in line *but still very sweet. Dorchen does not cause me worries, she is the quietest of them all. Helga is my Ebenbild (the image of me), sadly also in her personality. She is a bit moody and because of all the difficult experiences, somewhat spoiled. Other than that a lovely, cute little imp, a chatterbox.*

Heartfelt greetings to all our loved ones from your Werner, Liesbeth, Walter, Carl, Heidi, Dorli and Helga.

In July, when she had finally heard from the family in Canada, she again wrote at some length, relating our circumstances and asking about all the members of her family.

My dear Parents,
I must finally write and reply to your loving letter. You can imagine how pleased we were to have news of you direct. Our dear Hamburg Oma did not tell us that she sent you our address. We are particularly happy to hear that you are all well. We regret that you did not tell us more about your circumstances and what you are doing now. We wonder if you bought land or what other endeavours you might be pursuing.

She goes on to say that it took five weeks for their letter to arrive and they had likely received another letter from her already. The lack of news and time between letters must have been hard to bear. It is also at this time that she began talking of returning to Canada.

I nag Werner constantly and would really like to return to Canada, and of course preferably near you. I have to give it up though because we don't know what we might be able to do over there. It is difficult because Werner can't undertake heavy physical work because of his back injury. For the time being one can't leave here in any case.
I long for a normal family life. I particularly miss Sundays. Here we work every day. The people are very un-Christian and hardly anyone is interested in going to church. The whole church life seems dead and neglected, but at least there is no active work against the church as in the Nazi time. It makes me so sad that my children cannot enjoy the most beautiful and best that I enjoyed in my

childhood and that they liked so much. I do what I can, but it seems like so little.

So now I have ranted on at you which I did not want to do, but you understand this about me better than the people here. We do not have any good relatives or friends here.

Healthwise we are fairly well. Werner and I are often worn out and very tired but then it goes better again. Only Heidi worries us. She has a tubercular throat infection. The glands on her right side are very swollen and so far only one is infected. It is draining now and the doctor is hopeful that it will heal and not spread to other glands. So far her lungs are clear. She is very tall and skinny and she should have lots of sun, cod liver oil, calcium and good nourishment. We are doing everything we can for her and hope that she will soon recover her good health. She has school holidays now, so she can rest as much as she likes.

Werner's mother wrote that the brothers (they live on the same street) have to give up their apartments to the English occupation. Their part of the city was spared heavy bombing and now they have to lose their dwellings anyway. Next time I want to send a few pictures. Please send us some pictures too. We can hardly picture all of you any more, especially the children ....

She closes with birthday greetings, good wishes and blessings for all.

How Many Papa?

In her first letter following the long period of silence, Mother describes us children to her family in Canada.

We four older siblings were each born roughly eighteen months apart and as Mother points out, the boys were about the same height but there the similarity ended. Walter, the oldest, had very dark hair, a dark complexion and brown eyes. Carl was a redhead with the usual fair skin and freckles and blue eyes.

There was little resemblance between Heidi and me. She was always very slim with dark blonde hair and blue eyes, a head taller than I. My hair was more auburn than red and much admired by adults, but my eyes are a boring hazel.

Helga, five and a half years younger than I, was her very own person again. If she resembled anyone, it would have been Walter as she had the same dark hair and brown eyes.

Mutti wrote that Father had the good luck to take over the management of Goldenitz but also that it was very difficult.

This situation became more difficult as the Russians were still very much in charge. The Commandant was the top man, and his word was absolute law. Anyone could be accused of sabotage at any moment and no appeal was possible. Rumours of men being arrested and sent to Siberia were everywhere.

Whether as a gesture of goodwill or a matter of control by the Commandant, Papa was expected to attend his social functions when summoned. On one occasion, the Commandant told Papa that he, too, was a family man and wanted to meet our family.

In preparation, we were all washed and polished in our Sunday best and lined up for presentation from oldest to youngest. This was not a new routine for us. We had been presented to German dignitaries during the war. We knew to stand up straight and not to speak until spoken to and we knew Papa's steely, blue-eyed look that had us freezing in our tracks if we broke some rule of etiquette.

When the Commandant arrived, he greeted Mutti very formally and then stood back to look us over. He seemed very serious but not unfriendly as he looked up and down the line a couple of times and then turned to Mutti,

"Two black, two red, one blonde, how many papa?"

Mutti smiled and pointed to Papa. "Only one, him."

The Commandant shook his head and laughed. "Two black, two red, one blonde? No, no, no." He was still laughing and shaking his head. Mutti and Papa just smiled.

Under different circumstances, Mutti would have objected strenuously, but there may have been a look from Papa or she knew instinctively that you did not argue with the Commandant.

Fear and Desperation

Mother did not write again until three months later, when she explained her long silence.

Goldenitz the 23. 10. 1946

My dear Parents!
Now it is time that you should finally hear from us once again. You will no doubt be wondering why I have not written for some time. I know it is very bad of me, but I will make up for it and tell you everything when we are once again together, which we hope will not be too far off.

We have had serious problems and worries in the last few weeks. I hope we are almost over this hump. There has been a court case against Werner since the end of July for "Sabotage an der Volkswirtschaft" (sabotage of the national economy) which results in serious punishment. It is supposed to go before the Landesgericht (state court) in Schwerin, the third hearing.

Werner has entered 2 defences but is supposed to serve prison time as well as a fine. He has gathered a lot of supportive material in evidence and is hoping with the help of the district magistrate in Hagenow to end this so that it does not have to go to a higher court. Werner is innocent. The charge is an act of vindictiveness. Ingratitude is the wage of the world. I believe this to be the case more in Germany than elsewhere in the world.

Werner has completely collapsed under the stress of the difficulties and worries involved in the management of this estate. He was in bed for two weeks but is a little better now. As a result of all this, I too am very nervous but am trying to be brave. Fortunately, Werner was not re-elected as Bürgermeister in September. He also had to give up his position as the estate manager until his case is decided. If it goes well for him, he will be reinstated. He may not want it.

When this is all behind us we want to try and come back to Canada. Many have gone over and it should be easy for us. If our farm is still ours, which seems too good to be true, then we still have something of our own. We are all looking forward to this so much. The children picture all kinds of things and can't imagine that "everything" is available "und ohne Marken?!" (and without ration cards).

In the next letter to her sister, Mutti explains the sudden change of address, but her story of what happened belongs to Goldenitz.

Hamburg, November 25, 1946

My dear Helen,
You are surprised about the "Hamburg", aren't you? Well, we're here, the whole family. It wasn't possible to live under the Russians, so we struck out and sneaked across the line. But I must begin at the beginning.
Sometime during the summer "Gutsverwaltung Goldenitz" received a number of horses from the Soviet Military Administration. After a short time, not only some of these horses but also some of those that already were there, died of a disease the veterinarian finally found out to be anaemia. Most of the horses died as there is no known cure and the disease is contagious. The Russians are always blaming somebody and yelling "Du machen sabotage!" (You make sabotage!) The officer in charge said he would punish Werner for letting all the horses die, which means a trip to Siberia and no return. There is no possible chance of reasoning with them or defending oneself against them so Werner simply sneaked out.

Seeing our father's collapse and Mutti's constant worry was frightening. Papa had always been in charge. He found food and shelter for us when it seemed impossible and kept the family safe. We knew that the accusations and threats of punishment were serious. Other children's fathers had not returned after being arrested, and we had heard the horror stories of banishment to Siberia, torture, and death.

Suddenly, Papa was gone and no one was talking about it. Then a telegram arrived from Omchen in Hamburg with the announcement: *"Baby boy safely arrived. Mother and son doing well."* We laughed when Mutti explained that it meant Papa was safe in Hamburg with Omchen. She also told us not to talk about this to anyone.

Then they threatened to take everything we possessed and probably would have held me until they found Werner. One night I awoke and found light in the room. I jumped out of bed and stood face to face with two of these awful fellows and saw two flashlights and two pistols pointed at me. They had broken in through a window. They ransacked the whole house except one room upstairs in which the young widow lives. They took all of Werner's and my clothing that they had left us or we got back from them a year ago when they broke in.

Werner has no suit left, just an old torn suit of working clothes he had on when he left and an old pair of pants. They also took a pair of high boots and his best shoes but he fortunately had 2 pairs at the shoemaker and one pair on his feet. I only have an old winter dress and two or three summer dresses and blouses I had packed away and my coat. Werner's fur-lined coat also was left, guess they overlooked it. The last piece of bacon, about 5 lbs, my only supply of fat, also went.

When I tried to call for help, they beat me so badly that I can still hardly lift my arm and threatened to shoot me.

This is what my siblings and I remember of the night Mutti describes to her sister.

We five children were sleeping in a separate room from Mutti and were awakened by loud noises and shouting. Mutti cried out. Someone was hurting her.

Walter, the oldest but still just thirteen, jumped out of bed and tried to climb out the window to get help, but a Russian soldier appeared in our room, pointed a gun at him and ordered him back to bed. When Carl saw the soldier, he tried to hide under the bed, but there were boxes of our belongings under there. He had the gun pointed at him until he also got back into bed. Heidi and I huddled close under our blankets. Helga was asleep in her cot.

Mutti's cries stopped abruptly, but we could hear other noises coming from the rest of the house. I know I dozed off a few times, but the soldiers woke me with their rough talk as they took turns standing guard at our bedroom door. It seemed a long time before everything was quiet.

I don't remember what words the boys used to describe what happened to Mutti in the next room. We had heard the horror stories of what some Russian soldiers did to women and even very young girls. I knew about the physical act. I knew it was wrong, and Mutti had been hurt.

I am sure none of us ever forgot, but after the first few days, we did not talk about it. The silence around this event made it impossible to know what had happened. It was not until, as an adult, I participated in a volunteer training program at a sexual assault centre that I gained some understanding of the effect of what my mother had experienced. It seemed far too late to raise the matter with her, and I was left wondering if I actually knew that she had been raped or had I just surmised that so many years ago.

Recently in talking with Helga, I was surprised when she told me about a conversation about this with our mother. She couldn't recall how the subject came up, but Mom had simply said, "You could not stop those guys. So you just had to let it happen."

Mother recalls her desperation as she continues her letter from Hamburg.

> *With all the other worries, it was about all I could bear and I could only pray to God to show me the way I must go. As if someone had told me in so many words, it was suddenly clear that I should follow Werner.*
>
> *I packed all I could in trunks and sent them to Rostock, hauled them to the station on a hand wagon or wheelbarrow, mostly at night. What I couldn't pack, I sold. I couldn't do it all secretly and was in constant fear of something happening before I would be able to get away. It was awful, no peace day and night, constantly in fear and danger, all alone and not knowing what to do or what to expect.*
>
> *It certainly wasn't easy with all the children and our baggage on our backs.*
>
> *We tramped for four hours through mud in the darkest hours of night and were about exhausted when we were finally across the line and in the next village. We had a leader, of course, or we would never have made it. And I wouldn't have made it at all but for a loyal and brave friend I have here, the only one over here. She lost her husband in the war and is a refugee from Ostpreussen.*

Preparing to Escape

Mutti told us we had to leave Goldenitz as soon as possible. Again, we must not talk about it to anyone. We continued to go to school, but we did not dawdle on the way home, always a little anxious to get home to Mutti.

She was sorting and packing, so Heidi and I had to look after Helga and take on more chores. Walter and Carl helped her haul the heavy boxes and trunks to the train station to be shipped to Tante Hete in Rostock.

Mother described her decision and preparation to escape the Russians in the interview in 1989.

"I knew I had to leave, but how? The friend who had helped Werner escape told me, *"Sell what you've got so you'll have some money. I'll get you a guide."*

Mother explains. "She ran the telegraph and the post office with her father. He could manage without her so she came over to help me put on a sale.

"There were many refugees in the area who had walked from their homes and had even less than we did, but when I saw the prices she was putting on the things, I said, *"You can't ask those poor people to pay that much. They don't have anything."* She just insisted that I would need money to start over too, and we'd see how it goes.

"So we sold everything. I didn't think we had much, but I made about 6,000 Marks, all in change and small bills. (*At the time, that was about 2,400 in US dollars.*) It was much too heavy to carry with us, so I put it all in a bag and walked six kilometers to the nearest bank to change it all into bigger bills. I put those in my bag, and I was a little scared. Both coming and going, I thought someone might take it from me. The Russians were always back and forth, but I didn't meet anyone."

Her friend was also the one who acquired and packed some *Rucksacks* for us to carry our things. They were not backpacks with comfy straps and hip belts but canvas knapsacks with narrow leather straps.

Mother remembered even after all those years. "She got us some packs; each of the children had a pack. Walter's was much too big and heavy. He wasn't very strong, only about thirteen at the time; mine was very heavy too."

I remember Mutti telling us that she objected to the heavy bags, saying they could not possibly carry so much weight, but her friend insisted, *"Du kannst was du musst."* (Needs must.)

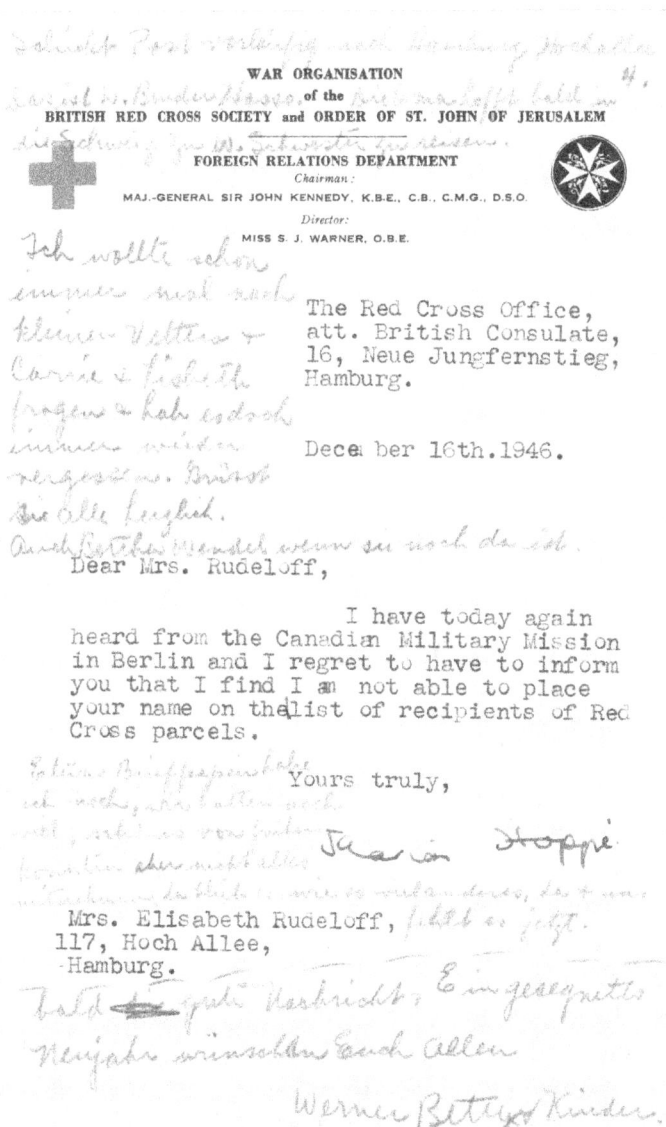

Mutti using a Red Cross Notice as writing paper.

See page 126

On the Move Again

Mother continues her story.

"When I met up with our guide, he told me it wasn't safe to go where Werner had crossed; the Russians had caught on to the place and he would not risk it with five children. We had to take the train south to a safer crossing. I can't remember the name of the place.

"He told me to sit in the last car of the train, get the children out as quickly as possible and walk around the end of the train to the far side away from the station."

Nighttime Escape

We caught a train in the early evening and met up with our guide out behind the train as instructed. He led us a little way into the woods where two other guides were waiting with a group of perhaps fifteen or twenty people.

The guides explained that we would be walking a long way, that we had to be quiet and ready at all times to get into the trees and onto the ground until we were told it was safe to move on.

They checked everyone's clothing. Any light-coloured clothing had to be removed or covered up. I was wearing an off-white hat and Mutti wrapped a navy blue scarf over it and tied it under my chin. The scarf was made of a silky fabric and kept wanting to slip off.

Two of the guides had bicycles and when they saw Mutti's pack, one of them took it from her and put it on his bicycle and carried it for her. Mutti very likely took Walter's pack.

In the interview, Mother remembered her worry about how she would manage the next part of our escape.

"Helga was only three years old and I was worried; how could I possibly get that child across? And then, one of the men offered to carry her. So then we started to walk and when she got sleepy, he asked if I had a blanket and luckily I had taken a small one. I folded it cornerwise and tied it around his neck and one shoulder to make a sling.

"She didn't fall asleep right away and she started to sing. He told her to stop singing. She turned to me and said, *"Why can't I even sing?"*

"I had to convince her that we had to be really quiet and the soldiers must not hear us so that we can go to see Papa."

During all our many travels when we were cold or hungry or scared, Mutti often said, *"Kinder wir singen."* (Children, let's sing.) It may have been because of this that Helga was always humming or singing.

Mother goes on to say that Helga slept all the way, but she may well have started humming again because, although she has no clear memory of this event she has a lifelong fear of someone putting a hand over her face to stop her making a noise.

I remember that when we were all ready to start out, Mutti said, "Carl, you look after Dorle. Walter, you and Heidi stay together. Be very quiet and stay on the path unless you are told to hide in the bushes." The path was not wide enough for us to walk as a family, and she wanted to stay close to Helga in case she cried or needed her.

We were pretty excited as we struck out into the woods. Carl kept me beside him, sometimes we talked in whispers. He stayed close behind me if the path was too narrow. It was dark, but there may have been a moon because we could see where we were stepping. It was also cold, but we had on quite a few layers of clothing, and we kept warm as we walked.

We could not see the road running parallel to our trail but after walking for some time we heard the rattle of a horse-drawn wagon approaching, loud voices shouting and singing. A warning came down the line to get into the trees. I was badly frightened, and I may have whimpered as we hunkered down to let the drunken soldiers pass. Carl put his arm around my shoulders and whispered, *"Nicht weinen, Dorle, wir schaffen es."* (Don't cry, Dorle. We'll make it.)

Back on the trail, we kept on walking for what seemed like forever. I think I must have dozed part of the time even as I walked, and I'm sure Carl had to urge me on as I stumbled along. Twice more we had to crouch in a ditch or in the bushes as patrols passed close by.

Suddenly, I was startled out of my stupor, ready to duck down again, when I saw someone coming toward us. It was one of the guides who had ridden ahead on his bicycle. He bent down, smiled and said quietly, *"Wir sind da!"* (We are there!)

A few more steps, and we came to a small stream with two wooden planks laid across. The men helped everyone cross safely.

We had walked for four hours. Suddenly we were all wide awake, laughing and chattering as we crossed no-man's land, a ploughed field between the creek and a big farmhouse; we were safe.

The whole group gathered in the big, warm kitchen where the wood stove was on, and there was a pot of coffee for the adults. We gathered on the floor in family groups. Everyone had packed what food they could carry, and when Mutti opened her pack she found a jar of canned meat had broken. She carefully picked out the glass and we ate the meat and shared it with the guides. We were ravenous, and it tasted very good. The few provisions that had weighed down Mutti's pack saw us through the next part of our journey, and we were grateful that we did not have to abandon them.

After our long hike, we slept well, everyone huddled together on the floor, some of us on a straw filled mattress in one corner. In the morning it was time to travel on.

Later, much safer in West Germany, we heard the news that our guide was caught with the next group he tried to take across the border, and they were all shot.

Bauernhaus to Hochallee

In the video interview, Mutti's story continues as she describes how we made our way to Hamburg.

"The next morning, the farmer drove up to the house in his one-horse cart and said we should put our bags on the back and he would drive us to the train station. It wasn't far, and we walked along as he drove.

"At the station, I sent a telegram to Werner at his mother's house to say we would arrive at seven o'clock. It was very early.

"We got on the train, and we went along a piece, and then it stopped. Nothing happened, we just sat there. The train wasn't heated, and it was cold.

"After a while, we started up and went a piece again; I've forgotten the name of the place where we had to change trains. We found our train and it was full, so full they were hanging out of the windows. Walter said, *"Mutti, you and the girls get on, Carl and I will get in somewhere."'* They went along to look, and the girls and I managed to get on. People made room for us. Then the call came, *"Doors closed!"* and there were my boys outside the window. *"Mutti, we can't get in anywhere, they won't let us in."*

"I pleaded with the people around me. *"Please be gracious once more; make room for my boys. I can't leave them here.""* Retelling and reliving the experience, Mother was moved to tears.

"So they did, and my boys got in, too. It wasn't much further to Hamburg. When we got off the train, there was no one there to meet us. I guess they hadn't received my telegram yet.

"I inquired about the streetcar that would take us to their street, Hochallee, and we managed to get there. It looked like no one was up, so I rang the doorbell. Grandmother lived three floors up. Werner's younger brother, Hans-Jürgen, and his family lived on that same floor. His wife, Anneliese, opened the window and called down, *"Who's there?"* When I called back, *"It's Betty and the children,"* she sent Werner down and it was a happy reunion, I can tell you."

As I watched my mother tell this story, I too was overcome by emotion. I had completely forgotten this part of our travels, and it gave me a new appreciation of the courage and determination she mustered when it came to looking after us. I know I often wished she were more assertive and would stand up for herself more effectively. She did so when it counted.

It also came as something of a revelation to me that the trauma of our escape did not end when we crossed the little creek and sheltered in the farmhouse. I have no memory of the crowded trains and the boys almost left behind. I wonder how I could retain so many details of our preparation and the long walk through the woods and completely block out the next phase.

I also don't remember the happy reunion at Hochallee 117, but my siblings and I had learned to make the best of any situation, and our brief stay in Hamburg was a good time for us.

Mutti told of ongoing hard times as she continued her letter.

> *After a very tiresome trip on this side we finally reached Hamburg and Werner. But that is by no means the end of our troubles. Having come this way, we can't get our ration cards and it's very hard for W. to get work. Our food supply is about exhausted. The British Red Cross promises to give us some relief and if there's no other way, we can go to a camp where we get free room and board. It isn't nice tho.*
>
> *I don't like to ask for it, but I know you'll all gladly help us when you read this. And if all of you send us a parcel only once in a while, it will be a great help. In the line of clothing, we need stockings and underwear for the children and stockings for me most of all, then, little things such as bobby pins, thread, toilet soap (don't send shoes, they're heavy and we can still get along). The main thing is food: bacon or other fat if possible, evaporated milk, fruit, vegetables, to save weight, cereal, cocoa, chocolate ...*

There could be no positive response to Mother's pleas for food in this letter to her sister in the US, nor the next one, on November 29, to her father in Canada. We were in Hamburg for only a short time and circumstances prevented us from receiving parcels from overseas for several months.

> *You see we are in Hamburg, a short step closer to home. The food question here is very difficult. Also living conditions generally. We had to sell everything in the Russian zone and have*

nothing to make a home with again. We are living with Werner's mother, one room, unheated most of the time. The boys are staying with Hasso and family. We don't know how things will develop further. We may have to go to a camp until further accommodations are found.

It would be a great help to us if you could send us a few food packages. Try to send coffee and cigarettes. We can trade these for potatoes and vegetables. You will surely find other things to send. We get very little milk here, if possible please send powdered milk and the children say "some chocolate please."

There's a long letter on the way. All good wishes for a happy and blessed Christmas to you all from

Werner, Betty and children.

Encounters in Hamburg

After our escape from East Germany, we were relieved and happy to arrive in Hamburg. While it was a very confusing time, we kids, as always, managed to find fun and adventure.

The boys were staying with Onkel Hasso and Tante Gitta who also had two boys. Dirk, the older one, was a bit younger than Carl, and Gert was quite small still and nicknamed *Püppchen* (Doll or Puppet).

I know they had a better time than Heidi and I because we were too young to play outside by ourselves, and they had much more freedom. Whenever we managed to be together, they told us stories about their escapades.

Hamburg had been badly bombed during the war and there were miles and miles of rubble and bombed-out houses. It was strictly forbidden to play in the rubble since there was no way of knowing if the remaining walls and floor were unstable and could collapse at any time, a serious risk to anyone climbing around in them.

The boys never let that kind of thing stop them, so the four of them—Dirk strictly admonished to look after Püppchen—explored the neighbourhood. They were very lucky that they never came to any harm, and none of the parents ever found out what happened, but this was another story that was told in our family for many years.

They were climbing around in the rubble, likely throwing bits of bricks, prying up boards, looking for treasure and not paying much attention to the little guy.

Suddenly Dirk realized that Püppchen was not in sight. Walter and Carl loved to mimic Dirk's panicked screams:

"Mein Bruder ist futsch! Mein Bruder ist futsch!" (My brother is gone. Or My brother has vanished.) He was found, of course, and the story ended well.

During this time, we talked often about returning to Canada. After encountering U.S. and British soldiers in the eastern zone before the Russians moved in, we always turned to Mother for answers when we were puzzled by them or their behaviour.

One day, the four of us managed to get together and struck out on our own, no doubt to the relief of the adults. It was a great day. We travelled on a streetcar and found a carnival with a Ferris wheel and other rides and attractions. It was very exciting, and I fell in love with the most wonderful thing ever when I saw my first merry-go-round. I still long to own a carousel horse.

When we were making our way home, we saw someone walking ahead of us who seemed somewhat strange. We argued back and forth.

"It's a woman."

"No, look at those legs and those shoes; it has to be a man."

"But he's wearing a skirt and kneesocks; it has to be a woman."

"No woman has that kind of haircut." And on and on. We couldn't wait to get home and ask Mutti because she knew everything.

We all talked at once, and when Mutti realized what we were describing, she laughed until tears streamed down her cheeks before she cleared up the mystery. We had seen our first Scottish soldier in a kilt.

I also saw my first Black man in Hamburg. We were on a train platform for some reason, and a train full of American soldiers pulled in. They weren't disembarking, but many of them were leaning out the windows smoking and some waving to us.

Then I suddenly saw a very big, very Black soldier in one of the windows. I had never seen anyone like that. In the German puppet theatres, the Black man was always the evil one, and I did not know what to think. I was fascinated, and I stared. We weren't allowed to stare, and Carl saw me and came over, nudged me and said, "Don't stare. You're being rude."

I guess I looked worried, and the big man smiled and reached down as far as he could and held out a small tin. I looked at Carl for permission to take it because we had been told not to beg for chocolate from the American soldiers when we first encountered them. Carl nodded, and I took the tin.

It was a Planters peanuts tin, almost full of peanuts, and I was very proud to share them with the others. Carl had to tell the story. I had no words to describe what had happened.

Leaving Hamburg

My mother wrote the following note (in English) on a small scrap of paper. It bears no date.

> *There is a letter on the way, but I hope to get this there faster. We're in Hamburg for a week tomorrow. It's a relief to have left the worries of fear we had in the Russian zone behind. If I never see a Russian again in my life, I won't miss them. Now, however, we have new troubles. The food problem is difficult.*
>
> *We are going to a camp in a day or two, that is the children and I. Werner has taken work in Hamburg so has to stay here. He will most likely go to live with his brother Hasso as there is no room here, neither in the home nor in the hearts.*
>
> *Hasso and his wife are nice, sensible, warm-hearted people. These here are just the contrary. It goes for a day or two and then everything goes wrong. It doesn't matter tho, we've been able to get along without them before and have met many people who were strangers to us but took us into their homes, so we shall get along without them further. Don't worry about us, we'll get along. We long for all you loved ones and for a home of our own. We think and talk so much about you. Your ears must ring!*

These here would be Onkel Hans-Jürgen, Tante Anneliese and Omchen. Mother always looked close to tears when she told stories about how she was made to feel like a beggar, especially by her brother-in-law, Hans-Jürgen, who commented every couple of days: "So, you are still here," or "When are you going to the camp?"

Thousands of people who had escaped the war zones and were

now escaping from the Russian zone, had to be housed and fed. As long as we were staying with relatives, we could not be placed as refugees or receive ration cards.

I don't know what the process was to get into a camp. I do know Mutti would not have stayed with the relatives any longer than absolutely necessary.

The distances from Hamburg to Hannover, then to Aurich would not have been more than an hour or two by car, but travel at the time was difficult by any means. Many refugees and army personnel were still being moved around. Our parents' story in the video interview explains our mode of transport.

Mom begins. "We had to leave Hamburg and so we went to where there was a camp for this sort of thing. We got there just at supper time and we had something to eat, but we didn't stay overnight."

"There was a train pulling out at midnight, and it was crowded, stuffed full. There were only boxcars," Dad interjects.

Mutti continued. "So we got in and sat on our bags and bundles. The first ones to get on were lying down, they had lots of room; they wouldn't move." Dad carries on.

"So we started out and then the train stopped. It was right outside a village, and the engineers went home for supper.

"There were five boxcars full of tired, hungry people. So another fellow and I went into the town and rousted out a town official, who helped us find the Red Cross, and we got five or six big soup pots going.

"We were there for the rest of the night. In the morning the engineers came back and we started out again for our destination."

There was another story from this trip that we children retold many times. The boxcar was dark and dank, and we tried to make ourselves as comfortable as possible sitting or lying on the floor as we got underway.

There was a group of people in one corner of the car who started to sing. One woman with a somewhat shrill voice could always be heard well above the others as they sang the same song over and over again. *"Bella, Bella, Bella Marie sei mir treu ich komm zurück Morgen früh. Bella, Bella, Bella Marie vergiss mich nie."* (Bella Marie, be true to me, I will return at dawn. Bella Marie, don't ever forget me.)

Eventually, they dropped off one by one; only the one woman persisted. She too must have stopped when we all managed to sleep for a time.

In the morning as the train began to move, Walter's groans could be heard even in the far corner as the singing resumed. I think it was also Walter who decided to name the lead singer *Bella*.

When this jaunt was well and truly behind us, we pondered whether the unpleasant smell of too many bodies, the discomfort of trying to sleep on the floor or the woman's singing was the most annoying part of that journey.

Bella and friends were also destined for Norderney and we saw her now and then during our stay in Norderney, but I don't think we ever knew her real name.

Aurich, Ostfriesland, 25. December 1946

My Dear Ones!

Today is Christmas, and I must write a quick greeting under the Christmas tree. It was a very modest celebration but very nice just the same.

I wrote in my short letter (which I hope the English lady sent by airmail) that we had to go into a transitional camp. We travelled to Ülzen, Hannover and were fortunate to be transported straight here to Aurich. I mean the luck was that we did not have to stay long in the camp. It is not at all nice there and very "Halt & Zug" (touch & go).

From here, we will all move on to the Ostfriesischen Islands where we will be put up in the summer hotels, etc. Several thousand are there already and if there is heating fuel organized it should be very nice. But we are "only" refugees! It is so sad that misery is still on the rise and the "Volkerwanderung" (relocation of people) is still in full swing. When and how will that finally be better!

While we were all feeling very defeated, Werner spoke with an official in the camps and asked if it would not be possible to be put up around here somewhere. The woman doctor who looks after refugees who are ill took me and the children straight into the "Kranken Baracke" (hospital barracks), where we are now.

There are no seriously ill people here, only children and adults recovering from various illnesses. Helga has just had the measles but is better now. The others had them already.

Everything here is very primitive, but it is adequately heated and we have enough nourishing food and at the moment we have no worries until Helga is completely well. What happens then and where we will end up, only the dear God knows and he will lead us on and keep us until we are back with you.

Werner was here for the holidays.

The lady doctor, her sister, the secretary and the nurses have gone to a great deal of trouble to make Christmas as nice as possible. There was a celebration of the whole camp with a tree and coffee and cake for everyone. In the rooms where there were measles or whooping cough, there was a small tree and also a celebration.

The children received a whole, the adults a half Stollen (it was simply white bread baked with milk, the raisins were missing), apples and sweets. Our children bought a little tree and decorated it themselves, it looks lovely. We sang Christmas songs and we happily talked about the Christ Child and that we were all together.

We talk about you all the time and how nice it will be when we are back with you. Ach ja!

Aurich – a Birthday and Christmas

Mother's letter of December 25, 1946 is written on the back of an official notice from the Canadian Military Mission in Berlin notifying her that as we are all considered to be German, there would be no assistance for us in getting back to Canada. In spite of how sad she must have felt upon receiving this news and sending it on to her family, she helped us celebrate the season as best she could.

She explains that it was Helga's measles that gained us admission into the hospital, and we were safe for the time being. My older sister, Heidi, had glandular tuberculosis, and I was always under the impression it was her illness that saved us from that dreadful camp.

Our beds were just army cots, but we were warm, and we could keep clean and we had indoor plumbing. We shared a large room with a number of other people, and we all got along well. There were some good times playing cards and other games, but we could never stay confined indoors for long.

It was already very cold but we begged to be allowed outside.

We explored the neighbourhood and roamed farther afield. My brothers thought it was good fun to lead us through a great maze of air raid shelters even though this was strictly forbidden. I imagine we could have gotten lost in what seemed like miles of concrete tunnels with most entrances and exits blocked off. The boys may have known of the danger, but I trusted them completely to keep us safe, whatever adventures they found, wherever we happened to land.

There was not much to do in the town itself, but I remember it best for the bartering shops. All sorts of wonderful items were displayed in their windows with notices on each item stating what would be taken in trade. There was nothing much to buy with money so none was charged.

Heidi and I were admiring many of the things in the shop window when I saw a beautiful pair of roller skates. I had wanted rollerskates since I was four years old and first saw a kid roller skating back in Rostock. The notice said men's white shirts were wanted in exchange. It seemed to me that my father had many white shirts. I saw Mutti wash and iron them all the time. I worked up my courage and said to Heidi, "Do you think we could give them one of Papa's white shirts for the roller skates?"

"Don't be silly. He'd never do that and where would you even roller skate? We are going to an island and there would be no place to use them."

I celebrated my ninth birthday in this place and while I did not get the roller skates, it was one birthday I remember most fondly. When the ladies in charge found out that my birthday was coming up, one of them asked what special treat I wanted for my celebration. Heidi blurted out, "*Buttercreme Torte*" which we had for birthdays in Ziegelhof. I sensed that I should not ask for cake. I knew everything was in short supply and asked instead, "Could I have white bread with butter and honey?" I couldn't quite believe she said yes.

I thought she was magic when she presented me with a huge platter of exactly what I had asked for on the day. I have never forgotten how good that tasted. We had had only very heavy, dark bread with a bit of jam for a long time so this was a rare treat. The children in our room were invited and we shared and it seemed we could not stop licking our fingers when it was all gone. There were even some presents for me to open which the family had bought in Hamburg.

After my birthday it was time to prepare for Christmas. In her letter home, Mutti wrote that we children bought our own little tree for our room. We had no decorations and no candles, but she taught us to cut many small snowflakes out of white paper with which to decorate our tree. I thought the tree was very beautiful even though we had no lights or tinsel.

With no piano or music, she called on her memory and experience playing the piano for choir practice as a young woman and taught us a fairly complicated harmony for a Christmas song.

We were very excited at the prospect of performing our piece at a Christmas concert for the whole camp. It was not to be. Even though Helga was recovering from measles, our dormitory was now quarantined for whooping cough. We sang the song, comparing the glowing lights on the Christmas tree to the stars glistening in the night sky, for everyone gathered around in our room.

It was a beautiful song that we sang and treasured for many Christmases to come.

Mother must have given up precious writing paper for us to make the snowflakes for our Christmas tree as the letter continues on the back and in the margin of a Red Cross notice dated December 16th, 1946 disallowing parcels to us. The shortage of paper is mentioned in several letters.

> *From this letter, which I am using as writing paper, you will see that we are not going to be successful. We are anxious to find out if you have had any success with anything over there. If not, perhaps we should try to get into the U.S.A. I believe it might be easier and from there to Canada. What do you think? We may simply have to wait until immigration is freer for everyone, but who knows what all will happen to us before then. I really hope to receive good news soon. We wish all of you a blessed new year,*
> *Werner, Betty and children*

For a while after Christmas we were able to stay in Aurich, and the boys got up to more exploits. My family lived near water for many years as we were growing up, and we continued to be drawn to it as adults. Carl and I once watched some tug boats towing what seemed like enormous barges at Spanish Banks in Vancouver, and he was reminded of our stay in Aurich and the tugboats and barges frozen in the canal.

"You know Walter and I were always after something new and exciting and we thought they were pretty interesting. We'd never seen anything like that before and this was our chance to have a look. It was hard to get up onto the barges and—once we got there—we were a bit nervous about actually climbing onto the boats even though there was no one around. The ice was really solid and we were able to climb down onto it.

"It turned out the most interesting thing we found was some peat piled up on the ice between the boats and the wharf where the barges had been unloaded.

"We knew it was fuel and we also knew there was never enough.

"When we got back home, we told Dad about it. It took him no time at all to get hold of some gunny sacks and he got Walter and me down on the ice scooping up the peat to take along to the island.

"I was kind of mad at him for making us do that, but he knew what he was doing. You remember, we were very glad to have the fuel that first while in Norderney and it didn't last nearly long enough."

Any kind of fuel, along with everything else, was in short supply and since it was a very cold winter, this would have been considered a real find.

There is a paragraph in Mother's letter that speaks to the shortage of food.

> *The Red Cross distributes parcels containing "Speck" or butter, sausage and sometimes baked goods that they confiscate from those who have. No German farmer gives anything freely or willingly.*

We received one of these parcels and our parents would have tried to hold on to some of that food for us to take along when we had to leave the hostel.

Life in Norderney

Norderney is one of the seven populated islands off the coast of Germany, called the East Frisian Islands (*Ostfriesische Inseln*) in the North Sea.

The last letter written by Mother on Dec. 25, 1946, from Aurich, would not have arrived in Canada by February 1, 1947, when my Canadian Oma wrote to Onkel Hasso in Hamburg looking for us. I have translated his very formal reply:

Hamburg, the 25.2.47

Sehr geehrte Frau Ulmer! (Most honoured Mrs. Ulmer!)
Your letter of the 1st day of this month has arrived here today. I understand that you are worried about Werner and his family. I believe in this instance the fault is not Werner's (even though he is very lazy when it comes to writing, we are constantly waiting for mail), but rather the problems are the conditions in Germany. We have an extreme frost at the moment which is seriously curtailing all travel and communication to the point where it is impossible for Werner to get a letter to you. Just yesterday, I received a telegram from him that they are relatively safe and that three letters from Canada that I forwarded to him have arrived. Other than that, I have received another letter from you as well as one from the United States. These have been forwarded to Werner's address. As far as the parcels you mention

are concerned, only one has arrived so far which I have collected from the customs office. I can however forward this only when conditions improve (meaning when there is a major thaw) as there is a danger that it will be left somewhere and may be lost.

As far as Werner's family's fate is concerned, I can give you the following news: As you know, Werner escaped from the Russian sector under extremely difficult circumstances and came to us. He and the family were then assigned to a refugee camp where they fared reasonably well and, as you know, celebrated a nice Christmas. They were then sent to a new location on the Island Norderney. The people who took them in, a master painter, are said to be very kind and have provided them with the necessities such as bedding, dishes etc. It continues to be very difficult for them as Werner is only receiving unemployment benefits and even the very barest of foodstuffs are available and those at enormous cost. Because of the severe weather conditions, the question of heating is critical, but I believe Werner will find a way to overcome this problem also. As far as we know, Betty takes the children to a large hall during the day, which is heated and made available for those who have no means of heating their own rooms.

During this extreme frost, the Island is completely surrounded by ice so that all connection with the mainland is cut off. As a result, as long as the frost continues, no letters etc. can be forwarded. I have attempted to arrange a telephone connection and will report on my progress with that later in this letter.

Should any more parcels arrive for Werner's family, we will, of course, keep them safely here until they may be sent on to them. I will discuss this with Werner if I am successful in reaching him by telephone.

As you will know, Werner is attempting to return to Canada with his family. The Canadian Consulate in Berlin has, unfortunately, advised that Betty, as she is married to a German citizen, is considered German and the children, as long as they are in Germany, will also not be recognized as Canadian citizens. In spite of that, there are ways and means by which travel to Canada may be managed. The most effective method would be for you to be able to procure the necessary paperwork and additional advice needed to obtain immigration permission from the Canadian Government.

I hope, my very, very honoured Mrs. Ulmer, that I have imparted all the information you desire. Should you have further questions, I am, of course, completely at your disposal.

With the best wishes for you and your family's well-being, I remain

Your Hasso Rudeloff

Unfortunately I was unable to connect by telephone today. I will attempt again tomorrow to relate your letter to Werner.

Hungry and Cold

The information Onkel Hasso had about us would have come from my father, and he may not have wanted to let his family know how unpleasant and difficult our experiences were after we left the facility in Aurich that Onkel Hasso mentions.

When Mother wrote her Christmas letter from Aurich she could not have foreseen the difficulties to come. It was one of the coldest winters on record, and we were soon to find ourselves in the worst possible situation.

Our family was part of an allotment of 1,000 refugees sent to Norderney, an island in the North Sea. There was a serious food shortage in all of Germany, and we suffered the additional hardship of being cut off from the mainland.

Hotels, pensiones and even private homes were required to take in refugees. We were billeted in a pensione in two rooms with one small stove and very little fuel. The smaller room had to be closed off because our stove was not adequate to heat it, and it became very damp and cold.

We were supposed to have the use of the kitchen and the gas stove for cooking, but this was rarely granted.

The *kind Master Painter* that Onkel Hasso mentions was only kind until he and his family found out that there were no special benefits from having the *American* family assigned to them. There were four of them living in the house, Herr and Frau Weierts, and two Fraeulein Weierts. I thought they were very old, but I imagine they may have only been in their fifties. They owned a pensione as well as the painting business and rented out rooms during the tourist season. In their defence, having a family of seven move into prime tourist rooms must have been devastating.

Mother writes that we spent two to three weeks in our beds, but occasionally we bundled up and hurried to the end of our street to a warming hall. We met other people there, some also with children, and occasionally we were given small amounts of food or fuel to take home.

What little food we brought with us from the mainland was soon gone, and we could only get our daily rations by lining up in the bitter cold.

Carl told this story.

"Dad and Walter and I had to go out each morning to line up for bread and milk. Sometimes we had to wait for two hours, and Walter and I took turns running home to crawl into bed to get warm while the other one kept our place in line. Sometimes we both had to stay outside because the bread was at the bakery and we had to get the milk at the dairy. When Dad was able to take one of the lineups, he would tell us to take turns."

Dad was often out scouting around for some fuel or something to put on the bread. At home, our parents made sandwiches with what they were able to get and divided it among us. I know there were times when they did not eat at all. They were both very thin.

Carl admired his older brother for his clever inventions and described how Walter and Dad built a hot plate.

"They moulded it from clay and I imagine the wire, which was coiled around a knitting needle to create the element, came from something Walter dismantled for this purpose. I don't remember where we found clay to mould the hotplate." This is where we cooked whatever could be found when we had no fuel and the electricity was on.

On at least one occasion, we received potatoes. We found that they had been frozen which gave them a foul, soapy, sweetish flavour. They were very hard to eat no matter how hungry we were. When I first heard of *sweet potatoes*, after coming to Canada, the very thought of eating them made me gag, and I did not try them for many years.

We could not identify the dried vegetable we received, but I believe it was dehydrated red cabbage. No matter how long it was boiled, it always consisted of stringy, leathery bits in a bitter brown brine. This was as disgusting as the frozen potatoes. Even as adults, Walter and Helga could always identify cabbage in dried soups or other dehydrated foods. Helga was only three and a half at the time, but some things the body does not forget.

I imagine the more interesting provisions did not arrive until the ferry was running again and some British personnel came to the island. Many of the German people took it as a grave insult when canned horse meat became available. We were still hungry much of the time and we did not complain.

It was decades later that I heard an explanation of how the hated cornbread came to us. In Germany, corn is called *Mais* and is grown on farms for livestock only and not considered fit for human consumption. *Korn* is the German word for grain.

The story goes that an official somewhere was asked, "What do you need to feed the people?" Since grain is a mainstay in the German diet, the answer was "*Korn.*" Once more, people were insulted to find they were expected to eat cattle food as corn flour was supplied to the bakeries to supplement rye or wheat flour to bake much-needed bread.

Mutti was delighted with the cornbread and, not being told otherwise, we children liked it too. It was Mutti's turn to be outraged when she heard that some people had changed the Lord's prayer and said, "Give us this day our daily cornbread."

Norderney
the 24. March 1947

Werner brought your loving, very comprehensive letter from Hamburg day before yesterday. Also a letter from Hans and two parcels from Lene and one from Hans. Everything arrived safely and you can imagine our joy at receiving the lovely, delicious things ....

The letters take forever to get here too. Even your airmail takes three weeks or more. That may be because they have been censored recently. We have written a number of letters from here that you should have received by now. I am so sorry that you worried about us so much. We live here very quietly and on the whole, things are not bad. We have several very bad weeks behind us.

While the ferry, which serves the island, was stuck in the ice, food was in short supply and we often did not even have bread, which is our mainstay. There were preparations made for this eventuality: flour, canned goods, milk powder, meat and vegetables in cans but it was not enough for the many people who were placed here during this harsh winter. We were often quite hungry but "He who feeds the birds in the sky" looked after us and we survived ....

The cold is also finally at an end. For 2 - 3 weeks we had no fuel and spent many days in our beds because it was simply too cold to get up. Sometimes we went to visit a young widow who came here with us. She occasionally received a little coal from her host family, while they still had some. Last week she did not have any more while we, fortunately, were able to get some so she and her three children came to us ....

Out of the Deep Freeze

When we were first told we were going to an island to live, I had no idea what that might look like. The only island I had seen was a small one in the middle of our pond in Ziegelhof. In the summer it was green, and we could see a few small trees and some flowers from the shore but could never reach them. In the winter we could cross over to it on the ice but it was covered in snow, and there was no sign of flowers or other living things.

Arriving in Norderney in January on the last ferry before the island was cut off from the mainland—and housebound for several weeks with very little food and not nearly enough fuel—was not a good introduction to island life. I wondered occasionally if it was as bad as I remembered.

When I found an article in *Magazin Norderney*, Winter 2006/07 in which Jürgen Rahmel describes the attempt to bring provisions to the island during this time, I knew that we had not exaggerated our plight in our memories. He writes:

"... on foot in temperatures of 12° C below with winds of 5 out of the east on a complete sheet of ice. Approximately 250 men were involved in attempting to bring food and fuel from the mainland for the 8,700 inhabitants of the island. They began on foot, then by sleigh and eventually by trucks. Regular ferry traffic did not resume until 21 March 1947."

During a similar icy grip in February 1996, Rahmel and two friends successfully completed a one-way reenactment of the journey undertaken in 1947. He describes the difficulties navigating the *Wattenmeer* between the eastern end of the island and the mainland. Unlike the white sandy beaches on the northern shore, the southeastern coast, the *Wattenmeer,* is made up of tidal shallows or mudflats at low tide. These areas, while unnavigable by boat, do not freeze solid. The men frequently broke through the ice into knee-deep water and struggled each time to regain solid ice.

Relating this test of his strength and endurance, Rahmel writes, *"I have to think of the man who died of a heart attack in 1947 while crossing the Matt to get food for Juist."* Juist is the island immediately east of Norderney.

The ground was becoming firmer when they were confronted and puzzled by what appeared to be an enormous stack of *Eisplatten*, (ice slabs), stacked like pancakes by a giant hand, creating a four-meter high iceberg. Rahmel marvels, *"How does an object of this size arrive so close to shore?"*

We also encountered these giant ice slabs when we were finally released from the confines of one room.

The weather finally relented and we eagerly bundled up to venture forth and explore the island beyond our small street. Looking to the right at the end of Kreuzstrasse, we could see shops and houses on the streets of the village. The view to the left was more mysterious, as the road rose slightly and seemed to end beyond a few large buildings. We could see only the sky, and I was a little nervous, wondering if the island ended there and we would drop into the sea.

When we reached the top of the rise, we found a large open area—still covered in snow—encircled by a road. We could not see what lay beyond until we crossed the road and followed a paved path to the edge of the seawall.

We were in no danger of falling off the edge of the island. We found steps leading down to a wide promenade and below that, we had our first glimpse of the ocean's enormous power.

All along the beach, huge, half-a-meter-thick slabs of ice were stacked two and three high, some tilted on edge, others still floating in the open water beyond. This is what had kept the boats from reaching the island.

We had a great time climbing around on the marooned ice for a time, and the boys were intrigued by the chunks floating on the waves. They had to concede that it was too difficult, and likely dangerous, to get onto the floating ice and abandoned the idea.

Mutti's letter continues with better news.

> Now it is quite pleasant outside. The children frequently go to the beach. In the summer it must be truly beautiful. I think the sea air will be particularly good for Heidi's health. Both girls are very delicate and too thin. They were x-rayed a few days ago and are both healthy. Heidi's tuberculosis was confined to one gland and it has healed well. The boys, especially Walter, are also very thin. I hope they can all recover better health here. Helga seems the healthiest of all. She is strong and healthy, has red cheeks and shiny, dark brown eyes. She looks so much like Margaret.
>
> The ferry is moving again, Werner received some help from his brothers, then we received the wonderful parcels, and now that the snow is gone, the children gather mussels on the beach. We finally have enough to eat again. We are not lacking in good appetites in this sea air.

Discovering Norderney

Climbing around on the ice floes somehow made us feel triumphant. The cold could no longer contain us. We were also happy when they finally melted and we could explore the sandy beach.

We took the same wide steps down to the promenade. A rounded brick slope took us down to the beachhead from which the breakwaters radiated out like the arms of a seastar. Between the breakwaters was the beach with the surf rolling in. Seagulls soared and screamed overhead. The wind blowing in our faces made us laugh right along with them.

Further along the northern side of the island, we found the bathing beach and sand dunes, pure white sand reaching inland as far as we could see. It was much too early to venture into the water but we knew this was where we would be headed as soon as it was warm enough.

We marvelled at all this space and, not surprising as it is a fourteen-kilometer (8.7 mile) long sandy beach, almost the full length of the island. After all the strange and confining places we had experienced, this was freedom.

Mutti mentions that we gathered mussels to supplement our diet. When the beach was finally clear of ice and we could reach the breakwaters, we were happy to gather a bucket full every day. At home we boiled them in a large pot and ate them right out of the shells. It was fortunate that we all liked them. There was still a shortage of food and we were often hungry, so the addition of this protein may well have saved us from malnutrition. We ate mussels for most of our stay on the island but less often as things improved and we were able to buy shrimp and fish from the local fishers.

The locals did not eat mussels at that time, but they are now considered a delicacy in Ostfriesland as well as elsewhere in the world.

We also found much of interest in the town. The streets were paved with cobblestones and the sidewalks and some roads were made of red brick. Most of the houses and many larger buildings were also built of brick , including the church and school.

We walked everywhere. The boys already knew where the bakery and the grocery store were from having to line up for food. The dairy store was in the opposite direction, and the greengrocer eventually also opened.

For transportation, colourful horse-drawn buses carried perhaps twenty passengers in comfort on rubber tires. It didn't take us long to learn to jump on the back of one of these to catch a quick ride. Older people, better off than we, could hire a closed carriage to take them to church or to go shopping. The only car on the island belonged to the doctor.

Life continued to present many challenges, but—in time—Norderney became as dear to us as our beloved Ziegelhof had been.

Mother's letter resumes.

> *Our efforts to obtain my repatriation were refused. We are not giving up hope that you will be more successful from over there. Our landlord heard on the radio about a new law in Canada which allows those who have close relatives there, being allowed to immigrate. If it is true, you will likely hear about it from your agent and then it should not take too much longer. The waiting is not so bad if one can hope that it will eventually happen. Werner will have work for the summer and we will manage.*
>
> *As far as the money for travel to Canada goes, there is no*

good news. I know this will be a great sacrifice for you and that it will not be easy but I also know that you do it gladly.

Dear Father, you ask about school and church here. The school has been closed for weeks because of a shortage of coal, and elsewhere the children have attended school only sporadically in the last 2 years and are behind in their education.

Starting School in Norderney

Not long after this letter was written, school opening was announced. I was excited but also worried. We had been free to roam and explore many new places with few restrictions for a long time as we moved from place to place. This would be a big adjustment.

Walter, Carl and Heidi had gone to school in Schwertburg, the nearest town to Ziegelhof before the end of the war, but I have no memories of starting school. I only attended for a few months in 1944 before we left Ziegelhof in January 1945.

Mother wrote in one of her letters in 1945, *from January until December 1945, we had no home.* Schools were likely generally disrupted during that difficult time as the war was ending. When we were more settled in Goldenitz, we attended school there for a few months. I enjoyed that time, and I think this must have been where I learned to read and write.

There was a scramble for school supplies. We had no notebooks, very little paper of any kind, and even pencils were in short supply. None of these were available in stores. I don't know what the others managed to find, but Walter got hold of what I believe was a receipt book and a stubby bit of an indelible pencil for me.

"I can't use this. What if I make a mistake? It won't erase. Couldn't I have a slate?"

"We don't have any slates. You'll just have to be careful."

I had used a slate before, and it turned out some of the local kids in the primary grades still had them. Those fortunate few wrote with a stylus made of slate; you had to be careful not to break it, but mistakes were easily dealt with. I eventually had one for a time, but by then there were notebooks and we used pencils. If we were lucky, we had an eraser.

Heidi was accepted into fourth grade and Carl joined grade five in the *Volksschule*. Walter, being the oldest son, went into grade six in the *Mittelschule* which was for students preparing to go on to higher education.

Because I had so little schooling, I again started in grade one at age nine. I don't recall being tested, and the discussion was more about which teachers were available rather than my abilities. Remembering some of the teachers from that time, Fräulein Gobel may have been the most sympathetic choice for me. She was a remarkable woman. I admired and feared her in equal parts as she moved up the grades with my class.

> *We try to teach them some English so that they know a little when we come back and do not have to start from so far back. There are no materials available, but they are learning a little. Walter already had some English instruction in school.*
>
> *There is a church and regular services here. We have not attended so far as it has been so cold and there is no heat in the church. The children are also behind in their religious education, but they are learning the catechism and know many prayers and hymns. It is a little slow because one can't be as strict with the instruction at home as it would be in school, but they all love their Saviour and have their childlike faith in God. When I despair, Werner often makes me ashamed with his firm faith in God, which makes me happy as he did not always believe as we did ....*

Mutti continued to teach us many songs in both German and English, which not only got us through the bad times but taught us to love music. When we had fuel, we spent our evenings sitting around the stove singing.

There was often only enough light for one person to read so we took turns reading out loud to pass the time. The attempts made at learning English through word games and songs sometimes had hilarious results. I remember feeling very shy when it was my turn to come up with a translation, and I proudly proclaimed the definition of *Ei* (egg) in English as Humpty Dumpty and everyone laughed.

> *Now I have chatted on for a long time and must close. God grant that we will soon tell each other everything that is in our hearts in person. Our most heartfelt wishes and love from all your*

very thankful Children.

The airmail paper arrived, many thanks.

Father's margin note: Heartfelt greetings and many thanks for your loving letters.

Your Werner.

Mother's letter, a few days later to her sister Helen in the US, is in English. She reports that the steamer is running again and that we have received a number of food parcels from various members of the family.

> *I wonder if you can imagine what our feelings were when Werner came & we opened your treasure chests. If you could have been here then, and since then, when our meals are so much better, I think you would know how thankful we are for every bit. It's like a bit of home to Werner and me, and ever new surprises for the children.*
>
> *The tea, coffee and cigs. helped in different ways and were also enjoyed. You'll understand me when I only say we thank you with all our hearts and "vergelt's Euch Gott!" (May God reward you!)*
>
> *I sent a long letter home a few days ago which I suppose they'll send around. Wish I could answer every letter I get but don't seem to manage. I'm so clumsy and slow at it.*
>
> *With love and greetings to all you dear ones from your grateful*
>
> *Werner, Betty, Walter, Carl, Heidi, Dorli & Helga*

Mother says she is clumsy and slow at writing letters, and she struggled with this all her life. What a shame that she did not realize what a treasure these letters are. She was intimidated by the German relatives and their apparent ability to write effectively and reply promptly.

I remember her remarking that she did not like to write to my Tante Gitta as she would get a reply almost immediately and then it was her turn to write again. The letters to the family in Canada were somewhat easier as they all seemed to suffer from the same affliction. Still, it is sad to think of how much of her life she lived at a distance from those she loved and how she struggled to stay in touch.

PS. An extra "thank you" for the thread. Comes in mighty handy.

If you get this before we start for home(!) (All the letters are censored now and take one awful time) and want to send anything yet, Werner says send tea. We can make a lot of people happy and get a lot of things we need for it. This is not black market trading but just one favour for another.

You were right about all the birthdays, Helen. We'll be thinking of you all and wishing you a Happy Easter.

A rare letter from Aunt Helen shows the care they all took to share any news from us with the rest of the family.

Sheboygan, May 5/47

Dear Parents,

Betty's letter came last week but I did not get at a reply. This evening I transcribed her letter (and made a carbon copy at the same time) and wrote to Walters in Wembley. Could you send a copy to Carl and Jacobs please? I will not get to it in the next few days and in the meantime, the letter is aging. Please also give it to Georgs to read.

I have been accumulating a pile of stuff that is growing but don't know if I should send it. Perhaps I will wait until she writes again.

Greetings from Marvin and the children, and from your Helen.

Another rare letter, this one in German from Dad, expresses his disappointment in the people of his country.

Dear Parents,

Again one of your loving letters, which always speak of your worry and uncertainty for us. Even if we reply immediately, our letters get there too late. We can see this in your letters. Your letter of 4 March arrived here on 12 April, so one must always count on 6 weeks. We believe you must have several of our letters by now.

We are not short of money here, and I am determined that we will try to pay our fare from here even if that means it will take a little longer. I hope you can help us arrange it in that way as I don't know how else we can do this.

I am working for the English as a host for English tourists in a hotel here. While there is not very much to do, it is at least a job. We survived the winter and hope we will not spend another one here in Germany. Betty already wrote about the parcels and we hope they will all arrive safely. I want to thank you all with all my heart as they filled a great need and made us all so very happy.

When I went to Canada in 1927 for freedom and the joy of work, I now go with contempt for my own people, their kind of freedom. Perhaps with God's help, everything will turn out alright again.

For all the good things you are doing for us, my heartfelt thanks. I hope these lines reach you in good health,
Your Werner

Mutti often wrote to her brothers and sisters in English since most of them were not nearly as fluent in German as she was. I am sure the circumstances she describes must have been very strange to her family at the time. They were accustomed to close quarters in a family of twelve children but, thinking back, I am amazed at how my mother managed in our situation.

The next letter is addressed to her sister Margaret but she seems to be writing to her sister Elsa and husband, Walter, as well.

April 23, 1947

My dear Margaret,
At last, you shall really have a letter from me and not one of my circulars ... I wish we could all get together once again and have a real gabfest, only I'm afraid we'd "talk our heads off." There are so many things I would like to know and so much I could tell you. My biggest difficulty is cooking. We've done most of it on the heater because we don't get enough gas allowance to do it all, and the folks here don't want us to use it. They don't want us to cook in the room tho either as it spoils the walls and makes the room messy. Even if we use our gas, you can imagine what it's like to cook with 2 other parties (one an old childless woman, and 2 old maids) on a gas range with 3 burners.

Cooking was very difficult at the time. One day when Mother was allowed to cook in the kitchen, she left a precious soup bone simmering on the stove while she returned to our room to prepare the few other items to go into the soup. When she returned to the kitchen, one of the women was skimming the fat off the soup. Fat was a rare and valued commodity, and it is hard to imagine mature adults taking it from children.

Often our evening meal was milk soup. This was most of our ration of milk plus a cup of rolled oats or cream of wheat. There was not enough to make porridge so it was a thin soup; we each had a bowl. This soup did not adhere to the sides of the pot but still, we took turns scraping the pot and sometimes there were arguments over whose turn it was.

Carl was devastated when a classmate, a relative of our hosts, taunted him at school about his family fighting over who could scrape the pot.

I don't believe it is possible to call up hunger pains long after experiencing them. I do remember that we seemed to be constantly thinking and talking about food at the time. I also remember our parents often going without food so we children could have a little more.

After expressing some concern for our fuel supply, Mother continues.

> *I guess we'll manage, everything "turns out" somehow, and time often solves problems that no amount of brain work will solve.*
>
> *Now I've rambled on instead of acknowledging the receipt of a wonderful food package about the 12th of this month. I really don't know how we'd manage without your help. Thanks to all you dear ones, our meals have improved considerably in quantity as well as quality. And can you guess how good everything tastes to us? It's like a bit of home.*
>
> *I wish you could have seen the children's faces when they saw the chocolate bars. The hot chocolate tin had lost its bottom and had spilled most of its contents thru the package, but we could save most of it.*

I am sure every last bit of hot chocolate was scooped up somehow as that would have been a rare treat indeed. Our ration of milk included three-quarters of a liter of whole milk for Helga, but it was always put in the pail with the two liters of the skim milk, which we had to pick up at the dairy store each day.

May 2

Of course it wouldn't do for me to finish a letter in one sitting.

This time I'm glad tho, that I hadn't mailed this yet when two days ago the parcel from Ell & Walter came. Also one, the first one, from the folks and one from Hans. They came just as our "cupboard was getting bare" and were greeted with cheers.

Thank you with all our hearts, dear Elsa & Walter, for all the goodies and the other useful things. Thread is a real treasure and I have quite a nice supply now from the different parcels ....

Mother acknowledges nine parcels, some of them CARE parcels, which she describes and expresses her gratitude.

...Each "CARE" parcel contains about 40 lbs of foodstuffs. May God repay you manyfold what we are unable to do.

CARE parcels contained the sort of staples still in very short supply at the time. Relatives and friends in Canada could pay a very reasonable amount to CARE Canada, and we received a heavy cardboard cube secured with metal straps and filled with forty pounds of nourishment. Unlike other packages, these cubes were difficult to pilfer and always arrived intact.

They were not as personal or exciting to us children as the ones packed by the family in Canada, but we could count on at least one special treat. Every package contained a large slab of semi-sweet chocolate which provided each of us a generous portion. I'm afraid my share never lasted very long, and I watched longingly as Heidi, who was much more disciplined, made hers last for many more days.

Hope you'll enjoy the little letters from the youngsters. I had to explain to them who you all are. Heidi asked how old you are, Marg, when I said you aren't married, she said: "Well is she never going to get married, can't she find someone?" How about it, old top, why not send some real news! Write sometime again, all of you, won't you? Again a thousand thanks from your sis,

The children's letters tell a little about our interests and our hopes. Carl wrote:

Dear Aunt Margaret, Aunt Elsa and Uncle Walter. I thank you many times for your parcels. The most important part for us children is the chocolate, the cocoa and the fruit. I dream of a cattle farm or a sheep ranch, but we are still wondering what we would do in Canada. Papa can't make up his mind. Greetings to all from your Carl.

In Mittelschule Walter attended English and French classes as part of the curriculum rather than the voluntary ones the rest of us took in the Volksschule, which were not a success. His letter is in English.

Mutti's note:
This with a little help, but he's doing quite well.

Dear Aunt Margaret, Aunt Elsa and Uncle Walter.
Thank you very much for all the good things you have sent us. I hope we may soon return home to Canada. We are learning English. I, also French. We also go to confirmation classes. We like to go to school again. We will be glad when summer is here and we can go bathing at the beach. We have been playing in the sand dunes. We have nice friends and have lots of fun.
We hope that we shall soon be able to see you all and thank you personally. Until then all good wishes and hearty greetings from your nephew Walter.

Helga was not yet in school so Mutti was holding her little hand as she wrote. She was a determined young person and would have been very clear about what she wanted to write.

Dear Aunt Marg., Aunt Elsa & Uncle Walter. Thank you for the chocolate, it tastes very good, do you have more? We would like to come to Canada on the big ship very soon and then we will visit you. A good wish and a kiss, from your Helga.

Heidi's note reads:
Dear Tanten und Onkel. I want to thank you for the very nice fruit and the chocolate. Mutti always puts a little of the "Speck" (bacon) in the food and then it tastes very good. We are going to school and that is nice. In the afternoon we get a meal at school. Many greetings. Your Heidi.

I wrote:
> *Dear Tanten und Onkel. I want to thank you most sincerely for the nice things you have sent us. Everything tastes wonderful. We would very much like to be back in Canada on a farm with chickens, cows and pigs. Loving greetings from your Dorli.*

In early June, Mother wrote to her youngest brother, Hans, who managed to send parcels from the US, where he was attending the Lutheran Seminary. She explained how helpful his efforts on our behalf were.

> *Isn't it a queer world? You have to struggle along and work practically day and night to be able to make your own way and to help us along, and here we have enough money but can't buy the bare necessities of life nor send you any of it in return for your help. Just take our good old parents. How much help and kindness have they given to others, often strangers, during their lives? Often they did not receive thanks and the Lord did not bless them with riches, but he blessed them in so many ways that their lives were full and rich. How much more that is worth, more than earthly riches, we have been able to see here again and again.*
>
> *For Heidi's birthday, I took the "biscuit mix" from your parcel, added a few things and made a cake, even "mit Rosinen" (with raisins).*
>
> *All three food parcels from you were quite badly damaged. The last one had been torn open ... something taken out as its weight was not as stated. Tea and cigs, is what they're after. The cardboard boxes alone don't stand the long journey, they should at least be wrapped in strong wrapping paper and gummed paper strips.*
>
> *The kids are writing too so I won't start another page. You'll be having your vacation soon. Are you going home? I had hoped we'd be there by that time, but it looks more "aussichtslos" (hopeless) than ever. We aren't giving up tho ....*

The description of the condition of the parcels no doubt inspired the family to work on a solution. Some of the parcels began to arrive sewn into unbleached flour sack material. These were much more difficult to pilfer quickly and unobtrusively.

I think I should explain the "flour sack" reference to younger generations. At that time in Canada, flour was sold in cloth bags and, as it was a necessary staple, every household had flour sacks.

Nothing was ever wasted, and the fabric was put to good use. Some of it came in pretty prints and was made into tea towels, aprons and children's clothing. The ones used to secure the parcels were unbleached cotton so the address could be legibly written. Mutti appreciated the cloth wrapping and used it along with precious thread, also sent from Canada and the US.

A Walter Story

Walter enclosed a poem in his letter to Onkel Hans and I have inserted my attempt at translating it. In June 1947, he was just a month shy of his fourteenth birthday.

Dear Onkel Hans,
   We have gratefully received your parcel and were delighted to see the lovely things inside. The chocolate was particularly tasty and we ate half a piece every day.
   I have heard that you are a poet and I have also composed three poems. I will send the nicest one along. It is called "Gedenke der Mutter" (Memories of Mother).
   That is the poem about a shepherd boy. You should send me one of the poems that you have written. It is too bad that I don't know English or I would write a poem in English. It will likely be a long time before I am able to do that.

A boy is lying in the meadow, all he hears is the hum of the bees,
He does not mind them, he does not glance their way.
So he lies and looks into the distance and dreams of pleasant things.
He'd rather be far away and sing a song with his mother,
But his mother is no longer living, she died a long time ago.
The world is now very empty, all comfort far away.
This is how the little boy dreams, and longs for his dear mother,
That she should cherish him once more, and say: "My precious boy."
But that is now all in the past, all shrouded in darkness.
He would gladly pass over to join her, were God to grant him His grace,
Then he would run to his mother and look once more on her face
And his heart would be full of joy.
He stumbles into the empty house and sobs "My dear Mama."

He longingly looks out the window and gradually falls asleep.
A raven caws on the roof of the house,
The boy wakes and his sorrowful face lights up.
He's had a glimpse of heaven and now knows what great joy awaits him.

> *We are doing very much better since we have received the parcels. The swimming here is very good and I have already gone swimming a number of times this year. School is also very good here and I have friends. But it will be much nicer once we are in Canada, don't you think?*
>
> *Your Walter.*

We were all crazy about swimming but when Walter mentions it here I am reminded of his great interest in *Dünenleuchten* (dune glow). There were rumours about one particular beach and, of course, Walter felt compelled to check it out, especially when it became clear that our somewhat straight-laced Mutti did not approve.

Düne Dreizehn (Dune Thirteen), as it was sometimes called, was some distance from the public beach, and Walter thought it was great fun and persuaded the rest of us to go a few times.

It was clearly a nude beach and there were indeed many people without bathing suits swimming, playing or sunning themselves in the sand dunes. We girls likely giggled to begin with, but the novelty soon wore off, and we were happy to swim closer to home. Many people went topless and sometimes nude on the regular beach as well, and I never saw a toddler wearing a bathing suit until we came to Canada.

In his letter to Onkel Hans, Carl also comments on the contents of the parcel.

> *Mutti makes hot chocolate from the Malskakao (I believe this was malted chocolate) and it tastes very good. We were allowed to snack on the raisins. We enjoyed that.*

In more than one of her letters, Mutti says Carl is the stronger of the boys, as tall as Walter since their early teens. He was also the practical one.

> We like Norderney very much, mostly because it is an island and in the summer one can swim a lot. We have already gone swimming many times.
>
> When we want fish we have to go to the harbour to get it. Sometimes we smoke some. My friend and I have acquired a square crate and have knocked the bottom off. Then we set it on rocks and that's how we smoke the fish. Smoked fish tastes very good. Most Norderneyers have such ovens.
>
> Many greetings and kisses, Your Carl

We had been eating mussels for quite some time, and they were our main source of protein. We didn't mind, but the mussels were just boiled and we welcomed Carl's efforts to introduce something new and flavourful to our diet. Since Norderney was a fishing village as well as a tourist resort, fish was readily available.

As he says in his letter, most Norderneyers had such ovens, and he learned the ways of the islanders and put them to good use.

I wish I could describe his smoker more fully. I remember he spent a lot of time and effort collecting wood to create the smoke needed. There was very little natural growth on the island, and driftwood was waterlogged and had to be dried out before it would burn.

We all loved the smoked sole we called *flounders,* and he kept us well supplied.

Mother's brother Walter stayed in the Peace River region of Alberta where he farmed with wife, Elsie, and their son, Jimmy. In her letter to Uncle Walter and Aunt Elsie she expresses her gratitude for the great benefit to us of the CARE parcels. She explains why they were particularly helpful.

> *Everything costs a lot here and what we get on ration cards is hardly enough to barely keep alive and is getting less all the time. Yesterday Werner bought a 3 lb. loaf of bread extra and paid 35.- Marks for it. It's very hard to get at that price. Fortunately, Werner is earning some money as cashier and publicity manager at the movie theatre for the British.*

Theatre Patrons

Dad's job at the theatre was a great source of entertainment for us. It was not just a movie theatre. There was a big stage where live musicals and operettas were put on. Papa would let us in, and we were allowed to sit on little fold-up seats at either end of the very back row. We learned all the songs and loved every minute.

After the shows at the theatre were stopped, a woman who had been part of the theatre troupe still had many of the costumes. She organized a group of refugee girls and choreographed a music and dance performance. We trained, separately and in a group, for some time before we were fitted with the lovely leftover costumes to put on a grand performance.

Heidi and one of her friends were the tallest girls in the group, and they were given lead roles supporting a very small ballerina who had been training with our choreographer for some time.

I was impressed with Heidi's grace and charm, but I too felt glamorous and hoped I was graceful at a time when our everyday lives were drab.

With some of the songs we had learned from the theatre performances and the dances the Fräulein had taught us, Heidi recruited her friends and organized our own little troupe.

We also had access to the English movies and while we could not understand the dialogue we enjoyed them anyway. It was there I saw my first cartoon. I remember it as being a lovely thing with all sorts of bugs and worms cavorting among the wildflowers. One image I have never forgotten was of two ladybugs hugged together, forming a ball and rolling down a leaf.

Mutti's letter continues.

> This sea climate is raw & we've had quite a few colds. In May we had about 2 weeks of hot weather. The kids went bathing and enjoyed the beach. I'm busy sewing so we have something to wear again so I couldn't get out much. Heidi is having trouble with her glands again. One opened below her ear last summer, now another one will open soon. It's due to her poor condition. She's quite tall for her age & skinny.
>
> Pa wrote that you had bought the Boyd farm and that all the others are earning good wages and getting along well. We're glad

for all of you, after the hard times we had before the war.

They don't really tell us so much in their letters and most of you never write at all. Won't you make an effort sometime and tell us about yourselves & Wembley news generally? You're the only ones who remained true to the old home.

Many, many thanks & "vergelt's Gott," if we can't ever repay you.

Love and best regards from Werner & Betty

In another letter to her father, Mother relays the latest news regarding our plans to return to Canada.

We have received permission from Berlin via Ottawa to enter Canada with the provision that we must have all necessary papers in order, and the travel costs must be guaranteed in advance. We enclosed a copy of these instructions and hope that you received the letter.

Werner got the information that we cannot do anything with German currency towards paying for our trip, as we had hoped. We are very sorry about this. I wish we could have saved you this worry. We are getting everything necessary to get our travel documents. I don't know how and where travel arrangements can be made. We are eagerly looking forward to news from you. Hope we will get started before winter.

A few days ago, our baggage arrived from Rostock, that is one worry less. As soon as we have anything new we will write again. Heartfelt greetings and looking forward to a happy reunion,

Your Betty.

When we were leaving Goldenitz and fleeing from the Russian occupation, Mother managed to ship some items to Tante Hete in Rostock which was in the Eastern Zone. I was surprised to see in Mother's letter that those things were sent to us in Norderney. We brought a number of trunks to Canada and perhaps those were the baggage.

The following is a rare letter from Opa in Canada. Most of the letters sent to Germany were lost.

>*Wednesday the 17 Sept/47*
>
>We received your letter of 19 Aug today. I have written two letters to you that you should have had long ago.
>
>I am sorry to say I have made no progress here. The local agent for the Can. Nat. Ry. has taken a lot of trouble on your behalf. He first wrote to the C.P.R. but received the reply that they can not transport you and as far as they know, no other Steamship line can do so and they are not allowed to deal with agents of lines in Germany.

He goes on to describe the many efforts of the Ottawa office of the CNR to make our travel arrangements.

>... the government will not oppose your return to Canada, but no steamship line can give a date etc. before you have your Visa as it often takes a long time to accomplish that.
>
>So that is the situation at the moment. We are not giving up, but you will have to consider that you will have to spend another winter there. The money is in the bank and can be paid at any time.
>
>The situation seems to be that the Canadian Military Mission will not give you your Visa until you can present your "travel documents" and the Shipping Line will only issue these "documents" when you have your Visa or know your port of embarkation ....
>
>We will, of course, continue to make every effort to make your return possible. I will write today to the Swedish-American Line, perhaps they can do something. There are many people here who want to bring relatives over and they are all waiting along with the C.N. Agent to see if our efforts succeed.
>
>We pray to God that He will soon bring you back to us. Please do not lose patience and trust in Him. He has saved you from great danger and helped you in many ways in the last few years and He will not forsake you now. We'll try to help as much as we can with parcels this fall ....
>
>>With best wishes from all.
>>Your Father, J. Ulmer.

Dear Father,
We received your letter of Sept 18 with a letter from your agent enclosed, on Sept 28. Werner was in Hamburg last week where he made enquiries ....

Mutti in turn, relates the same catch-22 dilemma that Opa described in his letter about visas and travel documents.

> *Your care parcel reached us about a week ago and we were very glad to get a little help again. In fact it is a big help & we were quite in need of it again. We are all well. I'm very busy sewing and getting winter things ready. It is quite a task, but we will all have enough to keep us warm.*
>
> *A thousand thanks and greetings to all ....*

My Very Own Coat

We were still living in one room of the Weierts Pensione. It was largely filled with beds where the seven of us slept, two or more to a bed. Finding even a place to sit down to sew was difficult; the added chaos of cooking, eating our meals, and all indoor activities, would have made it almost impossible.

The shortage of thread continues to be mentioned in many of Mutti's letters, and she never wasted a centimeter of the precious stuff. If she had to baste a seam before sewing it, she was very careful not to sew over the basting so that she could pull the thread out and reuse it for hand sewing.

She altered suits and jackets for the boys. She used the less worn parts of adult castoffs to make clothes for all of us, and I know there were many all-nighters in preparation for special occasions.

It was probably the following winter when she performed one of these miracles on my behalf. The stores were still devoid of anything useful, and I needed a winter coat.

She managed to find an old adult coat, and she salvaged the best pieces of material to make one for me. It was a lovely soft, hot-chocolate-coloured wool, and I was thrilled. This garment was made just for me and not handed down from my older sister.

I was very proud that Mutti used a special buckle from her sewing kit that I had played with and admired. It was dark brown and it had a lovely silvery shimmer if I turned it this way and that in the light. The belt—made of the same fabric as the coat—wove through the buckle and held my coat around me like a warm blanket. I did not mind that it had neither buttons nor buttonholes.

Mother hated making buttonholes. She was a talented

seamstress, but she was also a perfectionist, and consequently, she spent hours over details. A coat would have called for bound buttonholes and that was a daunting task. I needed the coat as fall turned into winter, and she let me wear it and promised it would have buttons eventually.

As the novelty wore off, I was less careful to avoid getting dirty and carried on with roaming the beaches, running headlong down the sand dunes and balancing along the breakwaters. I had to keep up with the others. I could not risk slowing them down for fear they would leave me behind next time.

One evening, when it was already dark, we were running along the seawall, hurrying home, and I had trouble keeping up. Instead of aiming for the stairs where the others had already arrived, I decided to climb onto the wall and take a shortcut. It was quite high for me, and there was no one to boost me. I struggled to get a grip on the top of the wall and managed to get one leg up when I heard, and felt, a snap. When I stood up, my belt was hanging by its loops, my coat open down the front. I had broken my beautiful buckle.

I clutched the front of my coat to hold it closed, and I cried all the way home. When I caught up with the siblings I would not tell them why I was crying; at home I quickly hung up my coat and hid in the bedroom.

Mutti found me, sat down and held me until I calmed down and told her what had happened. I think she was also pretty close to tears.

"Oh, Dorchen, I am so sorry. Please don't be sad. I should have made the buttonholes and sewed on the buttons. It's not your fault. I'll fix the belt. It'll be alright."

She lengthened the belt that night and in the morning she showed me how to tie it so my coat stayed closed. My hands were free, I could swing my arms, and I was able to climb and run and play again.

Mutti could relax too. I never really needed the buttons and buttonholes.

Mutti's next letter, in November 1947, is full of regret at the amount of trouble and expense we were causing her parents.

> ... and the high travel costs! That is a terrible amount of money. But the dumber the deed the higher the cost of the lesson. Or at least it seems so. If we had stayed there we would not need all of this now. And yet who knows if everything in life does not turn out as it should. We know you are not neglecting anything and not avoiding any sacrifice to bring us back and it will succeed but everything here is so disrupted one can easily lose patience.
>
> We have calmed down and have accepted the fact that we will not get away before next spring. We are also better equipped for this winter than the last ....
>
> I have so many letters to write and there is electric light only intermittently and in the early evening due to a shortage of coal.
>
> You siblings are all so letter lazy, especially you young ones at home. Elsa is so very busy and I treasure the fact that she took the time to write. You others, sit yourselves down and write to us. A letter from home, no matter from whom, is always a ray of sunshine in our dreary lives.
>
> Since last winter I have been making preparations for "die Reise" (the trip), in spring while we thought we would travel in the summer, in the summer for the fall and now I can again make plans and preparations for spring. I have to make the things anyway because we need them but have put several pieces aside for our trip. We don't want to arrive looking ragged ....

With the passing of each season, expectations had to be adjusted but we were all very much aware of the goal of all our striving.

While I wanted to go to Canada very badly, I began to dislike any talk of *die Reise*, the journey or the trip. We seemed to talk of little else and because Mutti did not *"want to arrive looking ragged,"* items were indeed put aside for the trip. This started not long after our arrival in Norderney, and the frustration for my mother must have been overwhelming at times.

Some of these spared items may have been worn for special occasions, but we simply outgrew some of them as our departure continued to be postponed.

A memory of a pair of pink panties my mother made for me may seem very silly now, but at a time when we had very little, they were pretty special.

Those panties were made of pink flannelette and were more like shorts than traditional panties. They were a bit bulky, but they were also new and soft and I liked them. Mutti said I should wear them only for good so that they would still be nice for the trip. So many things had to be spared, and I was disappointed when I outgrew them.

By the time they fit my younger sister, Helga, she would not have been thrilled to wear such things.

> *I have to even make the shirts and pants for Werner and the boys as no tailor will sew without a great deal of tea in payment. A "great deal" is actually not so much, a half pound accomplishes a lot. For the Ostfrieslander, tea is one of the essentials of life. It cost 650.- per lb., last winter 800.- to 900.- Butter in comparison only 200.- Mk. That is of course black market, otherwise there is no tea or coffee. For a pound of coffee, one can get 200 lbs of potatoes. For tea about double that. Don't think that we are black market dealers, I am only writing this to give you some idea of how things are valued here. Today I managed to get a lamp (petroleum) for tea. Werner got a pair of shoes, used, for Carl from the shoemaker who also wanted tea as part payment. I wrote to Margaret and Elsa asking that they send a parcel of a couple of pounds of tea.*

Tea, Please

The request for tea, coffee and cigarettes is repeated in several letters. Tea was particularly valuable, and it took Mutti quite some time to convince the Canadian family of the value of it in our circumstances. In this letter, she cites some of the items we were able to get with tea in particular. Previously she was careful to explain that this was not the black market but rather a means of bartering or helping each other out.

On a visit to northern Germany many years later, my daughter and I visited a tea museum and learned that the East Frisian people are noted for their consumption of tea and their tea culture. At about 300 liters per person every year, East Frisians drink more tea per capita than any other group of people. Strong black tea is served with breakfast, in the afternoon, evening, and whenever there are visitors to an East Frisian home or gathering.

The tea is sweetened with *Kluntjes*, a rock candy sugar that melts slowly, allowing multiple cups to be sweetened. We saw some of the older islanders hold a Kluntje just behind their teeth, through which they then slurped the tea. I have heard that this can also be done with sugar cubes if Kluntjes are not available.

In one letter, she makes it very clear not to put the tea on the customs declaration as it would certainly be stolen. One parcel arrived in which we found a package of tea in a bag of flour. Another one was concealed in a tin of lard.

Mother was thrilled to receive the lard. Any kind of fat was highly prized as so little was available. The lard came in a small lidded tin pail and Mother was reminded of her school days when they all carried their lunch to school in lard pails. The discovery of a pound of tea concealed inside added to the excitement.

After I met my grandparents, I had trouble picturing them buying a pail of lard with the idea of melting it, inserting the packaged tea and replacing the melted lard to conceal it. I thought it more likely to have been done by one of her siblings.

On the other hand, there was a family story of my sweet little Oma secretly distilling *Schnapps,* which she shared with friends and relatives. This was said to be mostly for medicinal purposes but was also enjoyed at special occasions and holidays.

Since hiding the tea was not meant to conceal a crime but rather to prevent pilfering of our precious tea, perhaps melting some lard to conceal the tea was something Oma and Opa could undertake.

Eventually Mother had her own treadle sewing machine, but there were many times she had to go to a friend's house to sew. The need for her own machine was great or she would not have continued to ask for tea, knowing that money was also short for her family in Canada.

In the next letter of November 30, 1947, Mother wrote at length about correspondence with a London-based steamship company and Opa's efforts in Canada with the Swedish American Line to arrange our passage to Canada. She had no idea how overly optimistic this planning turned out to be and all the obstacles that still stood in our way.

Her letter continues on a more personal note.

> *That is where I quit. It got very late and I didn't quite know how to go on. Everything is so difficult because it takes so long for the letters to go back and forth. Today your letter arrived, Father, which clears up some things, but it still contains nothing definite. Please don't worry about having to disappoint us. It is probably better if we don't travel during the winter months. When we hear the roar and thunder of the sea here, we are happy not to be outside. We still do not have our travel documents, or more accurately the definite approval. By spring we hope everything will be in order ....*
>
> *Your letter, dear Father, was once again so nice and long, loving and interesting. We are always so happy whenever one arrives. This morning, I had just said I would like to have a letter from Opa today and then it came. We are particularly happy about all the good news, especially the two new siblings that we welcome into the family. We can hardly picture Esther as a bride, she was still so young when we left. When we get home, we will all have to get reacquainted. Hans mentioned something about Carl's girl, but only a hint. Congratulations to both couples. We will write personally to both engaged couples.*
>
> *Winter cannot frighten us so badly this year. We are far better prepared than we were able to be last year .... Generally the plans for the coming winter on the island are much improved over last year in case the ferry is ice bound again.*
>
> *Last week, a parcel came from Elsa & Walter K. with the longed-for tea and a few other items which will also be a big help ....*
>
> *Our health is passable. Heidi seems to have recovered pretty well. Her glands still swell sometimes but not as badly. The doctor feels this will likely resolve itself during puberty and there should be no lasting effects. The glands that opened have left ugly scars but we are hopeful that she will develop normally and will otherwise be healthy and that is the main thing. Our most delicate one is now our Dorli. She is healthy, but when she gets even a little cold or some other minor ailment it really lays her low.*

We all had colds now and then; mine seemed to drag on. I loved our sessions at the swimming pool with my class, but Mutti, having had sinus problems, was concerned that being in the pool and then in the cold air in the winter caused my sinus headaches. I hated being benched, but it may have helped a little.

Things got worse when blinding headaches hit me even in spring and summer. I began to see colourful, flickering lights in front of my eyes and in my peripheral vision. I watched the dancing slivers of light with some fascination until I could not see anything beyond them, and an excruciatingly painful headache and nausea soon followed.

Mutti saw that I was in agony and took me to the doctor. I don't know if it was his experience as an army doctor or that his own children seemed particularly healthy and robust, but he had no patience for childish ailments. I wasn't given a chance to describe my headaches, and Mutti's attempts resulted in just another refrain of, "trying to get out of going to school." I liked school and I didn't like being sick. I only agreed to see the doctor because I wanted the headaches to stop. They stayed with me for another few years but then disappeared some time after we returned to Canada, likely at puberty.

I was in my forties when a young man my daughter was dating described the aura preceding his migraine headaches, and I realized that the headaches of my childhood had been migraines. I was reassured that I hadn't exaggerated their severity; the experience had indeed been as painful as I remembered. I am grateful that my migraines are rare as an adult, and I can usually forestall the headache and nausea with a hot beverage and pain medication at the first sign of the aura.

It is ironic that a hot beverage keeps my headaches at bay in adulthood, but something hot in the morning was not helpful to me as a child.

Once supplies were available, breakfast was often either oatmeal or cream of wheat porridge. I liked both. There was usually some sugar and milk to go with it, but we almost always had to eat quickly so we wouldn't be late for school.

Many days I finished my porridge, got my shoes and coat on and doubled over with stomach cramps. The cramps never lasted very long, but the school was on a shift system and—since the morning shift only lasted until noon—it likely didn't pay to try to get there late. My siblings were less than kind and teased me about wanting to get out of going to school. The problem may have been resolved when I switched to an afternoon class.

Years later, when Mom said hot porridge in the morning had

caused her the same problem when she was a child, I couldn't believe what I was hearing.

"Didn't it occur to you that what I was going through might have been the same thing?"

"Well, yes. But I thought it was important for you to have good nourishment in the morning."

I made porridge for my daughter's breakfast only once.

> *The boys are big, healthy and can eat mightily. They are both in confirmation class but I would prefer that they would not be confirmed here. The pastor is pretty good and struggles to teach the children the basics, but it is not as thorough as we were taught in our congregation and they have had little religious education. The boys' friends also do not have a good influence on them. They are coarse and tough and learn mostly how one can earn a lot of money with little work at home. The people here are so peculiar.*
>
> *The four children in school are eagerly learning English. Helga is still at home with me. I almost forgot about me, probably because I am fine. I am not so strong and all the work is hard for me because everything is so poor and difficult, but I am healthy and thank God for that.*
>
> *I always feel so sorry for Werner. He is very run down and seems very tired of life and he is still so young. He dreads the thought of having to start all over in Canada, which you no doubt understand. I hope that he will cheer up when he gets stronger with a better diet and when our life has more meaning and value.*
>
> *If possible could you send us elastic, shoelaces, hair pins, sewing thread (black and white) ...*

Mutti asked for these very modest items, and I have wondered if her family could grasp how difficult life was when they were not available. She also expressed more urgent needs.

> *Our greatest difficulty is getting shoes. The boys and Heidi are in greatest need. The length of both boys' feet are: 10 1/2 in, Heidi 9 1/4 in. They all have big feet, not wide but long. If you have to buy new shoes and they are expensive, don't do it, then we will get by. I would be very grateful for socks for the boys and stockings and socks for Helga, feet are 6 3/4 in.*
>
> *A long time has passed again.... Today (Dec. 12) is Dorli's*

birthday. She is ten years old already. She invited three little girlfriends. I baked a cake (in my own oven!) and made a pudding with chocolate sauce, and they had a nice celebration. There were quite a few presents, mostly little things. I knitted her a sweater of handspun wool.

That is enough for now, otherwise I will have to send it express. Our heartfelt greetings to all from your children.

Werner & Betty & children

Fräulein Gobel and Other Stories

Fräulein Gobel wore her thick, dark-blonde hair in a shoulder length pageboy—sensible, as were her clothes. I would guess her age at forty-something. In sturdy shoes, her powerful stride made her skirt swirl around her calves as she swept along the corridors of the school.

That image may have inspired a poem composed by my brother Carl's eighth grade class on their graduation for the teachers of the school. It compares her and her good friend and housemate Fräulein Friedrich. *Fräulein Friedrich ist ein stilles Wesen, und nicht so wie der Gobel Besen.* (*Fräulein Friedrich is a quiet soul unlike the Gobel broom*) Much is lost in the translation, but a sweeping broom was such an apt description that I have never forgotten it.

In her expansive manner, Fräulein Gobel shared her many talents with us. She was the most progressive teacher in the school and she inspired us to learn and to think for ourselves. She taught us how to draw and paint and read music. She was the only teacher who managed to get wooden recorders for everyone in her class. We learned to play these and performed as a group, in quartets, duets and individually—as talent allowed—for the rest of the school.

For one school year, we also experienced her unique religious instructions. These classes were part of the school curriculum and the Catholic kids, being in the minority, followed their priest to another room to learn their catechism, while we stayed in our classroom with the religious instructor. When no qualified teacher could be found, Fräulein Gobel was expected to teach this, as well as all other subjects. She was not a practising Lutheran, but if you were not Catholic at that time, you were counted as Lutheran.

Instead of bible stories and catechism she regaled us with stories of Pagan practices. She knew the times of the year and names of the festivals and kept us spellbound with her colourful tales of legends and customs. We could almost see the flaming wheel hurtling down the hillside at the Summer Solstice, and we wanted to be part of the Winter Solstice when a celebration around a bonfire was held for the entire night.

I may have come home with some of these tales and I imagine Mutti was horrified. I don't believe Fräulein Gobel was teaching us to worship Pagan gods, but the following year we had a practising Lutheran for religious instruction.

Fräulein Gobel also told epic tales during history lessons. The northern area of Germany, known as Ostfriesland and including the string of islands in the North Sea, is rich in folklore and seafaring stories.

Her favourite was the story about a pirate called Klaus Störtebeker. She explained that his name came from his practice of filling a very large *Beker* (beaker, beer stein) with beer and pouring it back in one go. Any man wanting to join his gang had to do the same in order to be accepted.

Fräulein Gobel added an interesting twist to the end of Störtebeker's colourful career. When he was eventually hunted down, and about to be beheaded, he asked that he be allowed to save some of his men from the same fate. His request was that they be lined up on one side of the chopping block, and whatever number of men he could run past, after losing his head, would be spared. She told us that he managed to stumble past eleven of his men, and was only stopped from going further when the executioner tripped him.

I wondered if any part of the story was true and was delighted to find that not only is Klaus Störtebeker's myth based on a real historical person, the legend has been immortalized in a 2008 feature film entitled *13 Paces Without a Head*, which dramatized his swashbuckling adventures. Despite his criminal tendencies, Störtebeker is celebrated by a memorial in Hamburg.

In a more recent time, the motto *God Bless Our Beaches*, inscribed on the arch above the altar in the Lutheran church in Norderney, has more than one interpretation. One would imagine that this prayer was meant to bring blessings on the fishers and their boats so that their hard work would be rewarded, but some measure of piracy may have lived on in the hearts of Norderneyers.

Before lighthouses were built, it was customary in coastal regions to light fires in strategic locations to warn sailing ships of dangerous waters and treacherous sandbars. The islanders were suspected of moving the fires to confuse passing ships and deliberately run them aground. They would then pillage and rob the helpless crew of its cargo. The two beautiful models of tall-masted ships hanging from the ceiling of the church may be the kernel of truth in this folk legend. They were not fishing boats, and the blessings sought on the beaches may have been ships with rich cargo, rather than nets heavy with fish.

I admired Fräulein Gobel's many talents. She had a good singing voice but could also sound like a sergeant major, which terrified me. She gave praise when it was due but did not hesitate to express her disappointment if she felt we were not doing our best.

Her passion for physical education was one source of my fear. Track and field were bearable. I was the oldest and tallest kid in the class, and I held my own at running and jumping, but I was in a complete panic in the gym when it came to tumbling.

We had to jump the pommel horse off the springboard, work on the parallel bars and chin ourselves on some kind of high bar, and she did not hide her disdain when she saw me freeze with fear when it was my turn.

The one skill I mastered in that class—climbing a smooth metal pole from floor to ceiling—did not seem to impress her. My only saving grace was that I could already swim when she took the class to the pool for swimming lessons.

Keeping Secrets

I only found out as an adult reading Mutti's letters that, while I was busy with my own little problems, my parents were dealing with much more serious matters. Actions brought about by circumstances during the war caused a serious impediment to our return to Canada.

New Years Day 1948

My dear Parents,

It is very difficult for me to write this letter as I know it will create new worries for you. Since the problem of our travel to Canada has gone this far we do not want to give up so I have to do this. I wanted to write about this in my last letter but wanted to await the reply from the Canadian Military Mission (C.M.M.) and if possible spare you this worry. The problem is not as great as it appears at first glance .... We are not worried but hope and trust that everything will work out and we should be with you by summer.

I want to ask you to keep all of this as secret as you possibly can as we are afraid it could be misunderstood and when we are there it will do damage. Werner is particularly anxious about this.

The problem is that Werner had to join the N.S. [Nazi] Party shortly after we arrived here in order to get work to support his family. Life was made very difficult for anyone who was not for the Party or tried to remain politically neutral. So many went into K.Z. (concentration camp) *because of that! It was a formality only and we did not disclose this in the forms we had to fill out to apply for our travel documents. The C.M.M. did some research and found Werner on a list that was still in existence in Hamburg. They sent the whole thing to the Dept. of External Affairs in Ottawa and very shortly we received the following reply:*

I am now instructed to advise you that the Director of Immigration has ruled that it is not considered that any facilities should be extended to your family in their desire to return to Canada at the present time.

Yours very truly
Jas. J. Hurley (Can. Mil. Mission)

He writes "at the present time", which does not sound entirely final. It is possible that a loosening of rules or new regulations will be implemented but that could take a long time. We don't know how else to approach the problem as we seem to have hit a dead end. It does not look like we can do anything from here as our only avenue was the C.M.M. and they get their instructions from over there.

Perhaps with the help of the Immigration Agent that was so helpful in the past you could initiate something. You will know best, dear Father. If there is nothing to be done we will, like so many others, wait until anyone is free to travel. The question of the "nominal Nazis" is not taken very seriously here any more ....

In spite of her disappointment, she shares her appreciation for the good times and her concern for her parents.

> We celebrated the holidays quietly with just the family. There was no shortage of presents. We were amazed at the many things that were gathered. Each of the children gave a gift to each of the others and also something for us. Mostly little things but they would not be discouraged from it. We also managed a nice meal, actually two chickens. We sang a lot and enjoyed festive church services and so it was a very nice celebration.
>
> PS. Please forgive me for not writing more from the heart, it was not on purpose ... What I would not give to spare you all of this and yet, I do want to see you all again so badly.

The following letter is dated March 3, 1948, and she is dismayed to realize she has not written home for two months. She wrote in English to her sisters, and also apologized for writing in pencil as "it goes faster."

We had fountain pens later on, received from the German relatives as gifts, but at this time, to write in ink would have meant pen and nib and a bottle of ink. So, pencil goes faster. Someone went over her writing in this letter with ink, perhaps to preserve it.

March 3. 1948

Dear girls!
   I shouldn't have waited so long before answering your joint letter, should have done it at once & told you how glad we were to hear from you, once again. Why is writing letters such a chore when getting them is such a pleasure ... This won't be a long one either as it's nearly supper time & we want to go to a show tonight. It's the last time and it's a good one, a Wien (Vienna) *film. There's always so much real clean humour in them and the Austrian accent is so gemütlich. We go to most of the pictures, it's the only bit of amusement there is here. We've seen, besides the German ones, which are mostly good & clean, English, American, French, Danish, Italian and Australian pictures.*

Written along the left-hand margin: *We didn't get to the*

*show after all. Instead of it, there was a play by local Plattdeutsch (*low German) *players. We didn't get tickets for it & I can only understand half of it anyway. The kids savvy it much better than I do and I didn't go.*

Your wonderful Christmas parcel came in February, in time for Carl's birthday. You should have seen the kids (& we're all kids when a parcel comes!) when we opened it. The cake & the homemade candy were best of all, but we enjoyed all of it very much. When I unpacked the little doll, Helga just took it in her arms and hugged it and didn't say a word. She calls it Susie. She has three homemade dolls, Lieschen, Hans & Erica. She can't sleep unless her dolls are with her & when she wakes up at night she asks about them.

When I asked Helga about the doll in the Christmas parcel and the ones Mom named in her letter, she said she does not remember all the dolls, but this reminded her of the fate of one precious *Püppchen* (doll) near the end of our stay in Germany. Helga tells the story of her ill-fated Püppchen.

"Remember catching a ride on the back of the horse-drawn coaches going to the hotels in Norderney?

"Most of the drivers tolerated this but there was one mean guy who got really mad when we tried to get on the back of his coach. He was chasing my friend Ulli and me off and in the process I dropped my *Püppchen* and split her head.

"I was devastated but I still loved her because she had such a sweet face."

Our dolls were not the much-prized dolls of the day. Those were the celluloid ones, much lighter and more talented. They could stand up or sit unassisted and had eyes that closed when they were laid down; when new, they wore shoes and pretty dresses. Others were baby dolls with cute little cloth diapers and knitted outfits; they all came in many different sizes. A big doll was, of course, best.

They had stuffed cloth bodies, arms and legs, and only their heads, hands and feet were made of a compound consisting of sawdust, glue, and other materials. The heads were lovely and smooth, the hair somewhat moulded and coloured. Their eyes were a pretty blue, they had pink cheeks, red lips and their hands and feet, complete with fingers and toes, were quite realistic. They were lovely when their bodies were covered in pretty clothes, but no one was ever tempted to check the nape of their neck to see if they displayed a small turtle logo identifying them as the most treasured brand.

We both remembered our dolls' noses being rubbed off from much loving play, and Helga wondered if my doll had been passed down to her, like so many of her other belongings and clothes. That was cleared up when we both remembered having to leave our precious dolls behind.

"When we were getting ready to leave for Canada I wasn't about to let go of my Püppchen, but Dad knew about this beautiful doll I had been admiring in the toy store and so he bribed me by offering to buy it for me if I would leave my doll behind.

"It was a harsh moment for me, that I could betray my beloved doll by buying a shiny new one."

Mutti continues.

> *You can imagine how anxiously we're waiting for word about the further developments of our trip ...*
>
> *You may think this funny, but I'll tell you about it anyway, just for fun. We met a young woman here, a refugee from Danzig, who can tell fortunes with cards. Early in December she told Werner's & mine & both were almost exactly the same. She didn't know much about us, nothing about our intended trip or anything connected with it. She told us a lot about it & also that it was still in the hands of the authorities & that there are still difficulties to overcome & it doesn't look too hopeful now. That we would overcome all hindrances tho & in not more than 1/2 year we would be at our destination.*
>
> *What was rather queer about it was that she also told us a lot of other things, most of which have already come true. Well, we wouldn't mind if she was right about the trip part of it too, then we'd be there in June or July. I'd be so happy, I don't know how I'd live through it. Then we'd be there for Esther & Carl's wedding and if all the rest could come too it would be a grand family reunion.*

Mother felt guilty over the fortune teller for some years. She knew how seriously her father disapproved of any sort of fortune-telling. She tried making light of it, and I imagine it helped her to keep from thinking that she was an instrument of the devil, which is likely what my grandfather would have said if he ever heard about it. She added to her letter.

> *This woman isn't at all witch-like or has anything uncanny about her. She's a widow working in an office here. Seems real nice.*
>
> *Helen wrote about her expected baby soon after Christmas. She also sent a snap of Lorry & one of the three girls in her last letter. They're certainly nice looking kids ....*
>
> *We're getting along fairly well. Since December we've been getting less bread, which makes it harder. It seems as tho bread is most important of all. The boys even talk about a Hungerperiode* (hunger period) *when they can only have three slices in the morning & one or sometimes two in the afternoon. Some days we have to do without any bread for supper too.*
>
> *We had to move out of the smaller room for the winter because it's so damp. Even in this room, where we have a fire all day, the water runs down the walls and everything is green with mould. It wouldn't be so bad if it wasn't so terribly crowded & if we wouldn't have to do all our cooking and washing in it. These stingy old cranks here won't let us into the kitchen so we can't use any of the gas that's coming to us. We don't get any extra coal for cooking tho' either, because there's gas in the house. As we're only Flüchtlinge* (refugees)*, we can't do anything about it. Hope we'll soon see better days again.*
>
> *We've had a very mild winter & are glad of it as our coal supply wouldn't have been enough to heat even one room. We'll be glad when spring comes so some of us can sleep in the small room again.*

The smaller room was off the main one, where we slept, cooked, ate and spent our days. Mother was not exaggerating. The wallpaper was falling off the walls, completely soaked. The very fancy lace curtains were looking grey and dingy. She cooked everything on a small wood stove, just big enough to hold one good-sized pot. The steam from that, as well as a certain amount of smoke from the stove, was enough to cause the damage.

It must have been very difficult for the owners, but the damage being done to their house was, in large part, due to their stinginess.

About two weeks ago we had a short cold snap and as soon as the pond was frozen over the kids went skating every afternoon. The boys learned two years ago & the girls just started now. I didn't see them but they claim "ich kann schon ziemlich gut." (I'm pretty good.) *I don't see how it's possible with the equipment they have, but they had a lot of fun while it lasted anyway.*

How are all of you, especially Mother & Dad? I hope they're well & not worrying about us too much.

Many thanks again & all our love to everybody,
your sister, Betty

The following single page, in English, may belong to this letter as the date seems right.

It fell me in (it occurred to me—a literal translation of the German phrase "es fällt mir ein" often used by Mom's family) *that I forgot to mention the March birthdays. I suppose they'll all read my letter anyway and so best wishes to all of you ....*

The children are looking forward to Werner's and my birthdays more than we are ourselves. We're getting so old that they are getting to be milestones on the road of life, more than joyous occasions to look forward to like children & very young people see them. Still, we always enjoy them very much because the children always find little gifts & surprises for us and they're always so happy about them.

Mother would have been forty-two on March 6th and Father forty-four on March 25th in 1948. It is sad that they thought they were getting old.

I didn't get this off last night anymore (this is Thursday the 4th). We're going to the Lenten service in a few minutes so want to drop it on the way.

I'm trying to do a lot of sewing but it's so hard to find time and a place to sit down here so am not getting much done. I'm making trousers & shirts for the boys and shirts for Werner out of worn ones that are too big. It's quite a job. You can't imagine how hard it is to keep all of them in clothes when you can't even buy a spool of thread. I don't know what we would have done without the help from home, other relatives & the Lady's Aid in Wembley.

Write soon again. Lots of love, Betty
W. & all the gang send their love too.

The next few pages begin on page two on small, flimsy airmail paper, with no date. The events mentioned would seem to be appropriate here.

II

I hope both of you, or all of you as the flu tends to go around, have recovered your good health. Fortunately, we are headed for spring and its warmth and sunshine. Here we get hardly any sun all winter. It will not really warm up until May ....

This morning we all went to church, except Heidi and Helga. The confirmants had their examination. There are 94 of them. They have not learned as much as we did and could not recite it as well either but seem to have the most important parts. The pastor explains a lot with parables and examples. He can't give these Norderneyers too much to memorize or they simply won't come. Confirmation is on Palm Sunday and they take their first communion on Easter Sunday.

III

This afternoon the children took their sailboat to the "Schanze", which dates back to Napoleon's time and is filled with water. The sailboat is a toy that they can't sail in the ocean because it is too rough. Werner and I went for a very long walk. I rarely get out into the air and really enjoyed it. We walked on the beach and in the sand dunes and I saw a part of the island that was new to me. On our way back, we went through the little pine forest. The pines are planted in rows and there are no real forests on the island and very few plants of any kind will grow here.

Mother did not get out very much. She was busy with housework under difficult conditions. Laundry was a huge undertaking often done by hand with limited facilities, and she was constantly sewing to keep us in clothing. She often felt cold even in summer, and she never went into the water.

We children played in the sand dunes and on the beach whenever we had free time. Many attempts had been made to plant grasses and other greenery to keep the sand from blowing and washing away in the winter storms. Eventually, this became successful and the dunes are now covered fairly densely in coarse grass.

This was both gratifying and disappointing to me when I took my children for a visit to Norderney in 1973. Having told them many stories about the good times in the sand dunes, it was disappointing that they could not experience the same play. The dunes surrounding the town are now enclosed by fencing to protect the growth from foot traffic.

"Das Wäldchen," the little pine forest Mother mentions, was another playground for us. We accepted the trees planted in rows as we had never seen another kind of forest. During the hard times when there was not enough fuel, the ground was completely bare. While not a branch or a twig could be found, and even the needles were swept up, no one cut down the trees.

On the final page, Mutti once again expresses her worries about our fate.

IV

We wonder what the verdict or decision regarding our immigration will be. Sometimes we feel it will surely happen and then doubt creeps in. We keep hoping that dear God will answer our prayers even if he has set us serious trials. He will surely not let all your worry and trouble go unheeded.

On March 10, 1948, the steamship company that had promised us passage on a freighter sent the following notice.

Since I have to send you this information I will use the paper to write a few lines. We are so very sorry that we have to present you with this great disappointment and to make it worse that it will reach you while you are both ill. Your short letter, Father, arrived on the 11th. Your letters are taking 10 days and are not being opened any longer. It is very annoying that our letters take so much longer and everything is going so slowly.

Written in the margin on the front of the notice: The birthday wishes will arrive too late but you will know, dear Father, that we are thinking of you. We hope to celebrate the next one together.

On April 8, she wrote again about her frustration with the authorities.

Your loving letter of 22. March, dear Father, arrived on 1. April. We were surprised that you had such a quick reply from Ottawa. We were also disappointed, but one can't really expect anything else. I don't believe, however, that your writing to them was of no use. The officials are now aware of the situation and this might also have made the road more level. We have no idea what else to try. Perhaps it is not meant to be and we have to accept that, even if that is very hard.

Walter's confirmation was a festive and solemn service on Palm Sunday. His Bible verse was: "Es ist ein köstlich Ding, dass das Herz fest werde, welches geschieht durch Gnade." (It is a precious thing for the heart to become firm, which is by grace. Heb.13:9)

We also celebrated very nicely at home. Georgs' parcel had recently arrived, the store owners added some things and we saved up some meat ration cards for a nice roast. I baked a cake and we even had apple wine. Walter invited a friend and it was a very nice day.

Otherwise nothing is new. We are all healthy and often our appetites are too big. It is too bad that you could not send more tea. Many people here have enough food and would gladly give it up for some tea.

Mutti tried to accept whatever came our way, but her despair is evident in the drastic proposal she made in the next letter. I don't believe this option was ever explored seriously.

My dear Parents!

We want to try once more to see if I could not come over with the children. I don't like to think of leaving Werner here alone. Who knows when we will see each other again. If it is possible we will do it only for the sake of the children. It is not just the worry about their nourishment, we would have worries there too, especially if Werner can't come for a long time. The upbringing and future of the children is what drives us to try it once more. They need an ordered life and later, goals and a purpose in life. Here it is as though one has lost one's way and wanders without goal and plan ....

We are fortunate that we can receive the CARE parcels in Norden which is on the mainland not far from here. Travel to Hamburg is very difficult. The few trains that move are so overcrowded that people stand on the running boards and climb in and out of the windows. Hundreds are often left standing on the platform. It must be hard for you to picture this.

There are still many shortages here and the predictions for

> the harvest are not particularly good. Since your parcels started arriving we are eating so much better. I fear that the clothes you send are leaving you without. You have sent so many things and we will have the most necessary clothing. I am particularly happy about your coat, Mother, I am wearing it as it is, 3/4 length, I only had to lengthen the sleeves. I wish sometimes you could be here when a parcel arrives and could see the happy faces. Everything tastes so good, just like home. We thank you from the bottom of our hearts. May the dear God reward you.
>
> The children are enjoying their holidays in spite of the bad weather. They will write soon. This letter is getting too heavy. We particularly enjoyed your loving letter, Mother. Will you drive to Carl's wedding? Father wrote that you have to have an operation? I am sorry that you have so much trouble and worries. I hope it is not anything very serious.

Mutti again explains the need for tea and suggests methods by which it would arrive safely.

> I am urgently searching for a sewing machine to borrow or a seamstress. Both work best if you have tea. Would it be possible to send 2 -3 pounds of tea? But it should not say tea on the declaration or it will be stolen. How would it be if you tuck the package of tea into a bag of flour or a carton of rolled oats ...
>
> It is late and I have to be up early tomorrow morning. I am going to Norden to pick up a CARE parcel and the ferry sails at 8 o'clock, so I will close for this time. Please give our love to everyone.

There were still so many worries at this time, but there were also bright days in spite of an uncertain future, bad weather and shortages. We looked forward to better times and the mood always began to change on May 1st.

May Day Celebrations

May Day in Germany is a special event. There may have been some years during the difficult time after the war when it wasn't celebrated, but I remember many bright sunny days when the town square was a riot of colour on the first of May. A tall pole was erected in the centre and a giant floral wreath—wound with red and white garlands—was suspended near the top of the pole.

We discarded our drab winter clothes in favour of spring and summer finery. A brass band, in full regalia, marched into the square escorting the dignitaries to their places on the stage. This was followed by the dancers in their *Trachtenkleidung* (traditional costumes) who performed their intricate dances, the highlight of the festivities.

May Day is generally the first appearance of the Trachtenkleidung each spring. The best-known, and recognized worldwide as German traditional dress, is the folk costume, with *Lederhosen* for boys and *Dirndl* dresses for girls. Originating in the Bavarian countryside, similar costumes are worn in many other parts of Germany and have developed differently from one region to the next. These differences may not be obvious to outsiders but have great meaning in rural towns and villages.

Many years later, as an adult member of Nanaimo's German choir, Chor Musica, I discovered just how distinctive the costumes are. We wore uniforms for formal performances, but we also had Dirndl for certain events of the choir and German Club. Many members owned authentic costumes from Germany, but some of us created or purchased Dirndl made in Canada, which do not necessarily adhere to any prescribed design.

On one occasion, I borrowed a striking, red *Tyrolean* hat from an acquaintance for our participation in the annual parade of flags at Nanaimo's Canada Day celebration. With no idea of its origin, I felt appropriately dressed as I wore it with my improvised Dirndl. When we were disbanding after our procession around the park, a man approached me and spoke to me in an incomprehensible dialect. He saw my confusion and asked me, in German, if I was from a certain part of Germany, which he named, but I did not recognize. When I regretted that I was not, he pointed to my hat and explained it was the traditional hat from his home in southern Germany. My friend had found it in a thrift store.

In Norderney, as in other parts of northern Germany, the local costumes are very different from the usual Dirndl and Lederhosen and resemble the Dutch traditions more closely. Accompanied by the clacking of wooden shoes, their folk dances are somewhat more sedate than the southern versions.

I remember one May Day celebration most vividly from our days in Poland during the war. Before the celebrations could get underway, we had to endure long boring speeches and presentations. My biggest trial was the singing of the national anthem, *Deutschland Über Alles* (Germany above all) while everyone stood at attention, right arm raised.

My little arm got very tired, very quickly. First I tried propping it up with my left arm. When that got hard, I raised my left arm, then propped that up with my right arm, and started the whole routine all over again, as all three verses were sung.

Since German reunification in 1991, only the third stanza, *Einigkeit und Recht und Freiheit* (Unity and Justice and Freedom), set to the melody written in 1797 by Joseph Haydn, is sung as the national anthem.

After the official ceremony of speeches and songs, a great crowd joined in a grand dance. The women and girls formed a large circle around the giant Maypole facing outward; the men and boys stood facing them. When the musicians struck up a polka, the dancing began with a bow or a curtsy to the person opposite. The couples linked arms and promenaded around the pole. When the music changed, they swung their partner. At another signal the couples parted, the two circles moved on in opposite directions and new pairs formed. Skirts swirled, hair ribbons fluttered, as round and round we went, amid shouting and laughter.

There were no special steps to learn, and I felt very grown up to be included, and was happy to hook arms with whatever partner approached, no matter how tall or elegant.

My sister Heidi and I were in our Sunday best and our everyday pigtails had been released in favour of long flowing curls, some of which were held back with a wide, white ribbon to form a big bow on top of our heads. In the year I remember most vividly, many of the men were in uniform for the occasion, and one rather imposing officer caused me some grief.

His large belt buckle, bearing the insignia of an eagle clutching a swastika in its talons, was just about level with my long flying hair, and as he took my arm and swung me around I lost some of my red locks as they caught on his buckle. It hurt like crazy, and I was dismayed each time we completed the circle and I was again faced with his large presence.

I have wondered if he had to untangle blonde and brown hair in addition to my red curls from his belt buckle.

While I remember the good times of the war years, the unfortunate consequences continued to plague us. In her letter on New Year's Day 1948, Mother tried to be optimistic about the fallout from Father's Nazi party involvement, but it was not until June of that year that they learned how the problem might be overcome.

> Dear Parents,
> A few days ago we were in Aurich, at the English security police. We spoke with the same gentleman who in January 1947 made a report which contributed to our permission for immigration being granted. He is very calm and helpful. He advised us that Werner must first apply for denazification, then we will have something to hand and he will be pleased to help us. We could have done that at the beginning but it seems everything needs time to ripen. We needed proof of exoneration and we did not have that at the time.
> About three or four weeks ago we received a letter from our last secretary in Ziegelhof. She left in the fall of 1944 as she felt danger was imminent and we had not heard from her since our flight from there. She did not know where we were but remembered the address of the summer home where Hasso's wife went during the war and sent her letter there. After a long time the letter finally reached us and we were astonished ....

The last secretary in Ziegelhof was Fräulein Klemm, or *Klemmchen* as she was affectionately called. She was one of the proxy sponsors, godparents, at Helga's secret baptism. The reference she supplied supported the idea that we did not have complete freedom of religion under the Nazi regime. The following part of the paragraph relates another happy coincidence in their struggle.

> Yesterday morning we went to church and met a man who worked with Werner before he took over Ziegelhof in 1941. He was in Norderney on business and neither of them had any idea where the other one was. Coincidence, or did dear God send us these people just when we needed them? We believe it in any case and trust that he will order things so that we may come home again.
> In addition to these references, Werner will be able to get

more from Rostock and Hamburg, and that covers the whole time and should suffice.

Hope and pray with us that we will all see each other again soon ....

Devaluation of the Deutsche Mark

In his letter of the previous year my father made the following statement about money to pay our way back to Canada.

We are not short of money here and I am determined that we will try to pay our fare from here even if that means it will take a little longer ....

That was the last time anyone in our family felt that we were not short of money. The disappointment was that while we seemed to have enough money, there was nothing to buy.

Massive inflation made our money almost worthless. In some parts of Germany, bartering or *cigarette currency* was most popular. In Ostfriesland, where we lived, tea was valued above cigarettes and was the most popular bartering commodity.

Mother's plea the same year to *"Please send tea to buy a stove ..."* was just one of many requests to her family to send tea.

June 20, 1948, the currency reform was introduced. Suddenly, overnight, there was colour and sparkle everywhere.

In a letter on June 24, 1948, she wrote, *The "reform" is changing a lot of things here and it looks as tho it will be easier to get along now ....*

The currency reform affected us all. Shop windows had contained the same dusty, faded items for the whole time we had been on the island.

This was particularly impressive at one store where beach balls, kids' sand buckets, shovels and other toys spilled onto the sidewalk. Helga wasn't quite five years old and had few memories of Norderney.

"I remember the huge, brightly coloured beach balls at one store. They were hanging in fishing nets from the awnings of the store, and I wanted one of those beach balls more than anything."

We all longed to own those, but suddenly there was no money.

Factories had been instructed to withhold the distribution of their goods until the currency reform could be implemented. It was hoped that the sudden flood of merchandise into stores would help the economy to revive as quickly as possible. Germans were allowed to exchange a limited amount of their Military Marks into Deutsche Marks, but most of their money was lost. Now goods would be rationed by the Deutsche Mark, not by ration coupons.

Heidi and I had managed to save a little bit of money before the reform. We gathered starfish, boiled and cleaned them and sold them as souvenirs to tourists on the promenade. In another venture, we took our little cart to the ferry and offered to transport luggage to hotels and B&Bs for people arriving for their holidays. We were not very successful, but there was nothing to buy so it was not difficult to hold onto what little we earned.

When the Mark was devalued and the stores were full of lovely items, the ten Mark we had managed to save were reduced to one. We may have bought one or two trinkets, but all I remember ending up with was a ping pong ball which eventually had a dent in it and would no longer bounce. We had no ping pong table or bats. I can only imagine it was a burning desire to own a ball that prompted us to buy the only one we could afford.

Any kind of ball was greatly treasured, but there were particularly precious ones. Some of the locals still had some items that we refugees had to leave behind when we fled. I not only coveted their slates when I started back to school, I also longed to play with their games and toys.

A favourite girls' game, one of those seasonal things that pop up every year, like hopscotch or skip rope, required a particular kind of ball. These were made of rubber, usually six to eight inches in diameter, with a shiny, colourful surface.

The game is played by girls standing a foot or two from a wall and batting the ball against it with various parts of their bodies without letting it hit the ground. They begin with hands, then arms, chest, knees or attempting to bat it again after a quick spin. Each manoeuvre had a name which was shouted out as the ball hit the wall and rebounded.

Heidi always had a lot of girlfriends, some of whom had the appropriate ball for the game. They took turns to see who could get the farthest in the routine before being *out* when the ball hit the ground. In time, and with her usual perseverance, she became quite skilled at the game until it was time to take up skipping rope or hopscotch, at which she also excelled.

A letter on July 13 acknowledges a glimmer of hope in a letter from Opa in Canada.

> *We received your letter of the 6.7., dear Father. We hadn't dared to hope that you could accomplish anything, considering how slowly anything in the government moves. The newsletter clippings give us hope that as your relatives we may soon be allowed to enter Canada.*
>
> *We have started another attempt over here. Last week we went to the English security officer with 5 exoneration certificates or references and asked for his advice in the hope that we could manage without this formality ... [the Denazification]. He sent us to the appropriate office and telephoned ahead to tell them that they should treat this as a particularly pressing matter. After that, things were set in motion and in about 10 days, by about 18 - 20 Juli everything should be in place. The security officer can then make his report which will go via the Can. Mil. Mission, Berlin, to the Can. Government.*
>
> *We hope by the end of August we should have news. In the meantime, we want to arrange the acknowledgment from the steamship company, get the children's passport photos etc. so that there is no delay in obtaining our visas if our travel is approved. Then when there is room on a ship we can, God willing, travel in Sept. Wouldn't that be nice? But we will leave it in God's hands ... if it should fail again, to yield to his will. Perhaps he has a role for us to play here.*
>
> *Many thanks for the reply coupons* that you sent. We haven't been to the post office yet, but I am sure they are the right ones. One has to use two for airmail because it is more expensive. The last letter was sent by Werner's boss, a nice man, with a German wife. I wrote in English and left the letter open but he said to seal it, he did not want to know what was in it. Sadly he is leaving here and a younger, single man will replace him.*

*An international reply coupon (IRC) allows a person to send someone in another country a letter, along with the cost of postage for a reply.

Because of the cold, wet weather this summer and the currency reform, very few tourists, English or German, came to the island. For the hotel and pensione owners this means a "failed harvest".

Tomorrow morning, if it doesn't rain, Helga and I will go to Norden to collect your CARE parcel. Helga is eagerly looking forward to this. She has not left the island since we arrived here. Our heartfelt thank you for the parcel! The other parcel with the shoes is likely lost, meaning it was stolen. What a shame. Since the currency reform, we are receiving clothing and shoe rations. There are actually all kinds of things available ... There is also more food available. Vegetables, fruit and fish are ration free. Everything is very expensive but those earning are doing better now. To begin with, everyone received 60. Mark Kopfgeld (head allowance).

At the beginning of August, when she had hoped much would be resolved, Mother followed up with another letter expressing concern for her parents' welfare and providing some information about our lives. There is some progress in our travel plans.

We thank you most sincerely for the detailed news about family events. You can imagine how pleased we are to receive every detail and it all interests us a great deal. When we receive these letters we do not feel so cut off ....

I am so sorry that you, dear Mother, have to have an operation ... How expensive that is! One should be a doctor in America. Here we have "Krankenkasse" (Public Health), a very good system that is of particular help to the poor. We pray with all our hearts that God stands by you ....

Werner was in Norden today to deal with his denazification papers. Everything is ready and in order. He is completely exonerated, there was nothing against him ....

On Thursday we will travel to Aurich with the English ration truck (free transportation) *to the Security Officer. We are confident that he will present a favourable report and maybe the Canadians can be convinced that we are not dangerous and that we want nothing more than to go home where we belong. When we are once there, everything else will fall into place. We are particularly happy that you want to start something jointly with us. The children say that if Opas go along, we will go into the* wilderness but there has to be a lake. We will surely find something to suit us. Werner is not enthusiastic about a very small farm and it would likely not support our large family without work off the farm.

We are all well. You always ask about Heidi. Her glands are better. Only the two broke open but she continues to be a worry. In the spring she looked better, with more colour and not quite so thin. She is so terribly restless, runs and jumps around too much. During 4 weeks of summer holidays, instead of improving her health, she lost weight. Now the doctor has discovered that she has a spinal curvature, just as I did at her age. It is not very bad but the doctor recommends therapeutic gymnastics but we cannot afford that. The public health plan does not pay for it as it is not a treatment by a doctor. We hope and pray that we will be allowed to come home where the children will have more milk and better nourishment.

We are having a very cool summer. It has rained a lot and the harvest is very good overall. Fruit, vegetables and potatoes are now available and a lot of other things are more abundant. The prices, however, are very high, much higher than Werner's income. We can only afford the very cheapest groceries. What will happen if we are still here come winter when the work ends again - well, kommt Zeit kommt Rat (time will tell).

Our most heartfelt greetings to you all ...

While Mutti constantly asks her family not to worry about us, she in turn expresses much concern, particularly for her parents. On the 10th of September there has been no news of her mother's operation mentioned in a letter in August.

My dear Mother!

This should still reach you for your birthday, for which I wish you many blessings with all my heart. May dear God give you many more happy years for you to enjoy in good health. Is the operation successfully behind you? We hope so!

We will write again soon ... Hope and pray with us that we will soon be able to send you good news.

We received this airmail letter blank for two of the "reply coupons". One has to write small and only the important items on one of these forms. You will have to wear your glasses to read this.

The *airmail letter blank* was a sheet of airmail paper that folded into an envelope and had prepaid postage. These were a blessing in speeding up the correspondence, but deciphering her tiny handwriting was indeed difficult.

In this one, each of us added a greeting for our Oma's birthday, and Mutti added further comments on the flaps folded into the envelope.

> *The children are not in school at present because of the threat of polio. I don't know if there are any actual cases here. I have borrowed a sewing machine in exchange for tea and will be busily sewing for the next while. The children are supposed to help with the other work but that isn't going so well as playing is so much more fun.*
>
> *Carl asks you to forgive his bad handwriting as he is in bed with two boils on his leg. Helga is not happy with her birthday wish, she thinks it should say - "von deiner 'lieben' Helga"* (from your 'dear' Helga).

The main part of the letter continues.

> *On 3. September, a week ago, our papers and letters left for Berlin. We supplied all possible endorsements and evidence with the request that the permission to enter Canada finally be granted. If the Canadian government rejects us again it can only be a lack of good will and we will have to give up for the time being. Then it was not meant to be. But we still have hope.*
>
> *Werner's work here is finished on 1. October. At that time the English are leaving here, except for a couple of occupation representatives, and they don't need any more "picture shows". Werner's boss introduced him to an English Major from Bielefeld who offered him a job as manager in a large auto repair works and parts depot. He will start with 400.- Mark per month and if they are satisfied with him he may earn from 600.- to 700.- a month and the job is good for 10 years, says the Major. If we can't leave Germany, Werner will try to find a home for us and then we can also move to Bielefeld. But that could take a very long time. Werner feels he can earn money here more easily than in Canada but for the sake of the children he wants to return. We expect an answer early in October.*
>
> *Werner heard or read somewhere that CPR boats are again travelling to and from Germany. We want to try to get more information about this in Bremen or Hamburg. Perhaps Father*

could try to write to the CPR. We are concerned about the many borders we have to cross by travelling with the Swedish-America Line. A direct passage from here to Canada would be much better

Please don't worry about us, we are all well and, thank God, Werner has good prospects for work.

As Mutti predicted, a reply to their efforts in September was received in early October and she again sent disappointing news.

Once again there is no good news to report. We did not know that there is a Canadian Consulate in Frankfurt, Main, and sent our letter with all enclosures to Berlin. The Canadian Military Mission in Berlin did not forward it to Ottawa as we assumed but to Frankfurt where the Consul will make the decision.

He wrote only very briefly:

"I am sorry to have to inform you that the view of the Can. authorities expressed in a dispatch to the Can. Mil. Mission, Berlin of 12 Nov. 1947 still holds. The statement made in the dispatch was: 'In view of the unfavourable security report on Rudeloff, the Director of Immigration has ruled that it is not considered that any facilities should be extended to this family in their desire to return to Canada at the present time.' When immigration of German nationals is reopened you should submit a further application."

A.J. Hicks, Consul.

Everything seems hopeless. We hoped to have a better report in light of all the evidence we presented.

Now nearly a week has passed again and we are in Norden. Werner is on his way to Bielefeld. The separation is difficult and costly, but there is no work on the island ....

The children are in school but do not learn enough as there is a shortage of teachers and classrooms. More refugees, who have been temporarily housed in Denmark, are being relocated here. The islands are expected to receive several thousand more, all the hotels are expected to be filled. Many others are still coming from the eastern zone and everything is getting very crowded here ...

I would like to remind my many siblings that you all owe me a letter. They should rattle themselves loose and think of me. Now that Werner is not here it is pretty lonely for me. But I am not

> alone. I have the children and have met a number of nice people through the children.
>
> Sunday evening is always an open evening at the parsonage which I almost always attend ...
>
> Last night I attended the evangelical Frauenhilfe, something like our Lady's Aid but not nearly as active. Last night a woman vicar spoke. They have them here in large congregations as assistants to the ministers of which there aren't nearly enough. They study theology and can do about all the work in the congregation but don't hold services. She spoke about her work in the prison for female prisoners in Hanover.

The role of a female vicar would have suited Mutti very well. As a young girl, she wished she had been born a boy so that she could study for the ministry. This would have been a close second.

Her unwavering faith is once again reflected in the following letter when she responds to news about an upcoming operation for her father.

> My dear, good Parents,
>
> When I returned from Norden on Thursday afternoon, the 12.10, I found Mother's letter here. I was so happy that one had once again arrived but what a shock when I read it. You poor dear ones, what all you have to bear ... You had already written that you needed an operation but I did not know that it was so serious. Forgive me for not writing right away but I can even now just say that I hope and pray that the operation is a success and you will recover soon. It is my sincerest wish to see you once again and to thank you, as far as that is possible, for all the love and goodness you have so generously given to all of us. If that is impossible then we will say it is God's will. I would often simply not know where to find my help and comfort if you, my dear parents, had not raised me in the Christian faith. For that, I thank you above all ....
>
> I have not had any mail from Werner but the children send their love and wish their dear Oma a speedy recovery. Thousands and heartfelt wishes for blessings for the Advents Season to you all, from your Betty.

On December 8, 1948, Mutti goes on at length about the many roadblocks standing in the way of our return to Canada but ends with some good news about our situation in Norderney.

We have moved and now live two houses down the street at Kreuzstrasse 10. The space is bigger and better but also more expensive and we have less and shabbier furniture. But we have gained a kitchen, a basement room with a laundry kitchen with a washing machine, wash kettle and laundry tubs all of which I am free to use. The owner is only here for the summer so we are alone in the house ...

The Boys' Escapades

The move down the street from Kreuzstrasse 8 to number 10 was a welcome change. The cramped space in the other house had become very confining.

Walter and Carl were both in their teens and they were too big to live in one room with their mother and three sisters. Mother tells of both of them working hard and contributing toward the household, but some of their efforts to earn money got them in trouble.

I have only vague memories of their activities at that time, and —in 2007, when Walter died—I needed information for a talk at his celebration of life. I sent Carl a draft of what I had written and asked him what more he could tell me.

"Once Walter was in the Mittelschule he had his own friend, and did not let me participate much. He and his best friend Schiko were always up to something, and when I insisted on coming along, he made me walk behind, out of hearing, so I missed most of what went on.

"While we lived at the Schütte house, Mom and I heard footsteps upstairs. There was no one else living in the house so we snuck upstairs to find out what was happening. We found Walter and his buddy Schiko in the process of removing a ventilation fan which they either needed for a project or wanted to sell for profit."

He adds, "Not things you'd want to include in your talk. Pardon me while I reminisce." Of course, I included it.

"Walter and Schiko were very enterprising, but sometimes they needed my help.

"The back of the empty lot between us and the last house on the block bordered on a plumber's business. We were able to reach some lead pipes under the fence which we liberated and sold to the recycler. He figured out where we got them and informed on us.

"The other recycle for profit issue was the abandoned Badehallen (Bathhouse or change room building). We pulled the old gutters off and sold them to the same guy who again identified them and told on us.

"I know Mother was upset when the cops came, and I always felt really bad about that."

The move to a new place with better facilities was exciting, but it added to the rush leading up to Christmas. On December 29, in her final letter of 1948, Mother described our festivities and how a gift went astray.

> *I did not keep my promise to write again before Christmas ....*
>
> *Your wonderful Christmas parcel came one day after Christmas, on the 27th. It was very good as we did not have everything all at once. Earlier we had a parcel from Omchen from Switzerland, where she has been visiting her daughter since September, containing chocolate and a few toys and games. Werner brought a few things also, and I managed to get some flour so I could bake a little. Each of the children always has to have something small for everybody else, we can't deny them that, so we had, once again, a happy and blessed holiday ...*
>
> *We received both your letters of the 6 & 9 December before Christmas. The $5 was confiscated and only a slip of paper, to which it had been glued, was in the letter. Another slip telling us that it is illegal to send money to us was also enclosed.*
>
> *We assume it is not lost and will be paid to us when German money once again has some value outside the country. It is a real shame but can't be helped.*
>
> *Werner just left this morning, very reluctantly. He likes it very much in Bielefeld. He says the scenery is much like Beaverlodge, hilly and forested. But he would rather be here with us; even more than that, he would like to take us with him. If we cannot come home by spring, Werner wants to try somehow to get us out of this water.*

On one of his visits home, when I was miserable with a bad cold and the weather was raw and nasty, Father vowed he would get us off the island before another winter. I believed in my Papa's ability to do whatever he set out to do and was very excited. I told my friend Brigitte that we would be moving to the mainland before the following winter.

She lived with her uncle, our family doctor, and Walter was friends with his son. The next time Walter visited they asked him about our impending move. He either had not heard Father's pronouncement or did not believe it and told them he didn't know anything about it.

It was generally assumed that I had made it up to make myself sound important. I was crushed.

The emotional tug-of-war between concern for Father's prospects for work in Canada and the desire to leave Germany is again reflected in Mother's letter.

> *We take it from your last letter that things are also very difficult over there. W. is very worried that he will have to do heavy physical work there, which we both know would not be possible, whereas here, he can work with his head rather than his back, and be paid better for it. It is very difficult and costly to organize a permanent home here and the worst part of that is that one does not know if one should try or hang on to the thought of one day returning to Canada. The general feeling here is that we have come through the worst of it and that it will soon get better in Germany. I have a hard time getting used to the idea that we will always live here and Werner would also rather come back ...*
>
> *We are very happy that you are doing so much better, Mother. I would like to write so much more but these pages are so small ....*

Mother managed to write a very long letter onto one of those flimsy airmail forms, and then complained she wanted to write more. I needed a magnifying glass to get as much of that as I did.

At times, I had the impression that she felt a connection to her family while she was writing, and that thread was broken when she stopped.

Her despair is evident as 1949 begins with yet another rejection letter.

> *Dear Parents,*
> *I have put off writing day to day and that is mostly because there is nothing good to report and my mood in the last little while is not good enough for me to produce a letter that does not sound dismal. Nothing seems to help, certainly not worrying and dwelling on problems.*

> *My main reason for writing is that we have finally received a reply from Ottawa which is, of course, once again in the negative! The reply is very brief and reads:*
>
> "Dear Sir, I wish to acknowledge receipt of your letter of Oct. 18 concerning your application for the re-admission to Canada of yourself and family. In reply I would advise you that the circumstances of your case have again been carefully reviewed but I regret to say no encouragement can be offered for your entry. Yours very truly, Laval Fortier, Assist. Commissioner"
>
> *So that is the result, or non-result, of all our efforts here and yours there. We can't undertake anything else. Your thinking that the Can. Gov't. did not want to let us come so that they don't have to reimburse us for the farm does not seem right to me although Werner has said the same thing.*
>
> *The gentlemen want to punish us by making us wait.*
> *Will we be forever "unclean" and shunned by everyone and for how long? Who knows. Why do they require denazification if it serves no purpose?*

After all their efforts to gather the evidence for their exoneration certificates, this was a heavy blow. Her despair is palpable.

On reading this letter, I am again moved by her strength. We children never knew the depth of her feelings of hopelessness. She was often frustrated, sometimes angry and resentful, but I don't believe she ever let us see this sadness and despair.

Throughout the war, she had to hide her faith. She sacrificed cherished, lifelong practices to keep her family safe from Nazi persecution only to be shunned by her own country on suspicion of collaboration with the Nazi regime.

Her sense of injustice is shared by others.

> *There is a new newspaper here for refugees called "Der Weg" (The Way) with an insert "Der Auswanderer" (The Immigrant) ...*
>
> *An article in the insert, entitled, "To Canada, but how?" asserts that refugees to Canada should have been able to come in the fall of 1948. There is only the one obstacle and all other countries have the same requirement.*
>
> *The article goes on to give the opinion that Canada is unlikely to allow mass immigration.*

In almost all her letters, Mother followed up disappointing news with expressions of hope and faith to reassure her family that we were not giving up. This time she cannot yield as readily. After a few brief news items and greetings to others in the family, she closes.

It is late and I can't write any more.
Good wishes, your El. & children.

In a letter in early February to her sister, she again voiced her many worries and doubts about our future but still found it possible to express her appreciation for small kindnesses.

I owe Esther, Hans and Elsa each a letter but it seems I don't get down to writing. I comfort myself with the thought that you can send my letters on or at least relay the most important items to each other.
We are, of course, very disappointed and I know you are too but who knows. Often, when we feel things are bad, we think of the countless number of people who have things worse than we do, who have a much greater burden to bear and then we are thankful for what we have. We have often found that when things seem very dark, a light shines from somewhere. A few days ago our Omchen wrote from Switzerland that Editha wants to send Carl his confirmation suit. That is a great help. We will manage one for Walter somehow.

Suits for the boys are mentioned a number of times in Mother's letters, and that may seem strange under the circumstances. One would think warm clothes of any kind would have been adequate when there was so little to be had. It was a different time, and a suit and a tie were considered essential for an event as important as confirmation. Pictures of us in Germany, as well as of our relatives in Canada, all had the men in suits from their teenage years on, so the Canadian family would have understood this need.

Mutti adds a reply to Opa's question.

You asked in your last letter how we are fixed for clothing and shoes. I don't know quite how to answer that because we can use many things. I have once again borrowed a sewing machine and can make many things with used material. I will list some of the most necessary items that are hard to get here, very expensive and not good quality ...

Her list of small items is long and detailed, and she added one larger item rather tentatively, as was her habit.

> *Walter badly needs shoes but I don't think it is practical to send them. One can sometimes find good shoes here and they would be expensive over there too. Better to send tea.*
>
> *Werner is mostly in need of summer underwear, two piece, or it could be long johns for winter. All the children also need underwear, preferably not combinations as they don't like to wear them. Summer underwear - I believe cotton is cheaper and more durable than silk ....*

My mother would be shocked by the skimpy, revealing undergarments randomly displayed in present-day advertising and magazines. I remember when it was not quite polite to mention underwear in public.

She is right about the *combinations*. We tried to avoid them at all costs. It seems they are not so well known anymore, but they were quite common, particularly in rural areas at the time.

They were called combinations because they were long underpants (also known as long johns) and long-sleeved undershirts combined, not unlike today's thermal underwear but all in one piece. Worn under your clothes, they could be extremely awkward at certain times, although a flap at the back allowed you to use the facilities without undressing completely. This was particularly important if you were required to use an outhouse in the winter. But the layers also made them bulky and visible.

The next items on the list are S*tockings for Sundays.* At the time, girls were allowed to wear pants to school, but we had to wear dresses to church.

Boys wore short pants summer and winter until they were well up into their teens. That was the custom in most European countries. Mutti could not allow bare legs in winter, especially in Ziegelhof, in northern Poland, where winters were bitterly cold, much like the winters of her childhood in northern Alberta. We had to keep warm, and so along with the customary short pants for the boys and skirts for us girls, she had us all wearing long johns, or combinations, under the long stockings.

I imagine Walter and Carl must have found that they could not risk letting on that they also wore long underwear. So they devised a system that achieved the smoothest possible stockings. I was pretty young at that time and did not attend school for much of our stay there, but I learned—and faithfully followed—the method devised by the boys.

Here is how it worked. You put on the long johns. Then you put the stockings on, pulling them all the way to the top of your leg and very, very carefully rolling each stocking down to make the perfect doughnut around your ankles. Next, on the inside of your leg, at the ankle, you carefully fold the bottom of the long john cuff over to fit as tightly and smoothly as possible just above the roll of stocking and gently tuck it into the roll. Now, carefully unroll the stocking doughnut up over the long underwear all the way to the top of the leg where it is attached to garters which were safely covered by the short pants.

The climate in Norderney was damp. The wind off the ocean could be cutting, but the temperature rarely dropped below freezing, and—except for our first winter—we did not feel the need for combinations.

In spite of the milder climate, Mother always felt it was important for us to wear warm underwear of some kind, and she made us girls wear what she called *snuggies*. These undergarments were made of cotton or wool and reached almost down to our knees.

The risk of someone seeing these granny snuggies was unthinkable, particularly to Heidi. If she was wearing a dress, she pushed them as high as possible up her thighs to keep them out of sight. Before we left for school in the winter, Mutti always checked to make sure our snuggies were pulled down. It wasn't always easy to find an opportunity to push them back up before arriving at school.

Mutti's letter continues with some modest requests for herself and Helga.

> *I could really use a couple of dark aprons and if Margaret could spare an old dress that I could still use as a house dress I would really appreciate that. If possible a bit warm with long sleeves. I think her things would fit me, she asked once.*

> *Helga needs a coat, maybe you have an old one that I could makeover for her. It can be for winter as they seldom wear coats in summer.*

Helga Needs a Coat

Not long ago, when I came across this note in Mutti's letter, I wanted to know what memories Helga had of the clothing she wore and where it came from. I hoped to jog her memory, and I wasn't disappointed.

She too remembered Mother never throwing out a piece of clothing if it still contained some fabric that could be made over into something else; at that time, this was common practice where we lived. Even the seamstress, who had a room on our floor and did some of our sewing, often said, *"das kann man wenden"* (that can be reversed) when the fabric of a well-worn garment was still good on the inside. When Helga needed a coat, Mutti made it work.

Helga was involved in Mutti's search through her stash of discarded clothing to find suitable fabric for a coat, and she spotted something special.

"I very much admired a light grey coat Mom had and wasn't wearing anymore. It had a herringbone weave and the lighter grey thread gave it a silvery sheen. I loved that fabric, and I wanted her to make me a coat out of it, but she said that wasn't practical. The light grey fabric would be dirty all the time.

"Instead, she found some brown fabric and made me a coat with a darker brown velvet collar. It was nice too, and I liked it, but I really would have loved that silvery grey one."

Helga and I went on to compare tales of woe about wearing hand-me-downs and other clothing we liked or hated. Having something made especially for you, no matter where the fabric came from, was pretty exciting.

I resented the ill-fitting cast-offs that were my lot in life, but Helga's story has an extra layer of bad luck from time to time.

"Most of my life, I had to wear not only your cast-offs but Heidi's as well. Sometimes you and Heidi had matching dresses and it seemed like I wore the same things for years, even if I didn't like them."

> *Otherwise there is nothing new here, we are all healthy. The children are back in school which reopened today (7.1.) I have a lot of work especially since Werner left. There is coal available and we have one warm room and use gas in the kitchen ....*

In a letter on February 15, 1949, Mutti wrote of a new worry added to her struggle.

> *Werner has had a serious eye infection for about the past 4 weeks. Two weeks ago he wrote to say it was a bit better and the danger of going blind seems to be past. Since then he has not written except a very brief note enclosed with a money order to say the left eye is worse and he can't write ... You can imagine that I can't be very calm about this ... He could, of course, not work the whole time. I don't know if he received his full salary ... He has sent very little money since Christmas and it is impossible to manage so we have had to add to our debt at the stores. As long as the merchants give us credit we can at least get the barest necessities. I don't know how we will ever pay it back.*
>
> *I want to take in some sewing but have not found anything so far. There is good money in sewing but if one is not a proven seamstress and is known, one has to be careful and not ask for too much. I have enough work and don't get my own sewing done but I want to try to earn a little money. The children will have to help more which does not hurt them.*

Helping with housework was our least favourite activity, and I fear we expended more energy avoiding it than doing the work itself required. We cooperated in one activity which I remember fondly.

In the evenings, we girls and Mutti sat and darned socks. Whether hand-knitted or purchased, socks were of poor quality and had to be mended after every wash. I like to think I became fairly adept at darning the socks without creating lumps in our shoes to give us blisters.

When my mother lived with us for the last two years of her life, I always asked her to match up the socks and tuck them together in the special way she had taught us. She was suffering from dementia, but she diligently checked them for holes and announced with some satisfaction, "There, not even one hole in that whole pile of socks."

Mutti's letter on February 21, to the siblings she feels she has been neglecting, was in English.

> *Dear Margaret, Esther & Ben,*
>
> I hope you won't mind if I write two letters in one, really 3 in 1. Thanks a lot for your letters. It's always so nice when you girls write. You write more of the family gossip and doings (but not nearly enough to satisfy my hunger) while Dad writes more of the important things.
>
> Werner wrote that his eyes are much better. He wanted to go back to work tomorrow provided they weren't worse. All my other worries aren't nearly as big when I know that W. is alright again. I was nearly worried sick, in fact, I was sick & the doctor gave me a tonic for my nerves & blood, seems to be doing some good too, also prescribed more to eat so I get a special ration card. Heidi gets it too.
>
> The snaps are old, but I thought you might enjoy getting them anyway. The girls have a film in the camera they bought for their own money last summer & still have a few to take so will fill it up and have them developed and printed ...
>
> We've had a very mild winter, hardly any frost. It's quite possible tho that the thick end is coming for us yet. It comes in February or even March sometimes ... When I think of the winter two years ago, I still feel faint, so I guess we should be thankful ...
>
> A mild winter has its disadvantages tho too. The milder the winter the heavier the storms. They've certainly done enough damage on the islands. It will take over a million Marks to build up along the beach what the breakers smashed up. The water level was as high as 8 feet above normal at times.
>
> One day an Italian tanker drifted onto a sandbank and had to throw off ballast ... For days there were oranges floating around on the beach, partly still in crates ... The boys got up one night at 2:30 and went out with two other boys and their mother. They walked about five miles and were back at 8 o'clock in time for school ...

Carl's Birthday Letter

Carl continues the story about the tanker in his next letter to Papa in Bielefeld after describing his birthday. It was written in a clear, bold hand, and translating it was a joy. It was a lovely break from trying to read Mother's efforts to write very small and fit as much as possible onto each page.

Dear Papa!

Thank you very much for your nice letter. My birthday was quiet and modest but when I received my presents in the evening it was very nice. Mutti gave me a case for my fountain pen and a shirt, Walter a comb, Heidi a change purse, Dorli a ruler and Helga a math notebook. I also received a silver tie clip and a card from Omchen. Mutti baked a cake with many raisins. It was very nice of Herrn Schütte (our landlord) *to give me five Mark. Tante Gitta sent a parcel and enclosed a fountain pen for my confirmation.*

Carl then describes the storm and the bounty on the beach.

A very bad storm washed up a lot of oranges on the beach. We went out at 3 o'clock and found 30 oranges. But because we went with another family we only got half .... The freighter usually travels only in inland waters and was not familiar with the North Sea. There were far more on Juist (our neighbouring island) *where they drove them home in sacks.*

Oranges! Can you imagine?

My older siblings may have remembered eating oranges before we went to Germany, but I certainly did not, and I thought they were the best thing I had ever tasted.

I think Mutti let us have one a day or perhaps we shared them to make them last as long as possible. I remember savouring the aroma first before I ever took a bite, and afterward, I licked the juice and the oil from the peel off my fingers. When the orange was all gone, we sometimes ate the skin as well. Mutti did not approve of this. She always believed that the white part was hard to digest.

I wonder whether at the time I appreciated the boys' effort to go out to gather oranges before dawn and get back in time to go to school. I'm sure they knew how much I loved the oranges.

We were not afraid of the storms. We could hear the wind howling and feel the vibration of the breakers hitting the seawall. At times, the whole island seemed to shake.

In the daytime, we loved to go down to the beach and watch breakers roaring in and great geysers shooting high into the air as they hit the breakwaters and the seawall. I remember Carl and I, in particular, never tired of the wind in our faces and the taste of salt on our lips from the fine spray. We stayed well back from the edge of the seawall, but if I was a little scared I never doubted that Carl would keep me safe.

His letter continues.

> *We start our Easter holidays on April 5 for three weeks. Mutti is spinning, she has filled the fourth spool this evening. At the beginning the thread kept breaking and the connections are not easy. Christa told Frau Dechow: "Frau Rudeloff can't spin at all", but now it is going quite well. The Spinning wheel is here again.*

Frau Dechow was the young widow mentioned a few times in Mother's letters. Christa was the oldest of three children and my friend, although she was younger than I. Carl goes on.

> *Walter is playing the Laute. He is trying to find songs for accompaniment so that we can sing and he plays.*
>
> *How are your eyes? I hope much better? Are the people still so nasty or have they improved? I hope we can somehow get to Kanada so that we can all be together and have a regular life, preferably on a farm.*
>
> *Today is Friday and a parcel arrived. Much love and kisses,*
> *Your Carl.*

Mother cannot let an empty page go so she added a note on the back of Carl's letter.

> *My dear Werner,*
> *Carl has written a nice long letter so I will just add a little ....*
> *Did I say thank you for your birthday letter? I don't think I did, so I will make up for that and thank you from the bottom of my heart just as your good wishes and love came from the heart. On that day I really missed you, more so than usual. It is quite correct that you did not send me anything. We don't have money for that. I also told the children they should not spend any money. Walter and Carl bought me a "Glockenkalender"* (bell calendar) *with their money, Dorli made me a paper cutting, Helga a bookmark and I think Heidi started to make me something but it didn't work for her.*

> On Friday we received the first parcel from the parents: 2 lb tea, 1 lb coffee, 1 syrup pail of honey, some rice, hot chocolate, that was ripped open and everything was covered in it. Margaret sent me a black dress which is very nice but very short but with long sleeves, a piece of cotton for the girls, 2 aprons, some flour in which the tea was concealed. Yesterday one came from Elsa with a wealth of things inside. Kiss, Betty

I believe my father must have kept our letters from Norderney when he was in Bielefeld. Opa would not have had these and yet, they were in the box with all the ones received in Canada.

Mother acknowledges greetings from her parents after her birthday.

> I have sent your two letters on to Werner. We both thank you for your birthday greetings and good wishes. We can't celebrate our birthdays this year as we have in the past but there is enough for a small cake and we are happy to have a loving family and that is something to celebrate on a birthday.
>
> I had company on my birthday. Two other refugee women who I visit for company now and then, and their children, and it was a jolly evening. We send our love and good wishes to all the other March birthday celebrants. I am sorry to have neglected the February ones. I had too much work and worry at the time ...
>
> [The parcel] arrived full of many wonderful things as well as a suit that I can take in a bit for Walter. It should do until he outgrows it. He is growing so quickly and is now taller than I. There are also good dresses for the girls and a coat for Heidi. The dress from Margaret fits me, just a bit short. And then the tea! That will solve several problems.
>
> Here I fell asleep and the pen made a funny squiggly line and I went to bed.

Mother was something of a night owl, which worked well for her for the most part. There was never enough time during the day for all she had to accomplish, and she stayed up late to get her sewing done. Sometimes she was so tired she would fall asleep while writing a letter, and we often saw her nodding off when she was reading a book.

In spite of falling asleep, she added a note about the money for the confiscated $5.

> PS For the $5.00 that you sent we received 16.55 Mark. So it is not lost and again many, many thanks.

The following letter, in German, was sent undated and contains a note in Opa's hand: *Angekommen.* (Arrived) *2 or 3 April 1949.* I am grateful to him for preserving these treasures by taking such great care of every little scrap. I have left the next one largely intact as it describes so many parts of our lives.

I am often touched by my mother's devotion to our family and the gratitude and concern for her parents and siblings. Her description of our pictures, our personalities and appearances match my memories of us as children, and I have some of the photos. Birthdays featured big in our family and this is, once again, reflected in her letter.

> *Dear Father,*
>
> *For your 69 birthday I wish you all the best blessings and pray that our Father in heaven will protect you and keep you in good health for a very long time.*
>
> *As a special greeting I am sending you these pictures of the children. I have been wanting to send them for a long time but Werner doesn't think they are very good. We had them made for their passports for the trip about 1 1/2 years ago.*
>
> *They already look bigger and more grown up, especially the boys. Walter's is a good likeness, that is, when he is serious as in the picture as he is usually making faces. Carl is more serious than Walter but friendlier, just like the picture. You wrote in your last letter that Dorli looks bigger than Heidi. Did you get them mixed up? Dorli is the one sitting on Werner's lap. Maybe she looks bigger because she has a bigger face than Heidi. She is much smaller and stockier and will likely not be very tall.*
>
> *Tomorrow is Werner's birthday. We sent him a few new things that Elsa sent, a small cake and a half pound of tea. He is away from home from 7 in the morning to 7 at night and travels in a truck for an hour each way. It will do him good to have a cup of tea now and then. Oh yes, and Helga sent him an egg. They now cost only 40 Pfennig each....*
>
> *It is very difficult for him, not the work, but with the Germans*

(because he speaks English and is working with the Brits, there seems to be much jealousy). I can tell from his letters that he is once again very nervous. He had a complete breakdown after his imprisonment in Goldenitz. His eyes are also not completely healed. It seems the climate is the cause. He writes that we should do everything we can to get out of here ....

I can't imagine the emotional conflicts my father was battling at this time. She went on to list all the various avenues he wanted her and her parents to pursue again, but she too was discouraged and felt it was of no use.

Sunday
I didn't get this letter done, and yesterday your 2nd parcel arrived. Many, many heartfelt thanks for everything. The shirts for the boys are, sadly, too small. The red one fits Heidi and she wants it to go with her slacks. The socks will likely also be too small after a couple of washes but then I will knit a piece on to make them bigger. I am very pleased with the underwear. There is nothing quite like it here.
The children all wanted to write a greeting but are in school. It is almost 12 o'clock and I still want to mail this letter.

Carl was confirmed on Palm Sunday, April 10, but much happened about that time and Mutti did not write until May 11, when she reported that the boys had their suits, and tea continued to be a blessing but also that the struggle was not over.

Werner came for Palm Sunday and stayed until Easter Monday, which made us all happy. Carl's confirmation and the evening service on Good Friday were very nice.
Yes, the boys had their suits. Elsa sent one of Walter's and I was able to alter it for our Walter. Carl received his from Tante Dita in Switzerland which also needed a lot of work but they both looked very nice ...
For the tea, which arrived safely, and by the way, parcels are no longer opened by customs here, I bought Walter and Heidi shoes. "Jedermann Schuhe" (everyman shoes?) for 25.- M. The others cost from 30 to 60.- M a pair.
Today I read an article about immigration that has completely discouraged me from making any more efforts to leave here, at least for the time being. That does not mean that I, and

Werner too, do not want to come if we can, because eventually we definitely want to come back, but at the moment it seems to be impossible. The article states that Canada will admit German immigrants but not until after there is a Peace Treaty. And if Werner will prove to be an obstacle, who knows. To the states it is not necessarily an obstacle but there are now so many applications ahead of us that it could take years if no exception is made ...

We have been having trouble with our rent. This is a tourist pensione also and, even though it is designated as a billet for refugees, the owner wants his regular tourist rates in the summer season. He knows we can't pay it but he says if the authorities force him to give us space they should also ensure that he gets his money. We don't have to pay it all ourselves but there is a lot of trouble and unpleasantness. In Germany one can, through no fault of one's own, do very little without getting involved with the authorities or the courts.

All of this means that we have to move again. We will have a bigger apartment in a small house where we hope to finally settle for a while.

I am so very sorry that I wrote about all the things we needed and have caused you so much expense. It was inconsiderate of me. Now we are able to help ourselves again.

*All my love to all you dear ones,
from your Eliz., Werner & children*

PS I received Father's letter of the 25.4 on the 3.5. There were "Antwortscheine" (reply coupons) *enclosed. Letters have not been censored for some time ....*

Another month passes and Mutti is anxious to reassure her family that all is well with us and she is grateful for good news about her Father.

the 15. June '49.

Dear Parents,

It is high time I answered your letters otherwise you will imagine all sorts of things. You can imagine how happy we were to hear that you, dear Father, came through your operation successfully. Now all you have to do is pass the test of patience required to sit still.

I am sorry, dear Mother, that you have to still work so hard. Does it have to be that way? The work will not run away or maybe tomorrow it is no longer necessary. You should try it sometime ....

When Father's letter arrived we were in the middle of our move. Even though we don't have very many things, moving still makes a lot of work. I had to clean and partly paint our new apartment.

It is Kreuzstrasse 13, a 1 1/2 storey house with 4 rooms, "hall" and 3 small rooms. The rent is only 20 - 25.-M. With Werner's raise in pay we can manage that.

We are arranging our little home as well as we can. Our new flat is not furnished but I have been able to gather a few things, borrowed, given or cheaply bought. We have also had some help with household items from the refugee assistance program.

Now we are quite comfortable and content. We also have more room and no one bothers us. We have a small kitchen, a living room, one bedroom for the girls and one bedroom for the boys and a long hallway. I sleep in the living room on the couch.

Kreuzstrasse 13

Mutti described our new home very well. It was small by today's standards but had *more room and no one bothers us.* It was a huge improvement from one or two rooms and no privacy for a big family.

We lived in an upstairs apartment at Kreuzstrasse 13. I don't know what she meant by a one-and-a-half storey house, but perhaps our apartment was actually the attic and not considered a storey. It had slanted ceilings and a dormer window in the boys' bedroom.

We reached our floor by way of a long staircase, open except for a railing on one side, which led to a hallway and all our rooms.

The living room was nice and bright and at the front of the house. It was roomy enough for a table and chairs where we had our meals, and a couch where Mutti slept.

The boys' room, off to one side of the hallway, was long and narrow with the beds placed end to end; their window made it nice and bright. They enjoyed their privacy, and we girls were not often invited.

Heidi, Helga and I shared the bedroom at the back of the house. Heidi and I in one bed; Helga on a cot. There was only a small window overlooking the flat roof of a shed or storage space; it was never sunny nor bright and almost always cold.

Helga, more than five years younger than I, was always put to bed before the rest of us, and she remembered being cold and somewhat scared and feeling left out of things. I'm afraid that was often the case and I was not as kind as I could have been. Being the youngest of the older four, my position was too tenuous. I could not risk also being seen as *a little one*.

We used a narrow space behind a wall on the opposite side of the staircase as our kitchen which had just enough room for a small wood stove, a narrow table to prepare food and wash up in a dishpan and some shelves. An even smaller space contained a toilet but no other plumbing. A wide shelf held another dishpan for washing ourselves.

I don't remember the last name of the people who lived downstairs. They were courteous but did not socialize with us. I can imagine five kids running up and down the uncarpeted stairs and floors above their heads were a trial.

They had two girls, Inge and Ulli. They were both always very nicely dressed and Inge, the older one, loved to lord it over all the other children in the neighbourhood. Ulli was a cheerful little tomboy who did not feel the need to brag, and she and Helga—both about six—became good friends. They were physically a mismatched pair. Helga was tall and skinny like the rest of our family; Ulli was shorter and of a much sturdier build, like the rest of her family.

Ulli and Inge's father ran a beer brewing company and beer was a common beverage in their house. I don't know if Helga tried it, but Ulli could often be seen wandering along, swinging a long-necked, brown glass beer bottle in one hand.

When they visited the brewery, Ulli usually came away with a bottle to drink on the way home. I thought I remembered something about one of those jaunts not ending well, and I asked Helga about it.

"I don't remember much about the brewery, but on the way home there were a few places where we liked to stop for a little break. Some of the stores had sort of a brick ledge below their shop windows, the perfect height for us to sit on. I wasn't aware of anything unusual happening that day and Ulli didn't say anything.

"I don't know if the police came or just an irate shopkeeper, but it seems we were in trouble because Ulli had cracked the shop window with her beer bottle. I hadn't done anything but, somehow, I was also to blame."

Walter enjoyed the dormer window in their room because of the easy access it provided to the roof. He was building ever better radios and this was the ideal place to attach his antennas. The slant of the roof outside the dormer window was very steep, but that would not have been a deterrent.

Late one night, Mutti heard unusual noises coming from the boys' room. She went to investigate and found Walter on the roof, hanging onto the window frame while reaching for the antenna connection. He was working on his pet project in his sleep. He had a history of sleepwalking and she managed to gently urge him back inside.

The boys' window faced a house on the other side of the empty lot where a young friend called Wiegel lived. He shared Walter's interest in radios, and the boys were back and forth between our houses frequently.

Carl told me a story about Wiegel when I asked him to help me with the talk at Walter's celebration of life.

"Walter and his friend Schiko managed to rig up a shared antenna with our friend Wiegel across the empty lot beside our place. They decided it would be funny to apply power to the antenna. We watched as Wiegel's window was flung open and a smoking radio came flying out."

Carl was more inclined to indulge in dangerous games for his own amusement rather than playing tricks on others, but he did not always use good judgement. At about this time, he acquired a BB gun. When he ran out of BBs, he loaded the gun with small pieces of bread that he had worked into balls to fit the barrel. I was sitting across the room from him when he shot his improvised BB and hit my knee.

He did not think it would do any harm and was devastated when the dough ball went right through my brand-new corduroy pants and embedded itself in the skin of my knee.

I know I revelled in some serious drama, having been shot, and while my knee healed without a scar, the hole in my corduroys remained. I hope I had the good grace not to point it out to him.

Pentecost was often the occasion for a visit from Papa, and

Mutti continued her letter after one of these visits.

> On the Saturday before Pentecost Werner came and stayed for 1 week ...
> The general manager told him before he left that on his return he would be taking over the management of the whole parts department. Someone else will be in charge of the offices, the books, etc. where there are about 70 workers. Overall, there are about 700 employees. Werner's income will go up to 600.-M which is a welcome change.
> In July I want to make a down payment on a sewing machine. The things from you are just lying here and I can't get them in order even though we need them badly ...
> Your last parcel arrived safely. The shirts fit Werner and the dress fits me, I like it and it suits me. Thank you also for the suit for me. I will work on lengthening the skirt. There is no hem to let down ...

We did not have a telephone and letters back and forth between my parents had to suffice. Waiting for a letter from my father may also have meant waiting for money, which was always in short supply.

On Friday, July 22, her letter begins:

> I waited until this morning for a letter from you but it did not arrive. You should have something from us for Sunday, it is high time ....
> I don't actually have much to write. Nothing much happens to us here except everybody wants money. Today we finished spinning a batch of wool which will bring about 12.-M but I will have to keep after her for it as she is not very reliable. We'll get it eventually. Now we are starting on the 8th batch.

Mutti did some of the spinning but she was not quick and had much other work to do. Carl was the master spinner and was largely responsible for bringing in the extra money.

She went on to share some news of the church rumours about Pastor Fischer, saying that ... *he is not carrying out his responsibilities in the congregation ...*

All I remember of Pastor Fischer was that he was tall and large and we all hated to shake hands at the door after church. The boys said it was like shaking hands with a feather pillow; his hands were so soft and cushiony.

> *Carl wants to add something so I will close for now. More next time. I am going to Frau Hofmann to sew, which is very nice. She reads to me as I sew and we have great conversations which means I sew less but what isn't finished she keeps and does it for me which makes it extra nice for me. Please write soon,*
> *Loving greetings, Betty*

Carl's addition is about a trip he and Walter took.

> *Dear Papa!*
> *This time it is my turn to write so I will tell you about our trip. We had an opportunity to go as far as Emden by motor boat. We travelled by night and sat in the mud flats a few times. It was fairly stormy and the boat rocked wildly. From Emden, we travelled to Aurich by train, then on to Sandhorst and set up our tent. The mosquitoes were terrible. To return we walked 15 km and then a man gave us a ride in his car all the way to Norddeich. His car was very new and he was driving it for the first time. When we arrived in Norddeich, the 3 o'clock ferry was just sailing so we had to wait for the 5 o'clock.*
> *This evening we are going to the swimming pool. We are getting in at no cost for a whole week ... We are working towards our life-saving certificates ... They threw our "Ting" in the ocean and it drifted away.*
> *Much love and greetings, your, Carl*

The boys had built some kind of raft from driftwood and whatever else they could find at the beach, which Mutti called a *thing;* hence Carl's reference to their *"Ting,"* which some other boys set adrift.

Swimming was one of our greatest joys. As soon as possible in the spring, we were in the ocean where we all learned to swim. The surf could be quite rough close to shore and, unlike my older siblings, I wasn't tall enough to go past the rolling waves, where learning to float was easier. I was determined to get out there with the others and struggled until I got my feet off the ground a bit longer at each attempt.

We loved the *Seewasserwellenhallenschwimmbad* (seawater indoor wave pool). We were overjoyed to find the pool was much kinder. In the saltwater, we still had the buoyancy of the ocean but in between wave sessions we were able to improve our technique. If the weather did not allow us to be on the beach and we could scrape up the price of admission, we were at the pool.

The locals did not believe in teaching their children to swim. Fisherfolk in cold water countries know that once you go overboard, you cannot save yourself by swimming. It seems many of the refugees had also not had access to lakes or pools. When Fräulein Gobel decided to take her class to the pool for lessons, only one boy and I out of a class of twenty-five or thirty kids were able to swim. By the end of the year, she had everyone able to stay afloat in the deep end in some fashion.

There were various certificates to be won. For the first certificate, we swam without touching the sides or the bottom of the pool for fifteen minutes. The second certificate required forty-five minutes of continuous swimming, and my teacher added a jump from the three-meter board as a requirement. I was so glad to get it over with, I just stumbled up that ladder and dropped off so I could get out of the water.

As Carl mentioned in his letter, the boys were working toward their life-saving certificates. Heidi and I joined the swim club. We worked on our breaststroke, were introduced to the crawl and learned to do shallow dives for races. We were also on the synchronized swim team where we had to learn a perfect float and worked on some underwater manoeuvres.

Heidi couldn't be kept out of the water. She worked harder than any of the other girls. We saw some of the Aqua Musicals starring Esther Williams, "America's Mermaid." These movies were colourful, elaborate, underwater panoramas. Heidi, age fourteen, worked for hours imitating the star's moves and perfecting them. She was very attractive in a bathing suit and had many admirers, even among the teachers and leaders.

Always very daring, Heidi taught herself to do what looked to me like a perfect swan dive from the three-meter board. I was very impressed, being much too scared to dive off the high board and rarely even jumping from it.

When talking about returning to Canada, we always stipulated that we had to have access to water. When we finally returned and settled in the Okanagan, we shocked our landlocked relatives by swimming across Kalamalka Lake without an accompanying boat.

In her letter in late July, Mutti apologized for the time between letters and, since this one was to be circulated to include her parents, for writing in English.

> *Yesterday I wrote to our former secretary in Ziegelhof. May seem strange to you but a farm here is such a complicated affair that one needs not only a host of working people but also a secretary. She's a nice girl, about your age, and she would like to go to Canada with us when we go ...*
>
> *I want to thank you and Ruth for that nice parcel you sent us and the lovely fabric. I've got a machine for about 3 weeks now and a dressmaker who is a saleslady in the leading style shop living in one of our rooms here so will have to see what can be done. If nothing else, I can make a dress for the winter out of it. It's awfully good of you Marg., to order some more dress goods, didn't mean to put you to that expense.*

This reminded me that there was another room at the very back of the upstairs suite, which did not belong to us. We rarely saw the woman who lived there except when she helped Mother with sewing. The machine was set up in the back hall just outside her door, an area where we often played, and she didn't seem to mind having us nearby or talking to her while she worked. She was not there on the one fateful day I will never forget.

We did not often include Helga in our games, and it was a mistake to involve her on this day. I can't imagine why we thought a game of tag, at the top of an open staircase, with one person blindfolded, was a good idea. I don't remember how many of us were playing, but it was Helga's turn to be blindfolded, and I agreed to stand at the top of the stairs to keep her from falling if she came too close. Suddenly, she was there, I froze and she rolled all the way down the staircase.

She was hurt but had no broken bones. We did not need Mutti's understandably harsh words to let us know how badly we had behaved

Mutti continues.

> *Thanks for the snaps you sent, they're nice. You've hardly changed but I can't associate pictures of Esther and Ruth with the kids they were 10 yrs. Ago ....*

She asks Margaret to congratulate her brother Carl and his wife, Dagny, on their baby girl and adds a comment about names.

> *Yes, Sherry Lynn is rather pretty but, personally, I like something a little more substantial. If I had another girl I'd probably name her Claudine or maybe Ruth. I had suggested Irene Margaret for Helga but Werner didn't like the idea because so many Polish girls are named Irene and we were living among them then ...*
>
> *"Today" is Monday, Aug. 1. It's terrible. I really don't know what I do all the time but I never get half the things done that I should. The kids aren't over-anxious to help either, altho they're not bad. The boys are growing quite sensible now, seem to be over the worst stage of Flegeljahre* (adolescence). *Right now the girls are in what I hope is their worst stage.*
>
> *It's harder to raise and keep a family in town than on a farm, I think. Walter is working at our baker's in the pm now and I'm hoping he'll need him for at least a few weeks yet as we owe him quite a lot of money and he can work it off. Carl is earning a little by spinning and the girls help sometimes too. Dorli is going on a 12-day tour of Ostfriesland with her teacher and the girls of her class. It's quite an expense but I don't want to break her heart so am letting her go. She earned a few Marks herself by taking care of a little boy several afternoons.*

Geschwister

Geschwister defines the bond among my brothers and sisters as no English word can. Our relationships were often complicated; we fought and scrapped, but it was us against the world, and we rallied when Mutti, or any one of us, was in trouble. After our parents died, Walter the oldest, often referred to us as the *Orphans* and somehow, that had a similar connotation.

The events Mutti relates in the previous letter, while factual, do not reflect the conflicts surrounding them and how they helped to shape our personalities.

Walter and Carl both worked at various jobs to bring in extra money, but I believe we realized even then that the situation should not have been as dire as Mutti describes in many of her letters. It wasn't until he was in his seventies, not long before he died, that Carl made this comment.

"I never wanted to criticize Dad, but I know he didn't send as much money as he could have when we were living in Norderney. He wasn't bothered by the credit mounting up at the merchants, knowing he could pay it off. The shortage of ready cash was really hard on Mom and she worried constantly."

Mutti very likely also did not realize that most islanders used credit in the winter when there was no income from summer visitors. She was much too modest in using the credit, and we lived very frugally. The baker did not hesitate to take advantage. In another letter, she deplores how hard he worked Walter to pay off the mounting debt.

Whenever Papa came home for a visit, he seemed to have money. He was always shocked by the state of our meagre store of supplies. Then he rushed out to the shops and brought home great amounts of food. We ate well, and the merchants were paid what was owed.

Those were rare times of plenty and Helga told me, not long ago, she thought Papa was right up there with Santa Claus.

Carl's spinning was mentioned in a letter earlier in July. Mutti was grateful, but I doubt Papa had any idea how consistent what *little he earned* was and how important it was to the household.

Carl was far more aware of Mutti's struggles and could not help but feel resentment when Walter was granted some privilege or given another musical instrument while his hours of work went unnoticed.

I also took Mutti's worries about money very seriously, and I was thrilled when I was allowed to go on the tour with my class. While preparations were underway, Papa came home for a visit, and suddenly money was no object, and Heidi also had to go on the trip. I'm not clear how the conversation went, but Papa talked to Fräulein Gobel, and it was arranged that Heidi be excused from her classes to help with the younger girls on the trip.

Heidi and I were good friends, and it wasn't in my nature to resent her for having the same benefit I was enjoying until I realized that the reverse was never allowed to happen.

Fräulein Gobel was also the only teacher in our school who arranged to have wooden recorders for her entire class. When I found out we had to pay for them before they could be ordered, I very reluctantly asked Mutti for the money. In spite of the fact that Heidi had no one to teach her to play it, she had to have one too. I couldn't help feeling some pride when, in addition to playing harmony in the choir, I performed a solo at a school concert.

More than once, Mutti wrote that I celebrated with Heidi on her May birthday because mine, in December, was not so nice. The weather was never suitable for an outdoor party and everyone was busy with Christmas preparations. I know Mutti felt bad, but there was never anything special for me at Heidi's parties. I was simply allowed to participate.

One year, just in time for her birthday, a parcel with five dresses, all in Heidi's size, arrived from Aunt Helen in the US. Hand-me-downs, good as new, all but one just cotton, but the full skirts, puffed sleeves and bright colours glowed in our drab existence, and I was envious.

I struggled not to cry, but when I could not keep my eyes from filling with tears, an adult (not my mother) told me I had to understand that it wasn't practical to cut any of the dresses down to my size, and I should be happy for my sister.

Heidi was hard on her clothes and only one of those dresses was passed down to me. It was the dressiest one which had been saved for *good*, to be worn only on Sundays. It was also the only one all in pinks and rose colours, which I had been told all my life, were not suitable for redheads. I hated it.

I was beginning to get the idea that I had to go after what I wanted for myself. I learned to sew on Mutti's sewing machine, first to make clothes for my doll, but—shortly before we left for Canada—I successfully fashioned a peasant blouse out of a tiered skirt Helga had outgrown. It was made of white flocked cotton and went well with a skirt passed down to me by someone. Mutti was surprised and pleased that I was able to make something nice for myself for the trip.

Heidi and her chums hiked out to the lighthouse here on the island yesterday but it rained in the pm so they came back by bus. The boys got a free ride in a motor boat to Emden about 2 weeks ago, camped in a pretty spot on the mainland a few days and hitch-hiked back to Norddeich and the steamer. They would have liked to go to stay with Werner a few days at least but haven't got bicycles, the cheapest means of travelling here and hitchhiking is too risky. It isn't as easy to catch a ride here as in America.

Werner hopes to get a 2 week vacation in August. Too bad it couldn't be in July. We've had about 3 weeks of rather nice weather, probably all the summer we'll have except odd days. There is very little sunshine here and yet this is considered to be a very healthy climate.

Ostfrl. is known as "das Land der Alten" (the land of the old) and there really are many people over 90 and even 100 yrs. old. Eighty yrs isn't considered very old. I think I'd rather only live to be 70 in a sunny, warmer climate tho. Werner says Bielefeld is much worse. It rains nearly all the time and there is a lot of TB, rickets and sickness generally.

We've had a lot of doings with the church lately. An old minister formerly of the Russian zone is giving lectures all over western Germany. It was like listening to some of our older ministers at home. We also had a very good Kurprediger (holiday preacher) for July. In summer, our pastor has help from ministers in need of a rest from other parts who spend their vacation here.

Last Friday a choir and orchestra of about 80 children sang and played in a special service and last week a quartet. A small fee was charged, proceeds go for church work. There is a lot being done and a portion more to do.

Paper's full. Give my love to all our loved ones at home and write again sometime to your Sis Betty.

A tiny little scrap of paper, in English, may fit in here somewhere.

Dear Esther,
I nearly forgot to mention the snaps you sent. You girls certainly look nice in your wedding togs. Werner said we older ones "can't keep up with your little sisters." We like both the boys too. Ben looks very serious & I can imagine that he's rather quiet. Len seems the opposite, looks like he would be lively & full of fun ... Send some more snaps. We haven't seen you for nearly 10 years.

Len married Ruth, and Ben married Esther. Mutti was correct about their personalities. Ben was older and more serious, and he was actually Len's uncle. There were many discussions, wondering if that meant Esther was Ruth's aunt and what were the respective children to each other.

In early September, Mutti acknowledges several letters which need a reply and explains her late response.

> *The bigger flat is partly to blame. There is far more work. Werner also sends his laundry because it is too expensive to have it washed where he is, and because he wears only white shirts there is always quite a lot, even if it is only every two weeks. I am very happy that we bought a washing machine when Werner was here for Pentecost. It is a very simple thing, really just a big galvanized tub with a three-winged paddle inside, the axle of which protrudes out of the lid which one turns with a handle. It washes easily and well and cost 45.-M. An inexpensive proper machine costs 136.-M.*

Mother was grateful for the washing machine, but laundry still involved a difficult process. The water had to be heated on the stove, first for the wash and again for the rinse. All of the laundry had to be wrung out by hand and then taken downstairs to the clothesline in the yard beside the house. This was very hard on Mother, and there was very little we could do to help.

Father's white shirts also had to be very carefully ironed as both my parents were perfectionists in their own way. She did this every two weeks. When I learned to iron the simple things, like hankies and aprons, I offered to try and iron some of Papa's shirts. I am sure I overestimated my skills, and she was right to say she did not think I was ready.

I didn't realize how exhausting laundry days must have been. When I was faced with washing my baby daughter's diapers in 1961, I had the luxury of a wringer washer and hot running water but it still took up the better part of a day. The clothesline in rainy Vancouver caused me the same problems Mutti experienced in Norderney.

In the past few weeks I have also helped out in a local pensione. The season is sadly rather short this year. There are not many people who have the money to pay the high prices in the Norderney Resort. I would have liked to have earned a bit to pay my debts. I didn't make it this month but maybe in October. Werner will receive an extra 100.-M a month starting in October so I hope to be able to manage some winter clothing for all of us. Walter still works at the bakery afternoons. He only wants to give him 30.-M and that is not enough as he works 5 - 6 hours and also on Sundays. He often brings home bread or buns that he is given.

Carl also earned some money but that seems to be past now. He carts bottles of wine and Schnapps to the hotels for a dealer and groceries to the stores for another dealer. Even Heidi is earning a bit of money looking after two little girls, 2 & 4 years old. When the weather is good, they spend the whole afternoon at the beach. I have to praise the children. They bring me everything they earn. When I ask them if they wouldn't like to keep some they say: no, we will just spend it, and if we need anything you give it to us anyway.

Werner sent me an article about ... immigration and employment possibilities. [It] reports that the Canadian Government has everything in order so that once Germany has a government, a mass immigration can take place. If the other part of our story doesn't stand in our way, we should also be able to return to our homeland. The German government should become a reality this fall.

We wish our dear Mother God's blessing for her birthday and a healthy and peaceful year. Much love to all,

your Betty and children.

I can hear my mother's voice, making suggestions for my letter to my grandparents, written in German on November 11, 1949.

Dear Opa and dear Oma,

Mutti does not have much time to write, she wants to sew and yesterday was Martini. It is the custom here for children to dress up for Martini and go house to house singing and then you get presents. Mostly Pfeffernüsse (gingersnaps) and Bonbons or apples. Heidi and her girlfriends were Schneeweisschen und Rosenrot (fairytale characters). Helga and I were little Japanese girls. Walter and Carl don't go anymore.

Martini

This *Martini* is not a cocktail, but a traditional event similar to Halloween, practiced mostly in *Ostfriesland* (East Frisia) and other parts of northern and eastern Germany.

We had not experienced this elsewhere in Germany and learned that we would dress up and go door to door for treats; it was something new and exciting.

We discussed and planned our costumes for weeks ahead. Some children dressed as animals or had traditional clothes from another culture, but fairytale characters were big favourites. I wonder how much of Mutti's precious time she devoted to making our costumes. I don't remember what Helga and I looked like as Japanese girls but I still have the little Dutch girl's cap Mutti made for my costume one year. Heidi loved dressing up as the glamorous fairytale characters copied from our storybooks.

When I wrote this letter, the boys didn't go out for Martini anymore, but—with Mutti's expert help—they had been cowboys, and I seem to recall a feather headdress another year.

Just as important as our appearance were our lanterns, and many of us had to make our own. Mutti loved that sort of crafting and was very good about helping us try our hand at it. Some were made of cardstock folded in elaborate shapes, others were glued and wired cardboard with suns, moons and stars cut out to allow our lights to shine. Mutti made sure the base of each lantern was sturdy enough to hold a candle, and she added a wire handle at the top. We carried our creations safely on a long stick.

As soon as it was dark on the day of Martini, the streets began to fill with children, and fairytales came alive. There were princes and princesses as well as a great variety of dwarfs and elves. Hansel and Gretel were great favourites as many of the children already had the appropriate clothes. The odd witch or ogre added a bit of tension to the excitement, especially if they were older children and wore masks so we did not recognize them.

We did not have to walk down long driveways or even knock at many of the houses as most of the front doors were at street level and already open, throwing a welcoming glow onto the sidewalks. The cobbled streets were narrow, but there were no cars and neither the horse-drawn coaches nor the carriages were out on that night.

Our lanterns helped to light our way on the wide brick sidewalks and so we walked, and gathered in small groups, waiting our turn or going on to a house where others had left off singing. When our hosts acknowledged us, we sang a song for them.

Even the youngest children knew at least one of the songs that was sometimes also sung as a lullaby. When Helga was quite small, she sang the tune perfectly but sang *Gaternchen* instead of *Laternchen*. I'm afraid we never let her forget it.

Laternchen, Laternchen, Sonne, Mond und Sternchen,
Brenne auf mein Licht, Brenne auf mein Licht,
Aber nur meine kleine Laterne nicht.

My little lantern is like the sun, the moon and the stars,
Burn brightly my light, Burn brightly my light,
But not my precious lantern.

We enjoyed the compliments of the adults, especially if they guessed which character we had chosen for our costume and commented on the clever lanterns we had made. When they handed us our small treats, the girls curtsied and the boys gave a little bow and we said *danke schön* (thank you), or *vielen dank* (many thanks), before walking on to the next house.

Of course, every year a few lanterns burned up and the owners were in tears. Helga very clearly remembers the heartbreak.

"*I don't remember any of my costumes, but I was so impressed and delighted with a lantern Carl made for me one year. He made it of black cardboard and lined it with red cellophane where he'd cut out moons and stars. I was very proud.*

"*Just a short distance from home, my beautiful lantern caught on fire and went up in flames. I was completely devastated.*" A childhood tragedy, not easily overcome or forgotten.

Toward the end of the evening, there was one song we sang only for the Lutheran minister at the parsonage. This was a big house near the church with a large paved area in front of the door. As we arrived in this forecourt, Pastor Fischer greeted us and exclaimed, "Look at all these lanterns and costumes. Be careful of the little ones, boys, we don't want any fires here."

When a large number of children had assembled and his housekeeper had handed out our treats, he clapped his hands and invited us to sing.

This was always the Protestant anthem written by Martin Luther, *Ein feste Burg ist unser Gott* (A Mighty Fortress is Our God) and traditionally sung at this time of year. For most of us, that was the grand finale to our *Martinisingen*. A few candles still burned in lanterns as we made our way home to take off our costumes, and treasure our small bag of treats.

I don't recall Fräulein Gobel commenting on Martini but if she had, I am sure she would have said it originated in Pagan times and was adapted by the Christian church.

This theory is shared by many, also regarding Halloween traditions. They were said to be influenced by Celtic harvest festivals, particularly the Gaelic festival Samhain, which is believed to have Pagan roots.

We were told it was called Martini for Luther's first name, but another explanation is that it was first named for the Catholic St. Martin's Day for Martin of Tours on the 11th of November and was brought forward and combined with *Martinisingen on* the 10th, the birthday of Martin Luther.

So, increasingly, Martini became a celebration of Martin Luther, and the motive of begging for food was explained as a tradition of the monastic orders rather than the original motive of begging by children to supplement winter food supplies.

When we returned to Canada I was past the age of going door to door for Halloween, but Mutti had told us stories from her childhood, and I was anxious to see how it would compare to our Martini. No doubt she took the same care making Helga's costume that she had done with ours, and Helga happily went off with her friends.

I could not believe what was happening when children came banging on the door, shouting "trick or treat," holding out pillowcases or big bags. When they had received their treat, they turned and ran to the next house with barely a "thank you."

In time, I found some of the magic in Halloween, and I certainly enjoyed my children's excitement as the day approached. One year when my daughter was about six, I washed and starched the little Dutch cap my mother had made for me, and I curled the corners just so, for her turn to be the little Dutch girl.

My letter to Opa and Oma continues.

> We are all allowed to make a wish list for Christmas. It rains a lot here and has been cold but a bit warmer again. We go to school every day, even Saturday. There is a shortage of teachers and school rooms so we don't go for as many hours as we should.
> There are approximately three thousand children in the Volks - and - Mittelschule. There are eight grades in the Volksschule and people start the Mittelschule in the 5th school year and go to 10th. Walter is in his 9th, the year before his last Mittelschule year, Carl is in 8 Volksschule year, Heidi in 7 and I am only in 4. We missed a lot of school after the war. The others were allowed to catch up and I wanted to also but the principal would not let me. People always think I am not very strong because I have very pale skin. Helga has started grade 1.
> On Sundays, Helga and I go to children's worship services. Mutti says you call it Sunday school. We have religious instruction in school. I received a 1 (A) on my report card in religion.
>   Greetings and kisses to all of you, Your Dorli.

Of Teachers and Fairness

My mother often said, "The Germans have no equivalent word for *fair* and they don't seem to understand the concept of *fairness*."

It may have been a sign of the times but there were incidents, primarily in school, that seemed to bear this out. Carl often told stories of teachers unfairly slapping or hitting him or his classmates when the punishment belonged to someone else.

Favouritism was common, and attempts to defend yourself were often met with more severe punishment, such as the strap, either on the hands or bent over for *a few of the best*. If a favourite student accused another of an infraction, that was enough to incur punishment. An unpopular student doing the same might get punished for tattling.

In the aftermath of the war, there were few male teachers, and, aside from the principal, I only recall one—Herr Koch—in the

Volksschule. He was not a very big man, but he was intimidating and his peculiar haircut added to that. He was the only man I ever encountered with a brush cut before coming to Canada. His hair was very short except for the *brush* standing up at his hairline and tapering to the back of his head.

When I heard about his nasty habit of swiping an eraser up the back of the boys' heads where their hair was very short, inflicting considerable pain, I always related that to his brush cut. He was the subject of many complaints. He never hit the girls, but Heidi related stories of his bullying tactics when she was in his class for math one year. He used ridicule and humiliation as punishment when a student did not meet his expectations.

In the letter to my grandparents, I related that there were 3,000 children in the school, which could accommodate perhaps half that number comfortably. We attended in shifts, and teachers coped in classes of thirty-five to forty pupils.

Big two-person, wooden desks filled the large classrooms. Some teachers had girls sitting on one side of the room and boys on the other. Fräulein Gobel assigned our seating according to our score from the previous week's dictation. We did not have spelling tests, but once a week Gobel held dictation. We had a special notebook for this and wrote with pen and ink rather than pencil as she paced around the room dictating some of the work covered in the previous week. She based our mark on spelling, punctuation, handwriting and neatness.

The person with the highest mark sat in the far left corner in the back of the room, others were seated in the rows to the right and forward as their marks became lower. The least able scholars ended up in the front rows.

I was almost always in the back row although rarely the top spot because I was careless and did not always dot every i or cross every t. I was good at spelling, but I could not seem to improve my handwriting, and I found neatness was difficult to achieve with a pen and nib.

I must have been particularly messy and careless at least once because I was seated in about the third row from the back on the day Fräulein Gobel had to leave the classroom for a period of time. She put prissy little Karin Trost, seated in the back row, in charge and told her to write down the names of anyone in the class who misbehaved while she was gone.

It did not take long for pandemonium to ensue, and when Fräulein Gobel was returning to the class, she heard the racket from a long way down the hall. A look-out gave the word, and all was quiet as she entered the room.

She was furious. She asked Karin to name the people who had misbehaved. It turned out my name and the names of the three quietest, geekiest boys in the class were the only ones on her list. We four had in fact made no noise at all but may have had a quiet conversation with a neighbour.

Dear Karin had several lists, all of which mysteriously disappeared. The troublemakers, seeing her spot them and write down their names, went to her and smooth-talked her into removing them from the list. I was aware of this, and I knew my name was on the list, but I had done nothing wrong and refused to play the game.

Fräulein Gobel was still seething as she lined the four of us up, made us hold out our hands and shouted at me, "I expected better of you, being the oldest in the class." Then she gave us each a whack with her very flexible stick. Had she reflected even for a moment she would have known that, not only was it impossible for the four of us to have caused the racket she heard as she approached the room, but it was completely out of character for us to have done so.

When I recall this incident, I often wonder if any of the people involved, including Gobel, ever had one of those moments when they remembered this nasty bit of work and cringed.

Next a little note, in Mother's hand - a bit squiggly - but the signature is printed by Helga.

Dear Opa, dear Oma, I want to send you and the uncles and aunts and cousins a loving greeting. What can Auntie Esther's baby do? What is her name? I am trying to decide what I shall wish for Christmas. I might ask for a little suitcase because I will need one if we come to you or to Aunt Lenes. Another big greeting from Heidi, Carl and Walter and a kiss from your HELGA.

Mother added:

> *My dear All, I have to add a short greeting ... I sent your last letter on to Werner. It seems he is regaining some interest in coming back and would like to have a farm. He has applied again for an apartment for all of us but it seems to be hopeless.*
>
> *I have been able to buy some winter clothing for the children but it has to come out of the household money.*
>
> *Our congratulations to Esther and Ben on the arrival of their baby girl and wish them good health. Please all stay healthy, write soon, and be in God's care.*
>
> *Your Betty*

On December 15, Mutti reports that our Christmas greetings and parcels from Canada have already arrived.

> *Dear Parents, Brothers & Sisters,*
>
> *Now it is high time that our Christmas greetings get underway ... We received your wonderful Christmas parcel yesterday and a card from Carl & Dagne with 2 pictures of Sherry Lynn on her baptism, and today your Christmas card that Ruth sent. So now I can acknowledge everything and thank you all from the bottom of my heart and most especially many thanks for our wonderful Christmas present.*
>
> *Who would have thought that we would have a turkey on our table this Christmas! And all the other wonderful sweets and confections!*

The arrival of any parcel from Canada and the US was an event but the Christmas parcels had us all jumping with excitement. We watched as Mutti worked to loosen each knot in the string before it finally came off. Then she carefully peeled back the brown paper, never wasting a scrap. It seemed to take forever to see what was inside.

We were not disappointed. There were presents, not to be opened until Christmas Eve, but the immediate feast for the eyes was the colour and sparkle of the candy and chocolate bar wrappings. Those were new to us, and, having few new or colourful things in our lives, we carefully flattened out the foil wrappers and treasured them. The new and tasty flavours inside were pure magic.

The *turkey on our table* was also something completely new. It came in a tin can and did not taste like anything we had eaten before. It was delicious. Mutti had to tell us about turkeys. We only remembered having a goose for Christmas dinner in better times.

> We can buy almost everything without coupons now except sugar, fat and flour. We spun a lot of wool for the owner of a big children's summer home and received groceries instead of money. So I had a bit of flour, sugar, fat and raisins. Also, money is a little more plentiful and now all the lovely things in your parcel. We also received a big CARE parcel from Elsa and Walter K. last week ... a letter from Werner today and he has also managed to get some items for us, 50 Pfund apples which are much cheaper there than here. You can see that we are not only very richly endowed for Christmas and can celebrate very nicely but also for long afterwards.
>
> The children are completely absorbed in Christmas preparations. In school, they are all practising for Christmas concerts and Heidi's class is preparing an evening for parents. The boys each set up the pins in a bowling alley once a week. They are earning some money for presents and have done quite a bit of shopping. The girls are knitting and sewing.

Our preparations for Christmas at home and in school were always a mixture of excitement and trepidation. Would Mutti get my new dress made in time for the concert? Would I remember the lines of the poem I was reciting? At home, it was important to have a present of some sort for everyone in the family and that became more difficult each year. Walter and Carl were able to earn money setting up pins in a bowling alley to buy presents, but I don't remember what they would have bought for everyone. Heidi and I had little opportunity to earn money for Christmas gifts, and we were past the age when decorated matchboxes and homemade Christmas cards were considered adequate. One year, we undertook to knit gloves for the boys.

We had both knitted socks and mittens before, but gloves turned out to be challenging and time-consuming. Mutti had some yarn we could use, and we made a valiant start; the cuffs and main parts of the hand were done fairly quickly, but most of the fingers required an irritatingly finicky manoeuvre.

The stitches for each finger had to be picked up and distributed evenly onto three double-ended knitting needles and were then knitted around with a fourth needle until the appropriate length was achieved. Time was running short. Mittens would have been much more sensible.

It was likely only days before Christmas Eve when we realized neither of us would get all ten fingers done. We could not present our gifts with knitting needles piercing the wrapping paper, so we got the idea to knit just a short piece of each unfinished finger before binding it off. The result was two pairs of gloves with several stubby little fingers on each hand and a promissory note that we would complete them after Christmas.

The boys took it well, and we all had fun trying on our creations and speculating about who might be able to wear them. I don't remember ever getting back to those gloves. Unless Mutti took over, I doubt that they were ever finished.

Mutti was always busy, and often frantic, trying to get everything done by Christmas.

> *I have made a little dress for Helga and a pair of pyjamas for Werner for Christmas presents. Since I had to give up the sewing machine last week I had to go to the home of an acquaintance to sew. She is good and helpful but a bit intimidating so I have to respect her wishes as to when I can come and sew.*
>
> *I guess Lene did not write to you that she found a farmer who was willing to bring us over and give us well-paid work for one year. If that had worked out we would have been able to spend Christmas with Marvins and Hans. Unfortunately, he could not wait so long. We were very happy about the idea but are once again disappointed.*
>
> *God is letting us wait a long time before he answers our prayers but he must know why. Now we wish you all, also Georgs, Bens & Jacobs, very happy holiday celebrations and a happy and blessed New Year.*

New Year 1950 was celebrated with great fanfare in Norderney. I remember thinking fifty years is a very long time and I would certainly not be alive to celebrate when the next half century rolled around.

Mutti was delighted with the contents of a Christmas parcel.

Thursday the 31 January 1950

Dear Parents, Brothers & Sisters,

We want to thank you again for all your very generous Christmas presents. The best surprise was your personal parcel which arrived one day after Christmas. It was really good to have good things for a bit longer. You really packed it in!

Our biggest joy was the picture of you, Father & Mother. You haven't changed much, Father, and don't look older at all. Mother looks a bit older and different somehow.

The children are enjoying the jigsaw puzzles very much, especially the map of Canada. The other one is pretty difficult. We have puzzled over it on and off for 3 days. Thank you so very much for everything.

Werner was here from Christmas Eve until Jan 2. He could have had two weeks but did not want to risk it as a new Major is supposed to be coming and some of the Germans, particularly his boss, would really like to be rid of him. It was fortunate that he went as 35 men were let go, including his boss. The depot will be further reduced by half in the spring and another 100 men will be gone. For Werner, there is no danger. The English trust him completely and have assured him of a position as long as the depot exists. He lives in an unheated attic but has been staying with a family that we knew in Ziegelhof, also refugees, for a couple of weeks.

Yesterday only one ferry came to the island, usually there are 3 but the ice is beginning to be a problem. We may be cut off from the mainland but it won't be as bad as 3 years ago. Last night it snowed a bit but today it started to thaw already. The children have been skating, even Helga is learning to skate. Carl received skates for Christmas. Walter would like some too, but he asked for a guitar for Christmas and there wasn't enough money for both. The girls have old ones received from acquaintances.

Wednesday, February 2.

We were at bible study, it is only nine-thirty, and I want to finish this quickly. A letter from Werner arrived today and he wrote as follows:

"I escaped death today by God's grace and protection. On Friday morning about 7:20, I was travelling to work on the streetcar. Suddenly, in a curve of the street, all three cars jumped the track and drove along the street. The second car fell over and was dragged 30 meters. I was in this car on the side that ended up on the bottom. The car was very full and I had the Landgrafs' boy *on my lap. (the people with whom he lives). They were very new cars and the windows were made of plexiglass which was fortunate for us. Two people were seriously injured, others only slightly or not at all. I sprained my ankle, it is getting better but I still have a headache. I want to see the doctor tomorrow and hope the headaches will pass as well. We have to be very grateful that it was not any worse ...."*

The rest of the letter was illegible.

Carl's Apprenticeship

Ever since our time in Ziegelhof, Carl wanted to be a farmer. It had made a great impression on all of us but him in particular. He had followed Papa around whenever he could, and he paid attention to what was going on and how things worked. He idolized our father and wanted to follow in his footsteps.

On an estate the size of Ziegelhof, everything was done at the appropriate time with manpower and equipment readily available. The horses were there to till the soil, seed fields, and reap and haul the produce to the railway depot. The cattle provided dairy products as well as meat. In addition, all the animals contributed to the enormous manure pile on the farm which was invaluable in fertilizing the fields for the best possible yield.

There was order and method and a rhythm to the year-round operation. Everything was utilized, put in place and maintained at the proper time. I believe Carl thought of this as the ideal farm.

Entering an apprenticeship was required for any trade in Germany at the time and was the logical step for Carl as he finished Volksschule.

Carl wrote to Papa near the end of the school year.

Ney. The 7. 3. 50

Dear Papa!

How are you? Did you recover from your accident? I hope your cold is better soon too. Have you looked for a place for me with a farmer? Please do it soon or it will be too late. We finish school in 3 weeks. I would like to start somewhere, please don't forget.

Our class was divided up into groups and each group was

given a question that they had to work with. I am in the wood group. We have to answer 12 questions and write a summary. Herr Lengerhues helped me collect some samples and identified the kinds of wood that I don't recognize. Another cabinet maker wrote to Frankfurt for us and asked: "What % of certified workers are in the wood industry and charts of production in various countries?" No answer has been received.

A freighter carrying coal ran aground on the sandbank near the west beach. A tugboat had to pull it off.

On Sunday we took some snapshots. If they are good we will send you some. I have also had prints made of some from Kanada and have organized my photo album.

My birthday was a bit of a muddle because I wanted to celebrate on Saturday. Mutti baked a Napfkuchen (pound cake) and yeast cakes with chocolate chips. Mutti gave me a shirt and fabric for another one and a pair of socks. From Walter, I received a ballpoint pen, from Heidi and Dorli an Alpenveilchen (cyclamen) and from Helga two little liqueur-filled chocolate bottles. Omi sent a briefcase and two pocket knives. Many thanks for your birthday wishes, heartfelt greetings,

Your Carl

I know there had been conversations before this about finding a place for the apprenticeship, but Carl was concerned that it would be forgotten. In his postscript, he urges Papa:

Please tie a knot in your handkerchief or a string around your finger so that you don't forget anything!

The meaning of Carl's second PS is lost in translation from German.

Did you notice that I used a small "d" for "Du" in the third line?

He pointed out his error in addressing his father. He was a very tidy person and he would not have wanted to cross out the incorrect form of address, or try to write over the lowercase *d*.

At the time, in Germany, it was correct to capitalize the pronouns for others, *Du*, the familiar form, and *Sie*, the formal address. It was bad manners to use the lowercase when addressing another person.

Among my German-speaking acquaintances here in Canada,

these customs are very much relaxed, and when I saw Carl's postscript, I did a search and found that the custom has evolved in Germany too. It was officially changed by the *Rechtschreibreform* (spelling reform) in 1996. The formal *Sie* is capitalized, *du* and *ihr* are usually written in lowercase, but some older Germans still capitalize them.

In the following letter to our grandparents, Heidi reported that Carl's apprenticeship was arranged in good time. Carl left for his placement on April 14th.

I have wondered if his sad letter reflected his homesickness or if the farm did not measure up to his expectations.

In one of her letters, Mutti regrets how hard he had to work, and Papa also mentioned that apprentices were badly used by employers. Carl loved much of the work and would have been willing to put in whatever effort was required. Heidi writes.

Ney., the 20. 4. 50

Dear Opa, dear Oma!

We haven't seen each other in a very long time and I can't imagine what it is like in Canada. But I remember what you look like and you have sent us such a nice picture of yourselves.

Carl left on Friday the 14. 4. for the farm. He wrote a kind of sad letter today. The other apprentices are all farm boys and know so much more than he. He will like it better when he gets more used to things. The work is divided up so that one apprentice looks after the horses, another one the cows and another one the pigs. Each week they exchange chores.

You asked in one of your letters, Opa, how we celebrate the holidays here. Easter, Christmas and Pentecost are celebrated for two days, all other holidays are the same as yours. Buss-und-Bettag (Day of Atonement and Day of Petition and Prayer) *and Totensonntag (All Saints Day) are also celebrated here. On Pentecost Monday there is a gold and diamond confirmation anniversary celebrated here, with communion. All those confirmed in the last 60 and 50 years will participate.*

For children just starting school, there is a special church service. The children and their parents go from the church to the school accompanied by the ringing of the church bells. Helga has now also started school. She was given a nice "Tűte" filled with sweets. I think she will like school and will learn well ...

Helga Starts School

The *Tüte* that Heidi mentions in her letter is traditionally given to children in Germany on their first day of school. Also called a *Schultüte*, it is a colourfully decorated cone-shaped cornucopia filled with sweets, treats and small toys or school supplies. They often have a lace or cloth closing with a drawstring or a ribbon to be untied when the time comes to explore the wonders inside.

Helga was very shy and never ventured far from Mutti, and the precious school cone may have helped ease the anxiety of the first day of school. Mutti would have been pleased with the church service and the procession to the school accompanied by the ringing of the church bells.

When I came across this description of Helga's first day of school, I had to ask her about it.

"I don't think I remember any of that, but I will never forget the second day. Mom walked me to school and left me to go inside with all the other kids. I was still trying to work out where I should go when suddenly I was all by myself in this huge empty hallway. Everyone had disappeared, all the doors were closed and I had no idea which one led to my classroom.

"I was scared to death and crying, of course. I don't remember how I was rescued. It took me a while but after I figured it out, I quite liked school."

She remembered the big classrooms where the boys sat on one side of the room and the girls on the other.

While on a family group visit to Germany and Poland in 2018, Helga and I and our two daughters took a side trip to Norderney. I was very happy to show Helga some of the places she remembered or had never had a chance to visit while we lived there.

Much had changed on the island since we were children, but the significant landmarks were all there and we toured around with the help of a map. We had just finished admiring some of the very old headstones in the cemetery when we rounded a corner, and I spotted the school. I pointed it out to Helga and she exclaimed, "It's huge! No wonder I was intimidated."

A barrier and scaffolding at the playground side of the school kept us away from the entrance we would have used to get to our classes. I was disappointed that we could not even get a glimpse of what changes may have been made inside.

Helga went on to tell me an interesting story about her school experience after we returned to Canada.

She had completed grade two in Germany but was put back into grade one because she didn't speak more than a few words of English. Her teacher, Miss Habermann, spoke German, but she made it very clear that she would not do so in the classroom.

"That was hard enough but what really got me was when she came down on me because she saw me writing. I started to copy letters and words from the blackboard in cursive writing, and she told me that was not allowed. I had to print. I didn't know how to print."

Helga has never had much tolerance for rules she considered illogical, and her indignation was evident even after all these years.

Heidi's letter continues.

> Mutti thinks that because you haven't written for such a long time that you are making another attempt at getting us permission to immigrate. It would be very nice if we could be there for the fruit harvest and could all earn some money. But Walter and I would really like to finish school here.
>
> Please greet Tante Margret and Tante Ruth from Mutti, Walter, Heidi, Dorle and Helga. Heartfelt greetings and kisses, sends your Heidi.

Mother's addition to Heidi's letter.

> *My dear ones!*
> *Now the already delayed birthday greetings are still lying here. I have a very guilty conscience because I did not write to you for Easter and especially you, dear Father, for your 70. birthday. Now Heidi has finally finished her little letter and we are sending it by regular post.*
> *The pictures are not especially good, too small and not clear. Films are not very good and so expensive that they get old in the stores ... But you will likely be able to recognize us and maybe you have a magnifying glass. The little one of Heidi you could send to Jacobs for now so that they have some idea what their godchild looks like.*
> *Love to all, from your Betty*

In the next letter on April 27, 1950, Mother acknowledges her father's efforts and the lack of accomplishments at our end. She may have become accustomed to Father's ambivalence because she only mentions it in passing.

> *I know you have taken a lot of trouble over our return to Canada and are perhaps waiting for a reply from somewhere. We have only been able to find out that there was an Immigration Mission for Canada established in Carlsruhe a few weeks ago ....*
>
> *Werner has lost his enthusiasm for going to Canada. I believe he will go when it is actually possible and the children and I want it. He has said he would ... We just have to wait and see how everything develops.*
>
> *Everything else is going along in its usual fashion. Werner was only here from Good Friday to Easter Monday but we hope he can stay longer for Pentecost.*
>
> *Carl is settling in well, has made friends with the other boys and seems to be quite happy. Since he left, it is quieter here and I have fewer aggravations.*

Mutti does not write again until July 9, and cannot hide her frustration at a new problem blocking our efforts to leave Germany.

9. 7. 1950

Dear Parents, Brothers & Sisters,

It is very late, but I want to make a start and the end will no doubt come. We received your loving letters and they made us very happy, especially because of your few lines, dear Mother.

It seems the authorities need to take their time. We don't quite know what to do with your suspicions, Father. Werner has had suspicions for a long time but over here that happens very easily with him ... Someone made that poisonous report in Hamburg ... Werner was never in Hanover nor in any position of authority. When he was in the "Reichs Umsiedlung" (relocation program), he was a simple civil servant and answered to Berlin. We don't know if there are other Rudeloffs elsewhere or if they have the name wrong.

It is difficult to know what we might do to clear up this misunderstanding. Werner is still waiting for his reference certificate, the gentlemen take a long time here too. I think it is best if we wait for your information. I think you are right. If they turn us down again they will have to tell the truth. I still believe

> we alone are to blame for all of this as we did not tell the whole truth at the beginning and they are saying we lied and are using that against us.
>
> Certainly, some things are nicer here than over there but the opposite is true too. We have put it in God's hand ....
>
> Werner is still in Bielefeld but we don't know for how long. If things don't work out with Canada, he would like to go to southern Germany to look for something and, of course, we would want to move there as well ...
>
> Tomorrow the summer holidays begin here ....

This must have been a particularly busy time for Mutti. It is not until November 2nd that she writes again, this time with news of a family mishap.

> When Werner returned to Bielefeld on Aug 20 from his holiday, he found that Carl had been in the hospital for 3 weeks with a broken leg. He did not write to us about it as he did not want to worry us and spoil our holidays with Werner. It happened the day after Werner left to come here. He and 2 other boys wanted to ride their bicycles to Herman's statue in Lentsburgerwald. He drove into the back wheel of one of the other bicycles and crashed badly.
>
> His leg was broken in three places, the shinbone had two breaks and was splintered, and the calf bone had one break. Poor Carl really suffered. He was 7 weeks in a cast and 9 weeks in the hospital.
>
> As he could not travel to Norderney right away, he returned to the farmer where he was put to work in the kitchen and had to cook pig slop. After a week he came here for 3 1/2 weeks and went back yesterday. It was exactly 3 months since the accident. We are grateful that his leg has healed well and is nice and straight. It is still a bit swollen and he limps but the doctor says that will pass with time.

Carl told us about cooking pig slop and also about peeling a mountain of potatoes each day in the farm kitchen. He was a pragmatist, and I picture him working out the most efficient setup and method for these tasks, possibly adding a chant or a song to stave off boredom. He did not mind working in a kitchen even though boys were usually not expected to do *women's work*. When he was still quite young he taught himself how to make porridge to ensure it was perfectly smooth. He hated lumps.

On the day he was to arrive in Norderney for a visit, I was so excited I ran all the way home from school. When I saw him, I was overcome by shyness. He looked different—smaller, or thinner or maybe just older. I didn't know how to greet him.

He laughed, *"Hey, Schwesterchen"* (little sister), and poked me gently with his walking stick and it was okay.

> *Ruth's letter arrived last week. I was so happy to receive it but it made me very homesick. She seems so happy and wrote so well of Len. I wonder if we will ever get to know all our new relatives? We also appreciated Elsa's long, newsworthy letter.*
>
> *Walter was recently in Hamburg for a week and wrote an application exam to be admitted as an apprentice with Siemens & Schuckert, one of the biggest electrical companies in Germany. Out of 53 applicants, eight were to be chosen and Walter's exam results qualified him for one of the eight. I am very proud of him as most of the other applicants were older and some had far more education than he. He has always been interested in electrical things and has built himself a radio. It is not very good because it was not allowed to cost very much but it works quite well.*

Family Stories

Father also mentions Walter's successful apprenticeship application. Our parents were justifiably proud and I think we were all a little in awe of him. Carl told me years later, "I was so impressed that Walter passed the test for this apprenticeship. He told me it was because he was able to accurately describe the function of a radio tube, the most advanced technology of the time."

In Norderney, Walter made friends with the technician running the movie theatre and spent many evenings helping out and learning how to run the projectors. On our return to Canada, Dad helped him get a job as a technician at CJIB, the local radio station in Vernon, BC.

Heidi and I benefited from his access to the theatre when he smuggled us into the prompt box at the front of the stage to watch movies.

Walter had a good time in Hamburg, and on his return, he had some interesting stories. He stayed with our grandmother and she was a bit of a mischief-maker. When he wanted to go out to explore the city one evening, she said, "Go ahead, but stay away from the Reeperbahn in St. Pauli. It is not a good place for a young boy like you."

That was all the incentive he needed and, of course, he had to find out what was there. He had no difficulty locating the area, and on one street he found sex workers displaying themselves behind windows, waiting for customers, just as in the red-light district in Amsterdam. He did not say whether he'd taken the adventure a step further or was content just to have a look around.

I found online that the *Reeperbahn* is now the centre of Hamburg's nightlife with the city's major red-light district. In German, it is also nicknamed *die sündigste Meile* (the most sinful mile).

Walter always chuckled when he told this story. He was convinced our Omchen had known exactly what would happen if she told him not to go there.

From time to time in our lives, Walter and Helga, the oldest and the youngest of the family, seemed to have much in common. They both learned to think for themselves at a young age while the rest of us went along with what we had been taught, without question, until we were much more mature.

Helga was the baby of the family and was often left out of our activities, but when we paid her some attention we were delighted by her cute ways.

Walter and his friends, considering themselves a cut above in Mittelschule, adopted jargon not commonly used by the rest of us. I imagine they held debates in school and so when any little disagreement arose among them, they said, somewhat pretentiously, *"Ich bin anderer Meinung; lasst uns diskutieren."* (I hold a different opinion; let us debate this matter.)

Helga, possibly already admiring her big brother, picked this up and when contradicted by someone, she repeated what she thought she had heard. *"Ich bin ein anderer Mann; lasst uns das quittieren."* (I am another man; let us write a receipt.)

The fact that Walter was the *cleverer,* as Mutti puts it in some of her letters, was not always reflected in his marks at school. Now I believe it would be said that he did not apply himself. Carl worked diligently to achieve average marks as it did not come as easily to him, but Walter would only work at what interested him.

Whenever Papa saw his poor marks, he was furious. He said Walter was lazy and told him he would never amount to anything. "You'll end up being a street sweeper if you don't work harder."

Before I was even in school, I piped up after one of these tirades and said, "And I will marry the *Burgermeister* and I will drive over your broom in my fancy carriage."

The irony was lost on me until many years later. It seemed I did not have to work hard to get the fancy carriage but must simply marry the right person, while his success or failure depended on his efforts.

Mother's letter continues with what would seem to be important news. I wonder, did she down-play this breakthrough because of Father's ambivalence?

> *You likely know that the restrictions in place since the war have been reversed and Germans are now allowed to immigrate to Canada as before the war. Werner is still undecided about what he wants to do. He often feels that he can do better here than over there and is hoping for some help from the government.*
>
> *Helga asks to be excused. She was cutting out pictures and did not notice that she was cutting into my writing paper.*

Elsa said she was planning to send some tea and coffee. We would be very grateful if you could send some as it would allow us to buy a little coal for the winter. A severe winter is forecast and coal is both scarce and expensive ... Werner can buy things much more cheaply where he is and has preserved beans, pears and plums in jars.

What are the feelings over there about the war in Korea? The opinion here seems to be that World War 3 is not far away and that Germany will be the arena. People are really crazy. Factories are already holding back goods with the result that there is more scarcity again and higher costs. When the war in Korea first started, there was all of a sudden no sugar available. People with money simply bought up all that was available. Now there is some in the stores but it costs 60 Pfennig per lb.

Please say hello to any brothers or sisters nearby ...

Some time in December 1950 it was again my turn to write to Papa.

Dear Papa

This week it is my turn to write to you but since nothing much happens here I don't really know what to write. My class at school goes to the wave pool every Friday but today the pool was closed for repairs so I will be going to school an hour later and have time to write to you. We can't imagine that Carl will not be here for Christmas.

Dear Papa, for my birthday I would like roller skates. They cost about 14 - 15 DM here. We are making many plans about what everybody will get for Christmas. The weather here is not nice and this morning there was hoarfrost on everything. When Mutti bought Carl gumboots before he left, she bought me a pair of high shoes (leather boots). *We would like to knit Christmas presents but Mutti has no money for wool.*

Lots of love and please greet Carl for me. Your Dorli.

Skates and Boots

Asking for roller skates was very daring of me. I was usually much more modest, but whenever Papa came for a visit he seemed to have money, and I hoped this time I might get my wish.

I had longed for roller skates from the time I was four years old and saw someone skating on our street in Rostock. For many years they would have been of no use but in Norderney there were ideal conditions and it seemed to me everybody had them.

Papa sometimes sent parcels from where he lived in Bielefeld, and I was very excited when one arrived shortly before my birthday.

My heart sank as the parcel was emptied, and I found my birthday present at the bottom of the box. It was a bathing cap wrapped in a bit of tissue paper. Bathing caps were required in the pool and some were lovely, in many styles and colours. Mine was a flimsy, off-white thing with no style whatsoever. I was often told I cried too easily, so I tried hard to smile and pretend these were tears of joy.

Ice skates were much easier to obtain, but in Norderney we could not always count on enough frost to make skating possible. Mutti mentions our ice skating in some of her letters; she couldn't imagine how we could skate with the equipment we had. To begin with, someone gave us what I think of as Dutch skates. They were described in the children's book *Hans Brinker And the Silver Skates*. Even novice skaters could keep from tipping over at the ankles.

Later we had ice skates that were clamped onto your shoes much like the old roller skates with a strap buckled at the ankles. These were higher than the others, and Mutti was concerned that we would damage our ankles. She declared that we would have to have boots in order to be allowed to go skating.

I always believed her, and when it came time to buy shoes I chose the *hohe Schuhe* (high shoes) mentioned in my letter to Papa. They were brown leather lace-up boots, not unattractive when worn with slacks, allowed in school at the time. I prayed that the coming winter would be cold enough to freeze the *Schanze* (lagoon) so that we could go skating.

The purchase was made in April of that year when Carl was leaving for his apprenticeship. We all went barefoot or wore sandals until fall, when it became too cold and closed shoes were called for.

That's when I was hit by the enormity of my mistake. The first time I got dressed for church on a Sunday morning, there I was, in a dress, socks and brown leather lace-up boots. Not even during post-war poverty and deprivation was it acceptable to wear brown lace-up boots with a dress at almost thirteen years of age. It was all I had, even for the Christmas concert where I had to recite a poem from the stage in front of many children and adults.

I was already self-conscious about walking into church or to the front of the class because Papa was always telling us to walk like ladies and I didn't know how to do that. Now, I could barely put one foot in front of the other as I tried to walk with my feet behind me to make the big brown lumps at the end of my legs less noticeable. It was agony.

Heidi made her decisions quite differently. She knew what was important and paid no attention to Mutti's rule about skating without boots. Her shoes for the fall and winter may not have been as fashionable as she wished, but they were far better than what I had brought on myself. My one consolation was that skating was good that winter, and I felt appropriately dressed; it was great fun. Nothing was said about Heidi's footwear.

I was grateful that my feet had grown by the following winter and I had to have a new pair of shoes.

Preparing to Leave

Early in 1951 we finally got the news we had hoped for, for so long.

I don't know just how the news came to us but Mother's letter, after a two month silence, leaves no doubt that it was welcome. She acknowledges two letters from her father on the day they arrived. Her opening paragraph seems to indicate that she was waiting for official confirmation of some kind.

> *Tuesday the 6. February 1951*
> *Dear Parents,*
> *We received your two letters this afternoon, dear Father. I can imagine you have been waiting for a reply and should have written sooner but wanted to wait for an answer from Karslruhe so that I might have further information or could report something positive. Since nothing has arrived I decided I had to write today. According to the news in your second letter there should be something here soon.*
>
> ***Do we want to? Yes, we want to!***

When your letter came, there was such cheering and happiness and I had trouble answering all the children's questions. I am sorry that I kept you waiting ... It never occurred to me that you needed to know if we wanted to come. I was overjoyed and just took it for granted. We are all healthy and pray that God makes this plan a reality.

Werner also wants to go now. When he was here at Christmas, he ranted and raved terribly against the Canadian government and didn't want to hear anything more about it. I think he just had to clear the air because he was so angry that we could not come back. He was also reluctant to give up his illusions about the opportunities here. But in his first letter after he returned he urged me to write to Carlsruhe right away .... shortly after that your letter arrived ...

When I read the first of your letters to the children, Helga whispered in my ear: "Mutti, I prayed for this last night and God hears us when we pray."

Heartfelt Greetings from, your Betty and Children
PS Carl's year is up on 1. April. The school year is over at Easter which works out well.

Confirmation and Graduation

In her letter of 6 February 1951, Mutti mentions that Heidi needs clothes for confirmation, which is somewhat reminiscent of the concern expressed in a number of letters about suits for the boys.

This was an important coming-of-age event in the life of a German young person at the time, and appropriate dress was essential.

Heidi's confirmation took place on Palm Sunday, which was March 18 of that year, and she was beautifully dressed for her special day. I don't know if Papa came home in time to have the dress made by a seamstress or if she chose the design and he sent the money to pay for it, but it was perfect.

In a black and white photo of her with our parents, she is looking very grownup and elegant. Her dress was navy blue with a white collar and a knee-length fine pleated skirt. At her neck, she wore a silver filigree pin in the shape of a bow, a gift from our Omchen.

Heidi's graduation from Volksschule was far less eventful. I imagine there was some kind of ceremony at the school, but the family was not involved and no special dress was required. After finishing school at age fourteen, it was customary for young people to enter an apprenticeship or go to trade school for a year to prepare for a job. I remember a friend of Heidi's describing some of the classes in cooking and other household skills. I don't know what the options were, but Heidi chose not to attend. Instead, Papa proposed that he would pay her an allowance if she helped Mutti with housework and preparations for our trip.

Walter also finished school at this time. I believe his graduation—at the end of grade ten in the Mittelschule—was more of an event than Heidi's, and there is a picture of his class taken on the occasion. Since our plans for leaving Germany were finally becoming real, he did not take up the apprenticeship in Hamburg for which he qualified. Instead, he and a friend went to work on a farm.

Mutti was surprised that it seemed to suit him so well and he *could satisfy his constant hunger with some good country cooking.*

Helga and I went back to school after the Easter holidays, but all other activities were directed toward getting ready to travel. It was an exciting time but not without some difficult decisions. We each had a suitcase for items needed on the voyage, but many precious items had to be left behind.

A letter from Father is undated. Opa made a note on the original: *Arrived on Karfreitag* (Good Friday) March 23, 1951.

My father's handwriting was difficult to read. The following letter was written on airmail paper, both sides, with one of the early ballpoint pens, the ink blobby and now faded with age, making it particularly difficult to read and translate.

After my own attempt, I came across the same letter in Opa's handwriting. He obviously had some trouble reading it as well and transcribed it for Mother's siblings.

Dear Parents, Brothers & Sisters

First of all thank you for all your help, I hope we can make it all up to you sometime in the future. I find it hard to leave my country but then again the people here are making it easier. Have I forgotten something or is it like this the world over? We are hoping for a better future in Canada after all our hard times and long separation.

We have received the cards from the Canadian Consulate in Frankfurt for the 4 Canadian children who will receive Canadian Passports. Betty has also been offered her Canadian citizenship which she can claim here or over there. If there is time we want to get it here. We have had no news from Carlsruhe but we have been told by Frankfurt that we will get an answer from there as well. So everything is in order.

When we receive the money for our passage from you, we can get our visas and must only wait for our departure!

Walter has secured an excellent apprenticeship ... but the apprenticeship years are not good. The boys are exploited and used. I am of the firm opinion that he will do as well in Canada in his chosen field.

For Carl it is certainly best as he will never own his own farm here. The girls will likely also have good opportunities there.

We are also hopeful for us, especially Betty. I hope she will be happy again because the longing never stops.

Greetings and good wishes, Werner

Mother adds her hopeful notes on the flaps of the airmail letter form.

Saturday morning

My dear ones,

It is fortunate that this letter is still here. A letter just arrived from the Immigration Mission, now located in Hanover, with an application for immigration to Canada enclosed.

The letter states: "After your travel arrangements have been completed an appointment will be made for medical and civil inspection." We will send the application immediately, although the papers for the 4 children must go to Frankfurt. How soon we can travel depends on the SS Line. We hope everything will not take too long. Werner would like to know if meals are included in the train trip in Canada ... Getting our own meals could be impossible if the fast trains don't stop long enough for us to buy the necessities.

We received your loving letters and thank you. I would have liked to write much more but ...

Mutti closes with a wish for a Happy Easter and does not write again until April 27, 1951.

Dear Parents & Siblings,

I keep thinking from day to day that something must surely come from the Immigration Mission in Hanover but they are very slow. We are still waiting for information regarding the examinations they require ...

There was a notice from the C.P.R. last week that we can travel on the 29th May if we have everything in order. They sent a receipt for the fare you have paid and gave this as our departure date.

At the Consulate things move more quickly. After we sent the registration cards in, we immediately received the application forms for the children's travel passes. They have to have passport photos taken and the applications must be signed by a person in Authority. I believe after that it will go quickly. We still have 4 1/2 weeks until the date so it could still happen.

Werner will likely give up his position by 1. May or maybe even by Pentecost. He wants to go to Hamburg then and sell his share of his grandfather's inheritance. There should be a couple of hundred Marks there, and that would help to get us the necessities for the trip. We are hoping to get free travel to our

> port of departure. I doubt that [our application] will succeed as I had to declare Werner's income and they always say with his income we can not expect any help or support.
>
> Walter and a friend left last Monday for Arnsberg, somewhat south of Bielefeld. They have both gone to a farmer there. After their first half day of work they wrote that they like it, especially the food. They had to milk right away, something I can not picture for either one of them. Walter will only be able to stay about a month but it pays and he can earn some money, can see some of the beauty of Germany and can satisfy his constant hunger with some good country cooking. He and Carl will then both come back here ...

Mutti's letter of April 27 continues.

> We are getting ready to break up our home here and are very excited, especially the girls. Dorli forgot yesterday afternoon that she was supposed to be in school and I did not remember either until it was too late. She goes most mornings except Thursdays when she goes in the afternoon ...

Anticipation and Confusion

The much longed-for journey was becoming a reality, and we girls, the only siblings still at home, were indeed excited.

The school year ended at Easter, and our two-week spring holidays started on the following Monday. When Mutti wrote, we had been back to school for about two weeks. Overcrowding was still a problem, and my erratic schedule made it rather too easy to forget to go to school.

I believe that Mutti put this down to the excitement of our preparing to leave, but there was more to it than that. At the start of grade six, we were told that Fräulein Gobel was finding some of the boys in her class troublesome, and she was no longer willing to teach all our subjects. As a result, we inherited the much-feared Herr Koch for math instruction and I was not enjoying school.

As I reached adolescence, the two-year age difference between me and my classmates had also become more troublesome. I had lost the only friend in my class when she moved away; I was lonely and unhappy.

For most of our time in Norderney, Heidi let me tag along with her and her friends and we shared many activities. We also squabbled and argued over chores, but we were good friends. After she finished school, she often went her own way, and I felt abandoned.

I loved spending my time with Mutti and helping her with our preparations. She seemed to enjoy my company and appreciated the help.

She told me the story of *Anne of Green Gables*, a redhead just like me, who broke a slate over a boy's head because he called her *carrots*. That made me laugh. Being called carrots was funny compared to my torment.

My brother Carl and I had been the only two redheads in our school of 3,000 students and after he left I was the only target for the taunts. One of the favourite ones was, *"Rote Hare, Summersprossen sind des Teufels Volksgenossen"* (Red hair and freckles make you the devil's compatriot).

I dreamed of a new start in Canada. I was convinced it would be a better place with nicer people.

At home, the excitement mounted. Omchen arrived for a visit amid a lot of bustle with her numerous bulging bags and was as entertaining as ever. Both Helga and I remember fetching her daily mug of foaming beer from the pub just down the street.

Soon after that, Papa came for a holiday and took Mutti and us girls to Hanover for final arrangements for our trip. We travelled by train and stayed overnight in a hotel and were pretty excited as the big voyage was planned for the end of May. Papa was still at home when Walter and Carl also arrived, adding to the turmoil.

Shortly after our trip to Hanover, it became clear that our departure for Canada was again postponed. Papa and the boys left on a trip to visit Tante Dita in Switzerland, but by that time I was not at all serious about attending school. I stayed at home and was happily sewing or reading; amid all the coming and going, no one seemed to notice that I had stopped going to school altogether, well before the end of June when summer holidays started.

Mutti continued her letter with hope for a grand reunion.

> *I hope all the brothers and sisters are coming for the golden wedding anniversary so that we will all be together once again. The last time that happened was probably Walter's baptism. 1933*

Heidi added a postscript to Mutti's letter of April 27 to thank the grandparents for their blessings on her confirmation.

> *Dear Grandparents! I thank you with all my heart for your lovely letter. I am looking forward to seeing you all soon and then we will have much to talk about. Your Heidi*

In his final letter on May 28, Papa sent news which the family in Canada would already have surmised.

> *Dear Parents,*
> *I took a holiday on 15.5. to get everything ready for our departure and during this time we are supposed to go to Hanover, Betty and the girls and I, the boys are both still on their farms ... We did not get enough information and now we do not have all our papers.*
>
> *We went a few days later but everything was too late ... We have had the Canadian papers for quite some time but the staff in Hanover delayed everything and now the steamship was fully booked and we have to wait until 12 July until the Beaverbrae sails again. We can't go on another ship as the money has been paid to the CPR.*
>
> *We are all very disappointed about this. I will make sure everything is now in order and we should be in Vernon by the end of July. We are all anxiously looking forward to that. We have been told in Hanover that we should be able to get the money for the farm so our beginning in Canada should be a happy one.*
>
> *I hope you are all well. Will you delay the celebration until we come or can that not be done? Heartfelt greetings from all of us and a happy reunion ...*

I am sure Mutti's addition to Papa's letter was punctuated with tears as she described the latest disappointments and activities before we could finally set out.

> *Hello All, there has to be another disappointment. The office in Hanover is a terribly muddled affair. It is also very annoying here. Werner has not worked since 1. June and both boys came home and it will cost a lot of money before we can get away, which should now be about 12 Juli. Werner wants to go to his sisters in Switzerland for two weeks, she will pay his way. Mother Rudeloff was here for Pentecost. She is very sad that we want to leave here but understands that we can't carry on as we have*

been, and that the opportunities to improve our situation do not exist here.

Please don't be too disappointed that it is taking another 1 1/2 months. Werner has tried to transfer the money to a different SS Line but it can only be done with additional costs.

We are all happily looking forward to the trip. It will be a big adventure but the very best part will be to be reunited with all of you. I can only hope that all the brothers and sisters can arrange their plans in such a way that we can still all be there at the same time.

In happy anticipation, your Betty

Sailing for Canada

Finally, on July 13 the day came. We packed the last few items, dressed in our travel clothes and set out. As we headed to the ferry, Mutti realized that one of us had forgotten a jacket which could not be left behind. I almost grasped the finality of our leaving the island when Walter jumped off the horse-drawn bus and raced back home to retrieve it. He caught up with us at the harbour just in time.

Once on the mainland, we boarded the train to Bremen where we booked into a bright, comfortable hostel.

I hear my mother's voice at peace in this final postcard from our time in Germany.

15.7.1951

Dear parents & siblings.

We've been here since Friday evening, 13th, in the Überseeheim (overseas hostel) in Bremen. Monday evening, 8 p.m., July 16, the steamer is scheduled to leave from here. Finally the time has really come and we hope, with God's protection, to be with you at the end of July. It is still unclear whether we will stop at Hans and Elsa's, at most 1 day each.

We have a lot of hand luggage, so it's very inconvenient. The next news will be of our departure from Quebec. We are eagerly looking forward to seeing you again.

Warm greetings to everyone, your Betty

We had a few days to explore the city of Bremen and we talked about the voyage and our plans for Canada until late every evening.

Monday morning we travelled on to Bremerhafen and had our first glimpse of the *Beaverbrae*. We watched as our trunks were loaded into her hold along with a mountain of other baggage.

In the evening of July 16, 1951 we sailed for Canada on the outgoing tide.

Passport Photos August 1948

Walter

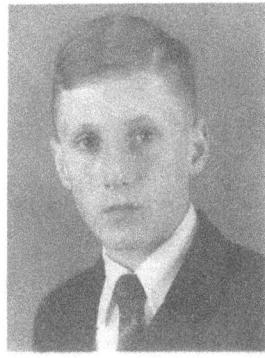

Carl

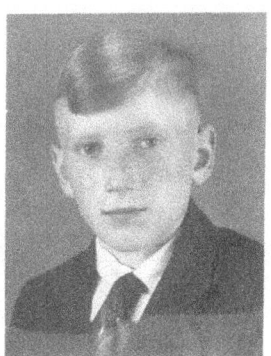

Heidi

Helga

Dorothy

Sources

Bauer, Ingrid. "German Compound Words Explained With Examples." ThoughtCo. www.thoughtco.com/german-compound-words-1444618 (accessed September 26, 2023)

Boyd, Jane E. "Celluloid: The Eternal Substitute" https://sciencehistory.org/profile/jane-e-boyd/

Leigh-Howarth, Jake "Klaus Störtebeker: The Bizarre Tale of a North German Pirate" https://www.ancient-origins.net/history-famous-people/klaus-stoortebeker-0016772

Taylor, Bryan. "The Currency Reform that Created Two Germanies." Global Financial Data. www.globalfinancialdata.com/the-currency-reform-that-created-two-germanies (accessed September 26, 2023)

Vorwald, Oliver. "Martini: Ein Nationalfeiertag für Ostfriesland." https://www.ndr.de/kirche/Das-Kirchenlexikon-Martini-in-Ostfriesland,martinisingen102.html (accessed September 28, 2023)

Map, by Richard Hoedl: Administrative boundaries: © EuroGraphics © UN-FAO © urkstatCartographer: Eurostat - IMAGE, 09/2023

About the Author

From the Canadian prairie to war-torn Germany, occupied Poland, and back to Canada, Dorothy Mandy's journey is marked by a unique tale of both Canadian heritage and immigrant experience.

As an adult, Dorothy has lived in a co-operative community, and she played an instrumental role in establishing Haven House, a refuge for battered women and children in Nanaimo, BC. She volunteered at the Sexual Assault Centre and served on the District 68 School Board.

Dorothy's passion for advocating women's rights brought her to represent Alberta Women at the National Action Committee on the Status of Women.

She now lives with her longtime partner in British Columbia, where she enjoyed the German Choir and served on the executive of the Canadian Society for German Culture to celebrate the culture and music of her youth. She has found her spiritual community with the Nanaimo Unitarian Fellowship.

www.ingramcontent.com/pod-product-compliance
Lightning Source LLC
Chambersburg PA
CBHW071337080526
44587CB00017B/2867